For Ann

IN SEARCH OF HOME

Joan Rowe

With love & best wishes

Joan

A gift from Frank.

First published in 2006 by
Joan Rowe
Box 133/2, Gylemuir Road
EDINBURGH
EH12 7DL

Designed and produced by

The Short Run Book Company Limited
Unit 1
Orpheus House
Calleva Park
Aldermaston
Berkshire RG7 4QW

ISBN
0-9552582-0-0
978-0-9552582-0-6

CONTENTS

Introduction	5
Acknowledgements	6
Birkenhead	7
Portland	23
Aldershot	31
Gillingham	40
Grays	51
Tottenham	55
Plumstead/Woolwich	60
Tinsley	74
Germany	86
Richmond	94
Sheffield	99
Nether Edge	102
Doncaster	120
Crookesmoor	140
Rotherham	154
Edinburgh	193
Bibliography	197

ILLUSTRATIONS

Birkenhead houses following an air raid, 1941	13
V.E. Day party, Tranmere Road, Birkenhead	14
Church Ope Cove	25
Army house, The Verne, Portland	26
Army house, Cove, Farnborough	33
Strover Street House, Gillingham	43
Arden Street School,Gillingham	44
Rock Avenue, Gillingham	46
Rook Hall, Dell Road, Grays, Essex	51
Bruce Grove, London N17	55
Ceres Road, Plumstead, South London	61
The Author and Church Manorway friend, Doreen	63
The first Sheffield house, 1958	78
Wedding Day with Anton, 1960	84
The Frenchgate house, Richmond, North Yorkshire	96
The Crescent Road house, Nether Edge, Sheffield	104
Sir John Barbirolli	106
The author, 1964	111
The author with Guards bandsmen,1966	114
First student house, Sunnyfields, Doncaster, 1967	122
Second student house, Doncaster, 1968	130
Third student house, Scawsby, Doncaster, 1969	132
Music class at Kelvin, Sheffield ... author and daughter, 1972	148
Rotherham house, Broom Road	157
College recital, Rotherham, 1982	162
The red-brick house, Moorgate, Rotherham, 1999	174

INTRODUCTION

The search for twenty six former homes has taken on epic proportions, far larger than I had imagined at the outset. Sometimes joyful, sometimes heart-rending and occasionally chilling and frightening. There were times when I wanted to shelve the whole project. Now I am glad that I kept going!

This book is about re-tracing steps, confronting a difficult past and attempting to gather some measure of self-nurture and understanding. It is an attempt to ameliorate emotional damage and try to find some positive good.

It is for my mother who died feeling that she had a wasted life. It is for my brother who took fifty seven years to articulate his feelings which were not dissimilar to my own.

It is also for my wonderful daughter, who gives me strength.

Each chapter describes a brief history of a former home and how we came to be living there, either as a family, or later when I had left the family home. I have described my return visits to all but one place and although it is a personal story I also see it as a social document which covers the past sixty years.

ACKNOWLEDGEMENTS

I am indebted to Birkenhead Library staff, Portland Museum, Book Boyz of Farnborough, helpful staff also at the Royal Engineers Museum, Brompton Barracks Chatham and Sandra Sparks who looked after us whilst we stayed at the Officer's Terrace, Chatham Dockyard. Thanks also to Victor Tucker of Thurrock Council Libraries and Cultural Services and John Ormston of Grays who took the time and trouble to write to me at length about present day Grays. My thanks to Bruce Castle Museum staff Tottenham and staff at Greenwich Maritime Museum and Greenwich libraries. Christine Ball, Hunter Archaeological Society Sheffield, Blackwell's Bookshop Fulwood Road Sheffield and Margaret Robinson of the Crookes Local History Group. Officers from the SSAFA and WRVS organisations offered valuable suggestions as did Anthony P. Munford, former Rotherham archivist and local studies librarian, and P.C. Sue Woods, South Yorkshire Police Press Liaison Officer. Sir Reresby Sitwell for additional information about the Renishaw Estate in Rotherham, Desmond Groves, F.B.I.P.P.,F.R.P.S., and also thanks to Lady Evelyn Barbirolli who both gave permission to print the photograph of Sir John Barbirolli, and Stuart Robinson of the Halle Orchestra Concerts Society.

In addition to professional contacts I also warmly acknowledge the invaluable help and support of personal friends, Doreen Cork (Plumstead) Yvonne Flora (Canada) Maureen and John Rumble (Australia) Rosie and John Grant (Sheffield) Jill Robson and Kate Napier (Sheffield) and Rotherham friends Elaine, Pam, Pippa and Alison and Barry, and in Selby John is in my thoughts together with fond memories of his partner Sybil Pentith.

My thanks and warmest wishes also to the hundreds of wonderful students who have given me such pleasure and taxing moments! – and importantly my thanks forever to Ellen Kelly, Betty Kerr, Marie Cakebread and Molly-Ann Smith who all believed in me. Finally I have to thank my amazingly wise, caring, patient and talented daughter who read each chapter as it was produced and gave me the benefit of her advice and perspective.

BIRKENHEAD

Birkenhead began on a headland jutting out from the Wirral and east of the River Mersey. The name, believed to be of Norse origin, is derived from birch-heafod (headland of birches).

Birkenhead is not mentioned in the Domesday Book, but nearby places such as Upton, Noctorum and Wallasey are so it might be assumed that Birkenhead was a very small settlement.

Recorded history of Birkenhead begins around 1150 with the founding of a Benedictine Priory. The Blackfriar monks, a charitable order, provided lodgings and kept a boat to ferry travellers across the Mersey.

After the founding of Liverpool in 1207 and the granting of a charter by King John, numbers on the ferryboat increased and proved to be a heavy burden on the resources of the monks who, in bad weather, also provided meals and lodgings for travellers free of charge.

It was in King John's interest to cultivate the people of Birkenhead and Liverpool since he and successive monarchs, realized the strategic importance of the location. It meant easier transport of troops in order to quell the troublesome Irish and Welsh Princes.

A significant historical development was that King John offered settlers to Birkenhead and Liverpool special privileges in the charter. They had to pay a shilling per annum but were absolved from various other agricultural services to the king.

They had the right to form guilds and to be trade members. These guild merchants controlled trade in the port and no foreign ships could discharge cargo without permission. The town burgesses appointed officials and a mayor who issued trading licences and lists of customs duties and fees for mooring and warehousing. Bailiffs collected fees or made arrests if necessary.

The Priory ferry continued to transport farmers, animals and goods to Liverpool on market days and eventually the monks were allowed to build lodging houses and charge for food. The monks themselves had a flour mill in Liverpool.

The Priory had a mostly peaceful existence until King Henry VIII ordered the suppression of the monasteries. The Priory was then closed and the land and ferry rights were passed through many different hands.

During the Civil War in the seventeenth century the old Priory was used to garrison troops. The Cavaliers surrendered the Main Hall to the Roundheads and it was then demolished. Only St Mary's Church remains. The stones were re-cycled to construct other buildings. The remaining monks needed help to re-build and the local population increased. However, it wasn't until the 1700s that Birkenhead people began to build individual farms and cottages in the Priory area.

Trade and shipping continued to develop for about five hundred years following King John's charter. No alterations were made to the docksides or to the improvement of navigational aids. This meant that continually shifting sandbanks on both sides of the river made the old docks unsafe, but shipping's problems meant escalating work for the town of Birkenhead.

In 1648 Liverpool is known to have been trading with the Americas and the West Indies. Trade in tobacco, sugar and slaves was lucrative business. The transport of coals and cotton from the Midlands had a great effect on Birkenhead where ships stopped off for repairs.

In 1801 the first British Census recorded Birkenhead's population a 110 and Liverpool's as 77,708. Birkenhead was still a small hamlet with just eight houses and the former prior's residence. There were a few farms on the outskirts.

By 1815 things had taken a very dramatic leap forward. There was then a steamboat ferry from Birkenhead to Liverpool and a hotel. Liverpool merchants now had an incentive to live in rural surroundings and commute across the river to their businesses. They built new villas in the surrounding countryside with excellent views of the river. By 1821 the population had doubled to about 200.

Three years later William Laird from Greenock in Scotland came to Birkenhead. He and his son John were to become a major force in shaping the future of the town. They formed the ironworks and shipbuilding businesses later known as Cammell Laird.

Trade and passenger shipping increased rapidly and by 1847 new docks were built at Birkenhead to ease the flow of shipping on the Mersey. It remained dangerous because the shifting sandbanks forced some of the shipping channels to narrow. Although written proof is hard to find, it was known that some unscrupulous people on the North Wirral shore were not averse to wrecking and looting if the opportunity arose.

They are purported to have used false navigational lights to lure ships onto the rocks.

The state of the docks on both sides of the river gave great cause for concern and in 1857 an Act of Parliament removed control of the docks by Liverpool Council and the independent Mersey Docks and Harbour Board was created. Improvements to the docks followed as safety was paramount. Individual owners who had seized and fenced off docking for themselves were made to adhere to more strict regulations. By this time Birkenhead had a population of 24,000 and industry and the docks were thriving.

Birkenhead was eventually linked to its North and Western coasts by a network of rail lines and to Liverpool by the rail tunnel. Birkenhead became a major part of the trade on the Mersey and developed its own trade in importing and exporting goods from the Midlands, cattle from Ireland and goods with the Eastern Tropics.

So what began as a hamlet of monks and farmers in time became a town of engineers and capitalists who developed the docks, marine engineering, flour milling, soap factories, detergents and pharmaceuticals. Many extra labourers were employed in the building of the first community housing project known as the Dock Cottages which contained three hundred and fifty dwellings.

The town's population grew rapidly and included workers for the railway companies, shipping firms, warehousemen, casual labourers, builders, landscape gardeners, shopkeepers and hoteliers in the town. Not all were manual labourers since the town also needed clerks, accountants, lawyers and policemen. The arrival and growth of families meant the establishment of schools, medical services, a cemetery, churches and in due course a library and leisure facilities.

Birkenhead Park was designed in 1847 by Joseph Paxton and involved vast amounts of landscaping, the creation of artificial lakes, cricket and football pitches and driveways. Such was its success that many of its features were copied in New York's Central Park following the visit of an American to the park in 1850. It is comforting to know that a hundred and twenty seven years later, in 1977, the park was nominated a Conservation area and a Grade 1 listed landscape by 1995. This means it will be enjoyed by generations to come.

In the late nineteenth century the design of Hamilton Square, resembling Edinburgh New Town was created by James Gillespie Graham. The gardens in the centre were for the private residents use, as were the Edinburgh and London Squares, the residents having their own keys for the iron gates. By 1903 the general public have been able to enjoy these beautiful gardens.

Late in the late nineteenth century remained precarious for the dock workers. Whether trade was good or bad, the problem of ocean going shipping could be irregular. Fog, storms and contrary winds could easily delay the passage of ships through Liverpool Bay. The docker would queue up at the quayside hoping to be picked for work. He was sometimes unlucky. Days of dispirited waiting could be followed by exhausting periods of work. Life could often be a hand to mouth existence for families. The time between work would be spent mostly in the taverns nearby.

Shipyard workers, often craftsmen, also had an unpredictable life. If world trade was booming the yards were too. When world trade slackened so too did the work and the men were laid off. Depression in trade would bring dreadful suffering and would repeat itself again.

In spite of Laird's building the ALABAMA – the infamous raider for the Confederates in the American Civil War and over 150,000 tons of war shipping for the First World War, only one vessel was under construction in 1931 and hundreds of men were out of work.

Ironically it took another world war to create work again and between 1939 – 1945 Laird's built one hundred and six fighting ships, an average of one every twenty days.

Many extra shipyard workers were needed and skilled engineers like my father were employed from all parts of the country. My parents moved from Sheffield.

My father's experience of working with men on the ill-fated submarine 'Thetis' was to shape much of his life and consequently, my life as well.

In June 1939 His Majesty's submarine THETIS was lost in Liverpool Bay during sea trials from Cammell Laird. Ninety nine men lost their lives unnecessarily, and four men escaped, two naval officers, a navy rating and a chargehand fitter from the ship yard. At the time it was the worst submarine disaster in British history.

The main cause of the disaster would appear to have been a half inch plug of black, bitumastic paint, inadvertently left obscuring the indicator mechanism on the inner door of the number five torpedo tube. The mechanism which was wrongly obscured was a small bore valve attached to the inner torpedo tube door which when opened would reveal the presence or otherwise of water within the tube. This had gone unchecked. Without going into too much technical detail, a decision was made to open the inner torpedo tube whilst the vessel was in Liverpool Bay awaiting the trial dive. What was not known to those on THETIS was that the Outer torpedo tube door on number five tube was also open. The sea came into the submarine with terrible force and those aboard sought refuge behind a watertight bulkhead between the torpedo space and the next compartment of the submarine. The fastenings to secure this door became entangled with their own housings, preventing it from shutting securely, so the sea came further into the boat before the watertight door to the next compartment could be secured. THETIS was dragged down into a position from which she was unable to right herself.

The appalling delays which followed were a gross series of 'unfortunate incidents and misunderstandings' revealing incompetency, a lack of urgency and a lack of will. The Navy way of doing things revealed also many examples of malpractice, cover ups and, because of the Official Secrets Act, a lack of public information and a secreting away of relevant documents for at least thirty years afterwards.

There was a feeling amongst the families waiting at the gates of Cammell Laird for news that 'they' could have got the men out. Several offers were made to do just that, and they were rejected. The submarine, flying a white ensign as it moved into the bay, was Navy responsibility.

It seems futile now to try to apportion blame to one person. Was it the painter/enameller's fault which caused the loss of submarine and the men? Could it be the fault of the navy overseer who neglected to check things properly? Did the rapid construction in the shipyard mean that several things went unchecked or passed as all right if not quite perfect?

From the telegraph boy at Gosport (the Navy submarine headquarters) who was fixing a puncture on his bicycle and not realizing that he had an urgent message to deliver, to the delay in sending naval rescuers to the scene, there were incredible delays.

People in Birkenhead and Liverpool had the feeling that the rescue of a whole, undamaged submarine, meant more to the Navy than did the lives of the men. Official reports and books by maritime historians have attempted to explain the THETIS story in much greater detail than is appropriate here.

The effect of losing THETIS in the first place and the subsequent way the grieving families were treated was in itself devastating. THETIS was eventually salvaged and the bodies of the drowned men were retrieved. The ship was quickly re-fitted and renamed (HMS THUNDERBOLT) and was despatched to war in the Mediterranean where four years and a day later she was sunk by the enemy with all hands lost.

The THETIS families struggled for compensation and an explanation. Financial support was very slow in coming and often derisory. In fact the naval rating who escaped the submarine in Liverpool Bay went to collect back pay from the Navy and was told they couldn't give him anything without his pay book. It was at the bottom of the sea! For many months he was forced to live on fresh air and the support of his friends.

Experiencing this whole sorry saga following on from the years of hardship and the Depression in the Sheffield steelworks, my father, then a young man trying to do his best, became angry and bitter. He became again a militant trade unionist and joined the communist party, thinking that he could contribute to making things better for working men and their families, and trying to ensure better safety conditions.

As a child I didn't understand how much this coloured everything my father did. He had always believed that if you were going to do a job it must be done properly the first time. Then you only had to do it once. He was a perfectionist at work and expected everyone else to be the same. This expectation and his disappointment to discover that life was not quite like that for everyone meant that he was very demanding, intolerant, and sometimes downright angry. This found its way into the home as well, and we grew up fearing him.

I arrived into the world on 10th June 1942 (a week before Paul McCartney!)

It had been a grim time for everyone since 1939.

Hitler's bombers had been relentless in bombarding Liverpool and Birkenhead. They had been aiming for the shipyards and the docks, but many homes were destroyed too. I discovered from my Father that the Home Guard at one stage crept out at night and laid some lights further away into the countryside, so attempting to lure bombers in the other direction.

Food shortages, financial restraint and health worries affected people everywhere, but those who lived in the target areas of shipbuilding, munitions, engineering and railways were most vulnerable and risked being bombed on a regular basis.

When my Father finished his shift at Cammell Laird's he would then be on Air Raid duties dealing with incendiary bombs which rained down on people's homes. Where homes were too badly damaged, the occupants had to be moved to 'safety' elsewhere. That is, if they were lucky enough to be alive. A number of Well Lane (Tranmere) residents were not so fortunate and there was a large area of devastation and horrific injuries with people losing limbs and some their lives.

My Mother lived in constant fear for her own and my Father's safety and feared she might have to give birth in an air raid shelter. She worried too about relatives living in Sheffield who had their own bombing blitz to contend with.

Birkenhead houses following an air raid, 1941

My Mother's fears for my Father's safety would be with her throughout the war years, later as an army wife, and right up to 1957 and the Suez crisis in the Middle East.

There must have been times when my parents wished they had stayed in Sheffield near to relatives and friends.

Following the death of their first baby from meningitis in 1939, my parents had their own personal trauma to deal with. It seems ironic to suggest that the move to Birkenhead might have been seen as a new start. How could anyone at that time think of new starts? I think it was a case of existing as best they could and trying to be a comfort to each other. They couldn't reasonably return home to Sheffield because Grandfather had re-married, my maternal Grandmother having died years earlier. There was a step-mother and her small daughter now occupying the family home.

I was born into much uncertainty, anxiety, noise and sometimes sheer panic. My Mother predicted that my life would always be like that and she was right. Apparently even as a small baby, I was startled and shivered in my cot or pram at the slightest noise. Sixty years on I cannot tolerate excessive noise, though what I think of excessive doesn't seem to bother my daughter in the same way. Background noise when I am trying to concentrate is worse. Traffic, blaring car radios, music in restaurants, even in the bank! People who shout, screaming children, sports spectators, the list goes on. Noise in the night when I am sleeping always wakes me and pigeons and seagulls really irritate me. Strange then that I should become a musician making my own noise. I suppose the difference is that when you are making your own noise it is under your control and if it becomes painful, you can stop!

I was too young to really remember the war years except for one or two isolated recollections. I remember the day my baby brother was born (in 1944) because I had apparently gone missing as my mother was in labour, and dozens of neighbours had been enlisted to help find me. What I remember about it is that people were 'chasing' me, and I was a scared two year old. I also remember VE Day. There was a party on the street outside our house. Everyone had pooled resources and their ingenuity to provide the children with party food. People were singing and talking loudly and laughing. I had been left in the care of older children and other mums. My Mum must have been looking after my brother, then just a year old. I think I remember it not for the joyous occasion it was, but because I had been left. Insecurity set in at a very early age. Once the merry-making was over life had to return as quickly as possible to a work orientated routine.

V.E. Day party, Tranmere Road, Birkenhead

After the war fewer ships needed to be built so the shipworkers had to find other work. The badly damaged docks had to be repaired so that food and trade imports and exports could move again. Trade had to be swiftly re-established. Since London docks had also been badly damaged and closed for a time, Liverpool and Birkenhead became of national importance as a distributing port for the whole country.

In time as shipping resumed a more stable existence, the hundreds of extra workers needed during the crisis were not needed in the same capacity. Many lost their jobs and the men who remained – dockers and labourers became very disgruntled with their low pay, long working hours and poor working conditions. It wasn't just the docks that needed re-building, it was people's lives too. Damaged homes were still in need of attention and families had to be fed.

The union and militant workers incited strikes and there were angry riots aimed at stating their case for better working conditions. Political meetings would mean that my father would disappear for hours at a time. My mother was not included in his activities nor was she expected to be. In fact heavily lectured most of the time, she was to believe everything my father said and kept her mouth shut. The only newspapers in the house were of a socialist worker nature as were the books on the bookshelf. I never saw frivolous reading matter at home. Sidney and Beatrice Webb were there along with 'Studies in Soviet Russia' and 'Democracy and its rivals.' We also had excellent dictionaries and a brilliant world atlas which provided me with many hours of pleasure, as a child.

My mother did manage to borrow women's magazines which were passed from neighbour to neighbour. The recipes and knitting patterns were often copied by hand. Eventually my mother found the public library and enjoyed choosing her own books to read during the many hours she spent alone. I know she had to be careful about which books she could safely take home, as I did much later. My father had very decided views about what constituted frivolous reading, and I know now that he was wrong to be so controlling and censorious.

My mother's childhood piano had survived and was her most treasured possession. In another time, another era, she might have been allowed to develop her skills as a pianist. She loved it and her music gave her a huge amount of release and pleasure. My father could have been a singer. He had a fine tenor voice resembling Richard Tauber's. My parents brief, happier domestic moments were spent making music together. They loved the songs of Ivor Novello and songs from the cinema – Broadway Melody, Jeanette Macdonald and Nelson Eddy, Fred Astaire etc., 'Little Grey Home in the West', 'Bless This House' and 'Deep Purple' were other favourites and if my father was a little the worse for drink he would give an ear-splitting rendition of 'The Holy City'.

A year after the war had ended life was returning to a kind of calm. There were still food shortages and rationing. Work in and around the docks was unpredictable, but at least the bombing and threat of war was at an end.

Clothing was scarce too and it was very much a case of make do and mend. Many mothers would sit and patiently unpick worn or passed on wool jumpers, rolling the wool into new balls and then re-knitting the wool into something which might fit a smaller child. If there wasn't enough good wool to save, then small amounts would be used to make socks, mittens or hats.

My mother once carefully unpicked ever stitch of my dead grandfather's best Sunday suit. She then made a paper pattern from brown wrapping paper and made herself a new skirt and jacket which became her best suit, used mostly for funerals, weddings and the like.

Childcare clinics which were run on very regimented and matronly lines were a godsend to mothers. They were given tins of National Dried milk for their babies, and instructed on how much to feed. Bottles of concentrated orange juice became available. Nurses regularly weighed and measured children and mothers were reprimanded if babies hadn't gained weight according to the 'chart'.

In spite of a wide inoculation programme in an attempt to raise more healthy children, there was an outbreak of Diphtheria. Both my baby brother and I contracted the disease and I almost died. My brother was not so ill but was deemed to be a carrier of the illness, so we both spent time in the isolation hospital.

My parents must have been out of their minds with worry, especially as they had lost their first baby from meningitis.

My father who until then had taken little notice of us sat beside my bed in the hospital peeling grapes, then attempting to squeeze minute pieces of fruit through my lips, encouraging me to swallow.

We eventually recovered and I began school in a class of over forty children.

My only recollection of my first school was during the big freeze of 1947. The third pint bottles of milk intended to be drunk by us every day were frozen solid, the tops forced off by the iced milk. We were all told to place our bottles on the heating pipes which ran along the bottom of the classroom walls and wait for them to defrost sufficiently for us to drink the milk. Knowing what we now know about bacteria it is a miracle we were not all extremely ill.

My father had been in a reserved occupation during the war and had been excluded from military service. As soon as it was possible for him to enlist as a regular solider he did just that. My mother had no say in the matter and we were to set off on the first of many moves.

JULY 2001

The start of the Magical Mystery Tour, revisiting and re-appraising.

My daughter, Rebecca, then thirty one years of age, together with Maria her stalwart, knowledgeable and interested young friend joined me on the first leg of my quest.

We were all convinced that this would be the longest chapter of my book and possibly the most interesting because it was my birthplace and because of the years involved.

The aim was to visit and photograph all the relevant places. Then we would visit local archives, libraries and museums hoping to add to the already substantial body of information we had amassed. I was to attempt contact with local community groups including appeals in the newspapers and local radio. I had hoped to find anyone who may still be alive from that time and who may have known my parents.

Although we set off with a clear plan and itinerary, there were inevitably a number of interesting diversions.

The outward journey from Edinburgh via Wigan was uneventful and took five and a half hours. By the time we found a taxi at Liverpool Lime Street and made the short journey to our rooms at the University, we had been travelling for more than six hours and were in desperate need of a cup of tea. Our three rooms were in a self-catering student flat which reminded me of how awful it had been leaving my daughter some years earlier at her university accommodation. I told myself that all things are relative, and pondered the fact that when I was born young people from our kind of background would not have been going to university at all.

I didn't ponder for too long. The rooms were clean and convenient, if rather basic. One room had its own sink, another sported a cover on the bed duvet. I drew the short straw and had neither.

Once refreshed we set off to find the ferry terminal, for use on our second day, in Birkenhead, and to seek out the Saveaway travel tickets and Museum Pass.

The walk downhill to the city centre was pleasant, and by now we were hungry. We stoked ourselves up with fish and chips at Wally Wong's Fish Emporium. Delicious!

The Saveaway tickets, giving us off peak travel on all buses, trains and ferries, was astonishing value. The Museums Pass for £3.00 was also amazing value allowing admission to eight museums and galleries for twelve months.

The Museums and galleries are brim full with interesting things to see and do and it would be possible to spend several days in each one. It is very impressive to see how Liverpool is attempting to preserve evidence of its past history and also appealing to all sections of the community, with programmes designed particularly for schoolchildren, older students and mature people.

The Maritime Museum at Albert Dock is housed on four floors of a former warehouse. The approach road via cobbled walkways looks pretty but is only comfortable if you wear flat shoes! Having said that, the Museum itself is phenomenal and worthy of several more visits. The history of the River Mersey, its shipping and other trades such as emigration, transatlantic slavery, merchant shipping and the river itself are all fully explored and explained, though some of the wall notes are rather small to read if you happen to be short sighted. Much space is allocated to the Mauretania and Lusitania liners, and of interest to me were the sad effects rescued from the sunken 'THETIS'.

Unfortunately we missed a whole floor of the Maritime Museum as it was near to closing time and it was vital that I visit the shop to seek local history books and information. The Museums Department has produced a fine series of in depth pamphlets about the history of the docks on both sides of the Mersey and there was a vast array of naval books and memorabilia.

The Museum has received funding from the Heritage Lottery Fund which has enabled archivists and others to mount a project named 'Generations Apart'. This is designed to bring young and older people together to explore the history and experience of people living and working on Merseyside. Using the Museum exhibits, archives, photographs, visual and sound recordings the Museum has provided reminiscence boxes for community use and for anyone interested in local history.

Liverpool has certainly learned how to re-generate itself from the ashes of wartime and depression. Rich in nautical and commercial history, it has utilized every possible historic building to good effect. H.M. Customs & Excise Museum, The Museum of Liverpool Life, a Conservation Museum, a Planetarium, even the football teams have their own tours and Museums. Architecturally there are some fine neo-classical buildings such as St George's Hall which has a spectacular Minton tiled floor and glittering chandeliers.

The two great cathedrals are rewarding and often have a summer series of concerts. We were fortunate to hear the superb Alessandro Bianchi give a splendid organ recital at the Roman Catholic Cathedral. Of interest to musicians is the Philharmonic Hall, home to the Royal Liverpool Philharmonic Orchestra. The Hall was originally opened in 1849 but later destroyed by fire. It was rebuilt on Hope Street just before the Second World War and miraculously the Hall has survived, unscathed by the bombings.

Of course Liverpool, like most cities, has its seedy corners but to the tourist visitors as we were, it seemed a pleasant, interesting and friendly place to visit. We saw little graffiti on public buildings and there were fewer street beggars than in Edinburgh. However I was duped out of a pound by a bogus Big Issue seller, on Albert Dock!

In general the shop assistants, bus drivers and populace at large were keen to help visitors and were good natured.

I was continually intrigued by the Liverpool accent. I guess if we hadn't ever moved that I would sound like that too.

The only down side was that we needed more time to understand the bus system. The maps and guidance on bus stops is limited and difficult to read, and the bus stations confusing. Still, the taxis were incredibly cheap and plentiful.

My father would not have approved of us travelling around in taxis.

No visit to Liverpool could be complete unless one considers the impact made on the city and the history of popular music, by the Beatles. Pop music was changed forever during the 1960's and many of the innovative groups and singers emerged from Liverpool, spurred on by the huge success of what came to be known as The Fab Four. John, Paul, Ringo and George have now become cult idols and in Liverpool a whole tourist industry has grown out of their popularity. People want to see the site of the Cavern Club and other places associated with their lives. The National Trust has now preserved Paul McCartney's childhood home as a 50's house and the 'Magical Mystery Tour' bus will take visitors to all the places associated with their songs. Strawberry Fields, Penny Lane, the church of 'Eleanor Rigby' and many more. It is a great delight to listen to the chap who drives the bus. He is a real enthusiast and loves telling people about the Beatles when he isn't singing along with the songs. Most people can't help joining in. It is a thoroughly happy experience and no doubt a great money spinner.

We heard during our stay, that Liverpool Airport is to be re-named John Lennon Airport.

On our second day we took the ferry across the Mersey, to Birkenhead. In spite of Gerry Marsden's sentimental song about the river, I have to say that I don't have any sea legs at all and when my feet leave terra firma the motion of the boat, however slight, reminds me that I can't swim. I am not a happy sailor and was greatly relieved to reach the other side.

My daughter whimsically suggested that had I been born on the other side of the river, I might have been the fifth Beatle.

The ferry boat has pictures in the saloons and the history of the ferry trade from earliest times and on high tourist days they play 'that' song.

We arrived at Woodside Terminal and found the yellow electric bus which does a circular trip up to the town centre and back again to the ferry. The driver, a gum-chewing lady with big hair and huge sun glasses, resembled Roy Orbison. She was unsmiling and spoke in a monotone Scouse accent. She managed to set us down at the best place for the start of our search.

Time was limited and we had to make the most of the day. It rained and rained and rained.

Although I was anxious to find my first 'home' and its environs, we had to be sensible and plan to be economical getting from one place to another. So our journey began on a logistical basis.

I had an appointment with a community social worker, at Age Concern. She was able to tell me about life in Birkenhead as it now affects elderly people. Unsurprisingly, the problems are universal. The local authority does not now have any residential care homes. People are either helped to stay in their own homes, or are placed in private care homes with government support if they have a low income. It was encouraging however to note that the extent of home care available is greater than my mother received in Sheffield. Even so, when the authorities fall short on their ability to provide, it seems that Age Concern in Birkenhead are often filling in the gaps and appear to be providing a wonderful service to the elderly population there.

There are day care facilities for those with no family carers, lunch clubs and a Home Support Service to offer respite to home carers if needed. Age Concern also offer a regular bathing service for those who cannot tend to their own needs and a telephone link service. This means that a trained worker will ring the 'client' at the same time each day, or weekly if they prefer. It is meant to be a friendly chat for people who have no other, or few contacts, and also to assess whether there are any problems. If the 'client' doesn't answer the telephone a designated contact in the locality will call round to see if all is well.

Active elderly are also offered many opportunities to get out and meet people, and to enrich their lives. There is a travel club, and day trips, or lengthier holidays can be arranged. There are a number of classes in art, safe exercise to music, tap and line dancing, cooking for one, a music hall group and aromatherapy.

Help with minor repairs and household maintenance for people on low incomes can be arranged and twice a month Age Concern organize a Senior Citizen's Forum, where any matters can be discussed.

With transport available to most activities, no elderly person in Birkenhead should feel isolated or lonely, but of course the person involved must ask for help in the first instance.

I felt happy and re-assured that if my parents had remained in Birkenhead they would have been all right.

Ten years ago Birkenhead was a rather neglected place. However, the evidence of a nationwide change in attitudes towards re-generation and funding of inner towns and cities is there to see.

Birkenhead boasts one of the largest undercover markets in the country and two quite different shopping centres adjacent to each other and close to the award winning bus station. There are thriving cinemas, restaurant galore, interesting shops and a wealth of culture and history.

The partnership between a wide range of businesses and other organisations has produced The Hamilton Quarter Project, an £82 million venture.

The once elegant buildings have been cleaned and restored, some being Grade I listed buildings. New homes have been created and a traffic scheme has been implemented to protect the buildings and limit the amount of pollution in the Square. Closed circuit television cameras have been introduced which, together with the Police 'Townsafe' scheme, makes Birkenhead a safer place for everyone.

The Hamilton Arts Quarter now hosts an International Jazz and Guitar Festival and a regular series of other music events. It also houses galleries and exhibitions, new shops and eating places.

We were in Hamilton Square when it began to rain heavily. We were on the wrong side of the road for the Tranmere bus, and short of time, so we hailed a passing taxi.

'56, Church Road,' we instructed the driver, excited at last to be going to find my birthplace, which my now very aged father remembered as a flat.

Father was wrong! The house numbers stopped at 54, when we found ourselves in a car park next to St Catherine's Church, on the other side of which was St. Catherine's Hospital. We later discovered at the reference library that number 56 had been the former Birkenhead Institution (or workhouse). Puzzled but undaunted I realized that I would have to do a bit more research into that. In fact it transpired that the hospital had taken over the workhouse during the war years and it had become a maternity unit, later demolished. Its present state is a car park.

We did find the little terraced house on Parkside Road where I first lived. It was a sweet little house in a row of very clean and tidy houses, now owned not rented from a landlord as in my parents time. Most of the houses had shiny red-painted brickwork. It seemed to be the trend, although I noted that the front steps were not painted white as used to be the fashion.

Sadly, I couldn't find any original occupants from the 1940's. I guess most of them will have died. Most of the present residents are not from the original wartime families. They now include young business people or couples who have jobs across the River Mersey. They either take the ferry to work, or drive through the tunnel. They cannot yet afford the smart expensive apartments in Liverpool, but are aspiring. Some of them will aspire to move further on into the Wirral countryside as the early merchants did.

The terraced houses were built for the ship and dock workers and often more than one family would live in the same house. They were built without bathrooms, and had outside toilets.

Now the houses have indoor facilities, new windows and doors and most have new tiled roofing instead of slates. Some have built on bay windows and porches and extensions at the back of the houses. The fronts still open onto the road.

Tranmere has a new Primary School and the old isolation hospital is now the site of the Europa Pools and Leisure complex. Birkenhead Park, and two smaller parks are still there and well cared for and appreciated. The many pubs are homely and friendly. However, I suspect that the young trendy owners of the little houses do not, on the whole, frequent the local pubs, but seek a higher class of entertainment in Liverpool, or further afield.

Birkenhead seems to be a clean neat town with a seemingly prosperous future, although the residents in the slightly out of town housing areas are on the whole a transient, upwardly mobile population. The old established close-knit communities brought together before and during the war years, and the old traditions and occupations have disappeared.

Life is moving on at a faster pace and jobs are no longer for life.

Birkenhead is an evolving town.

PORTLAND

The leaving of Liverpool and Birkenhead didn't grieve me because I was too young to realize what was happening and I was still recovering from Diphtheria. I imagine that my parents were relieved to be escaping the memories of the war years as well as the worry about mine and my brother's illness. The promise of fresh air and living by the sea was welcomed at first. Once again though, my mother's life was thrown into turmoil. The news of the Japanese bombing Pearl Harbour had incensed my father and he decided to enlist as a regular soldier in the Royal Engineers as soon as his reserved occupation in ship building came to an end.

Shipbuilding work declined towards the end of the war and conditions for the Liverpool men working at Cammell Laird were precarious to say the least. My father saw the enlistment in the army as a way of self development and personal fulfilment. It was also a way of providing a roof for us. Unfortunately, my mother saw it as a life of yet more uncertainty.

Having worked since the age of fourteen and lacking a grammar school education, my father expected the army to educate him. He was a more than willing recruit, determined to excel at everything he was allowed to do. He had been the youngest of eight children from a poor working class background. His mother was the daughter of eastern European immigrants who must have fled the various pogroms of the time.

Although my grandmother lacked formal education she certainly recognized its value. Only one child could be sent to Firth Park Grammar School (Sheffield) so Frank, the seventh sibling and maths expert, so we were told, was the chosen one. There was naturally some resentment since most of the other siblings had to go without things in order for Frank to have all the appropriate books and equipment.

My grandmother worked in domestic service. When she wasn't being a skivvy for wealthy people, she laundered, cooked and cared for the sick and needy in her own community.

My father's experience of a higher culture existed in his being allowed to join an award winning choir. Great efforts were made for him to have a clean shirt and boots for the journeys to Blackpool Music Festival.

Strict though my grandmother was, she tried to be fair and her family respected her for it. While under 'her' roof and eating at 'her' table, they would abide by her rules. There was a definite pecking order in all matters. If my grandfather, a furnaceman, was home and not in the betting shop or the pub at mealtimes, he was always served first. He received the largest portion. Then came the eldest son, then the next and so on, until the eighth, my father. His was the smallest portion, served last after which he often had the job of clearing up after the others.

He used to remind me that he also had the last hand me down clothes and belongings. However, when he found himself running errands for his parents and siblings he quickly learned how to manipulate things to his advantage, especially when girl friends appeared on the scene and they wanted him out of the way.

My grandfather, who was a law unto himself, needed no encouragement to stay out of the house. Nevertheless he too was given his orders when first Lily, then Flora, Lily number two, Rose and Ada were by turns invited to tea. The best cloth was laundered and starched and home baked bread or scones were produced. No efforts were spared in order to convince the girl friends that they were being welcomed into a respectable home where good manners and hospitality were the norm. It was a disciplined but caring home.

The house was a two up and two down worker's terraced house with a shared lavvy in the yard outside. Until one or other of the brothers left home to marry, the boys shared beds or bed space. It wasn't the only thing they shared. The eldest son Jack (John) was a genius with the horses and he eventually lived a prosperous life in Brighton on the proceeds of his winnings on the Derby. Some of the brothers became his 'runners' in their spare time and the grammar educated Frank became an accountant serving the turf. I never actually knew what that meant until I was in my late teens.

My grandmother died in 1932 following a stroke. She was fifty two. My father was eighteen. To this day my father will not talk about her, except to say that she worked herself to death and he was glad that she had not had to experience the Second World War.

My father began to accompany his father to union and political meetings, or spent his spare time swimming, walking the Derbyshire hills and boxing for money in amateur fights.

With this background it is easy to understand how my father became such a diligent solider. He already knew how to live by his wits and his fists and he learned early about social issues, political ideologies and how to argue a point. His socialist beliefs and his willingness to join the working class struggle marked him out as an industrial agitator.

I find it difficult to understand why he didn't stay in Liverpool and fight the worker's cause. Perhaps he thought it was futile or maybe he was thinking about us and what a precarious living it might be.

The only thing my mother knew about Portland was that it was near the sea. She was unprepared for the terrain and the harsh weather. It was with a great leap of faith that she accompanied my father, hoping for a better life for us all.

Our first army home, or married quarters, was at The Verne. It was a simple wooden bungalow, little more than a temporary pre-fab type of building.

The Isle of Portland is not really an island. It is four and a half miles long and a mile and three quarters wide, a limestone peninsula adjoining Chesil Beach, a slender shingle arc which over thousands of years has receded across Lyme Bay. The Isle is in two distinct parts. The escarpment facing Weymouth is a huge slope of ancient rock, curving in dramatic concave and convex land shapes around Portland's summit, Verne Hill, site of our house.

Over the hill the remainder of the island descends gently southward towards the extremity of Portland Bill. Tophill is the surface of the geographical strata containing the famous Portland Stone

Church Ope Cove

Army house, The Verne, Portland

beds. The Portland beds date from around one hundred and forty million years ago and are of marine origin, containing many fossils from a subtropical sea. This stone has for centuries provided some of the world's best building materials.

The first inhabitants of Portland lived there about fourteen thousand years ago. Stone tools and animal remains from that period have been found at the Verne and at the Bill. Bronze Age tools and pottery have also been found. Iron Age occupation of the Verne as a hill fort has been confirmed by many finds including sling stones, spindle whorls, a mirror, a bronze collar, ingots and pottery. Complete examples of these can be found in the Portland Museum at Wakeham and at the County Museum in Dorchester.

The Romans extensively occupied Portland between the first and fourth centuries A.D. Pottery and coffins as well as floors of buildings and Roman wells have provided much information about Portland's inhabitants. Later dwellers also left much in the way of evidence of their existence, including Rufus Castle (named for William the Conqueror's son) at Church Ope Cove.

Portland Castle was built by Henry VIII as an impressive tudor fortress, part of a chain of defensive fortresses along the south coast, to deter invaders, notably the French. The Castle's importance was understood by several later monarchs and there was much activity there during the Civil War.

There are buildings on Portland which still retain features of the Elizabethan and Jacobean periods, particularly in Reforne and Weston. The ancient mediaeval field systems at the Bill are also of considerable interest.

Portland's landscape is unique in being almost devoid of trees and bearing the scars of extensive quarrying, but the sense of isolation is its very beauty and strength. Tiny coves along Portland's coast, flanked by cliffs, once provided cover for smugglers and looters who dared the rough seas to pilfer anything of value from the many ships which foundered there. Piracy there has been well documented.

Thomas Hardy used Portland as the location for his novel 'The Well Beloved', calling it the Isle of Slingers, the name derived from the islanders skill of slinging stones at strangers to keep them away.

In our own time Portland and Church Ope Cove in particular, was the setting for high drama when it was revealed that Harry Houghton, a former naval attache's clerk in Warsaw, later employed at the Underwater Detection Establishment in Portland, had assisted Russian spies to enter Britain. Church Ope Cove was chosen as a suitable place to land the spies because it meant the boat would not have to enter Portland's breakwater. The Cove was not visible from the Coastguard lookout or the Portland Bill lighthouse. With a calm sea and the right wind, a boat could land on the pebbly shore, which was exposed at most states of the tide.

Harry Houghton, who was living in a caravan further along the coast, knew the place well. He knew the man-made steps down the cliff to the beach would be a good place to bring the alien spies. He parked his car at the top of the cliffs and placed two red leading lights to guide the boat in. There were a number of beach huts in the vicinity, but from late Autumn until early Spring there was rarely anyone around after dark. Three alternative nights were arranged for the landing, when no naval exercises were taking place. The moon and the weather had to be just right. Mission accomplished, Harry Houghton drove his passengers to Blandford Forum where they were passed on to the next person in the spy chain, to continue their clandestine activities.

When Harry Houghton had been stationed in Poland, he had a girl friend called Karytzia. Since living in England he had corresponded with her and this may have enabled agents from eastern Europe to put pressure on him. Eventually he came to supply naval information to them. He had manipulated his friend Ethel Gee, an unwitting accomplice, to help him. In time they were exposed, along with Gordon Lonsdale and

Peter and Helen Kroger, in the affair known as the Portland Spy Ring. Houghton and Gee were sentenced to fifteen years prison in 1961.

The navy dominated Portland for centuries but perhaps the greatest human story occurred in 1944, when as one of the world's largest man-made harbours, Portland was a major assembly and embarkation point for the thousands of British and American troops destined for the Normandy D-Day landings. On Weymouth Esplanade there is a memorial to the 418,000 men who embarked on D-Day. The Naval Cemetery situated on the slope below the Verne bears testament to many lives lost at sea or on land during war time or in shipping disasters.

Our arrival in Portland shortly after the war was so that my father could join the number nine regiment of the Royal Engineers. Here he learned to build Bayley bridges, and how to handle a rifle and grenades.

My brother and I thought it was great fun living in a bungalow, that is until our first misdemeanour. We found that if we climbed onto a chair we could get out of the window and jump on the grass outside the house. This we did very early one morning before our parents were awake. Unfortunately we had not thought about the return. The window was too high to reach from the other side and reluctantly we had to bang on the door to make our presence known. We were in deep trouble.

The winter at Portland was awful. The wind seemed relentless at times and biting cold. We were taken to school by soldiers who held us tight as we clambered into the trucks, and then steadied us as we alighted at the other end, clutching the rope to get us safely down the hill to school. (Nowadays there are iron rails). I remember the wind being so fierce it almost took my breath away. It was very frightening. I remember nothing about school, just the ordeal of getting there and back again.

My return to Portland was during the summer of 2001, fifty two years after we'd left. The day was blazing hot. Thanks to Dr. Beeching there is now no train service to the island. There is a very efficient bus service which tours the island. Alternatively one can pay a taxi driver £10 - £12 for the journey from Weymouth.

I headed first to Wakeham and the Portland Museum which is housed in a collection of thatched cottages, formerly the home of Marie Stopes. The adjoining cottage is the 'Avice's Cottage' used by Thomas Hardy in his book.

The museum is rich in local, naval and smuggling history. In the gardens lie the remains of a German bomb, an unexploded bomb, discovered long after the war, beneath a football pitch! When the bomb was discovered the people of the village had to be evacuated until the Bomb Disposal Squad could make it safe.

A few yards down the path to the left of the Museum I re-discovered Church Ope Cove with its winding steps down to the beach, with Rufus Castle nearby. The place was deserted and I felt strangely privileged to be enjoying it all by myself. It evoked vivid memories of the spy scandal. This was the exact spot where the red guiding lights were set for the Russian boat. I walked up the very steps the spies has taken up the cove. The atmosphere also evoked childhood memories of an age of innocence. I remembered the smells of the wild flowers and grasses, the bright hot sun on my face, and the shimmering silver sea below. I lingered on the cliff top for some time until I sensed my face was being burned by the sun. I was thrilled to see a number of different butterflies and Red Valerian growing in profusion.

The gentle walk back to the village of Wakeham was truly relaxing. The white painted cottages standing back from the road along with the more recent, but elegant stone houses, exuded an air of calm gentility.

There were no visible signs of tourism or trash. There was one amusing, neatly hand written notice in one cottage window. It read, DO NOT LET YOUR HORSE FOUL THE PATH, FIND A FIELD . . .

I loved the whole place and will most certainly return, if only to pick the brains of the curator of the Museum who seems to know every detail about Portland. I felt uplifted and glad I had made the journey. However, the reality of actually living there now is something else. In the winter the place would be as inhospitable as I remember from my childhood. For someone like me, with badly arthritic knees and dodgy blood pressure it would be very difficult unless one was prepared to be housebound for several months of the year.

I wasn't able to find our former home, though I found the site of it. All evidence of army and navy occupation has now disappeared. In its place is Portland Prison.

The island maintains an Air-Sea Rescue station and a sub-aqua training school. These days Portland is geared mostly to tourism. Visitors come to admire and study the flora and fauna along the magnificent cliff walks. They come also for the watersports and to learn about the dramatic history of the place.

Quarrying of stone and masonry was once the major source of employment for local people. Although some quarrying is still done here it is no longer the main occupation of Portland workers. The Portland Sculpture Trust has set up a study centre and visitor centre as part of the Jurassic Coast Project, to explain the geology, quarrying and working of stone. As well as receiving educational groups the Portland Sculpture Trust is now running BA electives and an MA level degree course in partnership with the University of Brighton.

Disused quarries have been re-claimed by nature and are a haven for wild flowers, rare butterflies and birds. The cliff plants differ considerably from those found inland and some of these plants are scarce and so of international importance.

Special to Portland is the Sea Lavender. Red Valerian grows everywhere among the rocks and in late Autumn it is possible to find Autumn Lady's Tresses, a delicate late summer orchid.

The joy of possibly finding such rare treasures certainly merits a further visit.

ALDERSHOT (COVE AND FARNBOROUGH)

Archaeology and history have shown that the area around Aldershot in North East Hampshire had a pre-history community and is mentioned in records of 885. The isolated hamlet seems to have been a staging post for coaches using the desolate stretch of the London to Winchester road. Small groups of pine trees, gorse and bracken will have provided good ambush cover for highwaymen such as Dick Turpin who is said to have had his cottage headquarters near Farnborough.

In 1850 Aldershot was still a small village, but within a hundred years of the end of the Crimean War Aldershot had grown into the country's chief military centre. The Crimean War had emphasized the need for Britain's soldiers to be grouped and trained during peacetime in units larger than a battalion or brigade.

Farnborough, which merges imperceptibly into Aldershot was also a village become the coming of the army, but until the building of the Royal Air Force College, later the Royal Aircraft Establishment, its main importance was that it witnessed the end of the long story of Napoleon Bonaparte.

After the defeat of Sedan in 1870 had brought the Second Empire of Napoleon's nephew, Napoleon III down in ruins, the ex-Imperial family took refuge at Chislehurst in Kent, where the fallen Emperor died in 1873. After his only son the Prince Imperial was killed six years later in the Zulu War while serving in the British army, the widowed and childless Empress Eugenie moved to Farnborough, bought and enlarged the house called Farnborough Hill (later a convent school), and lived there until she died in 1920.

In 1887 the Empress Eugenie had built a mausoleum in the French Flamboyant style, for herself, her husband and her son, whose tombs she had transferred there. To serve the Mausoleum she also built an abbey, called St Michael's, parts of which are modelled on the Abbey of Solesnes in Normandy.

The Benedictine life was established at Farnborough under Abbot Fernand Michel Cabrol, Prior of the Abbey of Solesmes, who at the funeral of the Empress Eugenie said,

'You have built this church in stone, not in order to pass on to distant generations the memory of the glories of France, but because you understand that there is something greater than man's glory, more lasting than stone, the daily sacrifice of Christian prayer. This sanctuary raised on English soil will not only speak continually of the memory of the Empress Eugenie to all who come after; it will be an eloquent witness to her faith and piety."

To most people Aldershot, Farnborough and Cove, where we were next stationed, still means 'the army', with its barracks, and married quarters, tattoos, horse shows and pageants; all inspired and watched over by the great statue of the Duke of Wellington on horseback. There are many military museums, each with its own character, from nursing to paratroopers. The stories of the various regiments are revealed with great pride. Battles are re-fought in model form and deeds of heroism recounted. Mementoes are exhibited, uniforms, flags, silverware and regalia are all displayed. Sombre reading though are the Rolls of Honour and memorials to the fallen that line the walls of the garrison churches.

Before 1914 Cove was a typical Hampshire village serving two masters, sandwiched between two large landowners and dependent on one or the other for employment and housing. Most villagers worked for the War Department or the Currie family's Minley Estate. Two World Wars caused great social upheaval and skilled workers were attracted to the burgeoning aircraft establishment and larger enlistment in the army meant that new housing was needed. The old communities and communal open land would continue to be eroded.

The day we moved from Portland to Cove was the first time I remember seeing my mother cry. We were almost marched into the house by the Quarter Master. He had a list of furniture and household items and he read from the list in a loud voice. When he had finished my mother had to sign the list thereby acknowledging receipt of goods and her responsibility for them. Nothing in the house could be painted. The army decided when and if premises were to be re-painted and the army chose the colour. There were still dense blackout curtains at the windows, left there since wartime. My mother was allowed to stitch a length of coloured braid along the hem of the curtains by way of decoration.

We had little of our own furniture, but we still had my mother's piano which was placed in the parlour, as our sitting room was known at that time.

Army house, Cove, Farnborough

We lived mostly in the kitchen and used the parlour at the weekends or when visitors came. We children were not allowed to play in that room by ourselves and in due course I had to ask permission to go in the parlour to play the piano.

No one had a television set or even a gramophone but we did have a radio. It was a 'Ferguson' wireless set!

My father used to listen to the news and the football results. We were not allowed to talk when the radio was on. Sometimes my brother and I were allowed to listen to Dick Barton, Special Agent or Journey Into Space, but we weren't allowed in the parlour. We sat on the bottom of the stairs which divided the two rooms.

I didn't like 'Journey Into Space'. It was frightening!

My little brother used to say, 'It's not real you know!'

The army houses were built in short terraces and the back gardens faced each other, with a wire fence separating them. A narrow path ran through the centre of the development. We could run from one garden to the one immediately opposite, or along the central path past all the gardens. I had a friend who lived across the path whose mother has just had a new baby. Although she was happy to show the baby off we were not allowed in the house when the baby was being fed. Breast feeding babies was done quietly and in secret in those days. We had no idea what happened. It was a mystery. To the front of our house was a large expanse of common land bounded by hawthorn and oak trees. The side path which ran behind the Tradesman's Arms public house and the small parade of shops lead to the main road and to the right of the path was St. Christopher's Church. We played for hours on the common, climbing trees, flying kites and gathering up bunches of purple clover.

To the left of the army houses and a more secret playing area, was a large field which adjoined the Primary School grounds. The School was on the other side of a wicket fence and some boundary trees and bushes, mostly blackberries. Alongside the field was the path to school. Parents could watch their children walk the path to school and back again at home time. We had strict orders to go home the proper way. We were not allowed to go through the fence or the bushes. It seemed a bit strange to us because at the weekends and all through the summer holidays we were allowed to play in the field for hours. Groups of us would play in the long grass sometimes tying bunches of grass together to make a kind of Indian tepee or den. We would make up all kinds of games, even battles between warring 'gangs'; 'tribes' or 'armies', and when we tired of that we'd see who could pick the most blackberries from the bushes at the far side of the field. We carried pounds of luscious fruit home to our mothers, stopping along the way to eat a few.

Three years after the Second World War had ended food and clothes were still rationed. Anyone with a garden was encouraged to 'dig for Britain', and grow food. My father in true military fashion measured every inch of the garden, sometimes enlisting our help to hold the string while he carefully marked the precise spot for the planting of potatoes, peas, beans and carrots.

Harvesting and shelling the peas was great fun and they tasted so good. We must have eaten as many raw peas as we managed to pop in the pan. My mother was grateful for the vegetables, some of which were salted and preserved in jars for use during the winter.

In time we kept chickens and rabbits though these were not such a good idea. The feeding of the animals was fraught with problems and the slaughtering was extremely traumatic. Then there was the real job of plucking feathers and skinning dead animals. I used to wonder if all that effort and trauma was really worth it.

Our wonderful field was eventually ploughed up and planted with a potato crop. When it was time for the potato harvest casual pickers came to do the work. We had strict warnings to keep away from the field and the workers, who we learned were gipsies. We didn't really know who the gipsies were except that some of the women would come round with baskets of pegs to sell, and some of them offered to read people's palms and tell the future. When that happened mothers gathered up their children and scurried indoors whispering as they went. There were hushed conversations about babies being taken away and one of our neighbours, I think it was the Quarter Master's wife, put a large notice on their gate. It read,

'NO VENDORS, HAWKERS OR CIRCULARS'

Towards the end of that summer everything changed. School was especially busy one day as we were changing classrooms around. I was helping Miss Tyrell to put books away. We were a little later than usual finishing school but Miss Tyrell thanked us and told us to hurry home and not to dawdle.

A couple of my friends ran towards the forbidden wicket fence and squeezed through, running across the field to their houses. I held back slightly not wanting to incur my father's wrath, but then, realizing that I was already late I knew that it would take me longer to walk round the proper way.

I squeezed through the fence as my friends had done and felt a tear in my dress. Stopping to examine and then worry about the damage I hadn't noticed the man sitting in the grass. He smiled at me and asked why I was crying. He took my hand and drew me on to the grass beside him.

'Come and see what I've got,' he said, inviting me to touch his fully exposed and erect 'thing' which I, a totally innocent and unsuspecting seven year old could only stare at with incredulity. I couldn't imagine where he kept the 'thing' or what it was for. God only knows what might have happened. Just at that moment my mother, anxious for my lateness, was shouting me from the school path only yards away. She sounded frantic, and suddenly scared I ran from the man and towards my mother. I was more terrified to admit that I had come through the fence than admit to my encounter with the man. My mother, unaware of the man, was cross but relieved that I was home. I didn't feel I could compound things by telling her of the strange encounter. More to the point I did not wish to incur my father's wrath which was more fierce than my mother's. Everything was decided by father. Every misdemeanour was relayed to him and anything we wanted to do always received the same reply from mother.

'You'll have to see what your father says.'

My mother rarely made any decisions. I mostly remember her being anxious and I mostly remember my father as being cross. I remember too how he could make your legs sting.

Cross he certainly was the day following my encounter with the man. I had been sent on an errand to Munday's grocery shop on Cove Road. This meant that I had to walk the path beside the front field and then turn the corner into the lane behind the shops. There, lurking at the corner of the lane was the man, staring at me and grinning. This time I didn't hesitate, but ran as fast as I could to the shop. Preoccupied with worry and trying to think of a different route home I inadvertently left the Ration Book in the shop.

In 1948 my mother lived the true reality of being an army wife. My father was to be shipped out at short notice to an unknown destination and for an unspecified period. The men guessed that it would be to the Far East, possibly Korea. They would not know their destination until they were on board their troop ship.

The night before the soldiers left felt very weird and quiet. My father, a tough and seemingly insensitive man who denied that religion was of any importance, took me to the garrison church, leaving my mother and brother at home. Prayers were being said for the men about to go to a war zone. My father was not in uniform, but wore his best overcoat and gloves and a hat which he took off in the church. It was the only time in my entire life that I felt loved and cherished by him.

The next day my father sailed, not for the Far East, but for the Middle East, to the Arab/Israeli conflict which had arisen since the founding of the state of Israel. When he returned he seemed a harder man than he had been before and although he told us about Egypt, Libya, Tobruk, Benghazi and Jerusalem, we didn't really understand what he had been through until we were much older.

A temporary respite from the fear of my father being sent abroad again was provided by the Farnborough Air Show. We could see everything from our garden and it was thrilling to see the red, white and blue trails left by some of the displays. On one rare occasion we were able to see the Bristol Type 167 BRABAZON plane fly directly over our house. This was a plane designed as a passenger plane specifically for operating the direct London to New York service without having to re-fuel en route in the West bound direction. Eventually a Mk. 2 version was made with more powerful engines and the Mk. 1 version which we saw continued to be engaged in experimental flight research on problems associated with very large aircraft. My father knew the names of all the planes and we would try to draw them.

The best thing I remember from that time was that I began to learn to play the piano with Mrs. Gould, a kindly, elderly lady who lived in a picturesque cottage on Bridge Road. She had plum trees and apples in her garden and I often went home with fruit as well as a new Strauss waltz.

When I transferred to the Junior School I had to pass by Mrs. Gould's house and cross Cove Brook to walk under the bridge to school. I was in a class of forty five children and I found it very dull. The journey home was fraught with danger as I was continually bullied by two older girls who sometimes pushed me into the brook.

'Army kid, army kid! Push her in and watch her swim,' they would chant.

On one such occasion I took refuge at a surprised Mrs. Gould's house, and when the girls had moved on I was sent home to face my parents. It was no use explaining what had happened. My father was always cross with me because I hadn't hit back and mother was cross because I had messed up my clothes.

During a subsequent piano lesson I tried to hide the mend in my dress, and noticing my embarrassment Mrs. Gould thinking she would make me feel better, exclaimed what beautiful stitching it was!

School was a miserable experience on a daily basis. I worried about getting there, avoiding the bullies at school including the teachers and I worried about the journey home and then about my father's reaction when I couldn't do the homework. At the age of eight I had attended four schools and all had large classes. We received little individual help. Arithmetic, particularly times tables were like a foreign language to me.

Away from school I was really happy to have my music and the few books we had were read over and over again. I needed no encouragement to read. I even tried to read my father's newspapers, not easy for an eight or nine year old to understand such things as were written about in the socialist Daily Worker, but I tried. I'm certain that my mother's fascination with crossword puzzles helped me to spell words correctly.

As a family we were made to go on long walks at the weekends around Farnborough. Occasionally we would visit friends of my parents who lived at North Camp, a place I now remember with horror. My father took us to see soldiers boxing. I was very distressed to see grown men hitting each other until they bled or fell down. I think I was most distressed to discover that the spectators actually enjoyed it and cheered the men on.

My father just didn't know what to do with small children. As a girl I must have been a big disappointment to him.

I was not tough or athletic. His attempts to make me swim in the Olympic size swimming pool at Aldershot were agonizing and fraught with tears and protests. He had no patience.

I realized later in life that I would never teach children anything through fear, whatever the circumstances.

Revisiting Farnborough and Aldershot on 12th September 2001 was strange and not a little painful. Memories of nasty things came flooding back and I struggled to contain my emotions at times.

The day before my visit the whole world was reeling from the shock of a terrorist attack on the Twin Towers in New York. Terrorists had hijacked two planes and simultaneously flown them into the skyscraper buildings which collapsed killing thousands of innocent people.

The government, unsure of what had really happened had placed all army bases on Amber Alert, the highest stage of alert ever mounted in peacetime. Nevertheless I was able to wander around freely, taking photographs without being apprehended.

I arrived at Farnborough Station early in the day and although it was busy it was not chaotic at that stage. I took a taxi for the short journey to the army houses. We used to live at number 54 Married Quarters. I found the house, but it was now in a re-named road called Hunter Road and the house had become number 11.

The houses looked the same as when we left in 1952 except that I thought how dingy and unkempt most of them appeared. Many of the gardens were overgrown and neglected. None had neat rows of vegetables growing there, and few of them sported any flowers. I observed a few plastic garden chairs lying around amongst children's toys. The same type of wire fencing was separating the houses and this competed with the weeds which no one seems to mind.

The houses were still occupied by army families and now most of the army wives have jobs in the town. When I was a child growing up in Farnborough none of the wives worked, but stayed at home to care for the children.

I found the little primary school and the 'proper' path was still there but the adjoining field had disappeared. In its place was a small development of private house and bungalows with lovely gardens and shrubberies. The place by the wicket fence where I had ventured that afternoon as a scared seven year old was now completely obscured by huge Leylandii trees and rhododendrons. I was glad. The other surrounding field paths had been widened and were now paved roads, though the route of some of the original paths are still traceable as they converge on the short path that runs behind the Tradesmen's Arms public house.

The front field where we had flown kites and climbed trees has completely vanished. The Council have seen fit to build blocks of very ugly flats there which are covered in graffiti. Only the side path to the shops remains as it was and I hurried along it re-tracing the frightened steps of all those years ago. My heart was racing as I remembered it all.

St. Christopher's Church on Cove Road was bigger than I had remembered and there had been a lot of additional new building there. The church was obviously thriving and looked cared for, not like the army houses or the council flats. I found Cove Brook and observed that the water level was low and it now journeyed through some newer housing. Mrs. Gould's 'Potter's Cottage' was still there, still pretty, and still had fruit trees in the garden. I stopped and looked at it and remembered the happy hours I had spent making music there and I remembered her warmth and affection.

It was significant that I felt seeing the cottage again as a kind of healing. It wiped out the disappointment of seeing the rest of the place.

My final sojourn in Farnborough was at the 'Old Courthouse' pub on Cove Road, where I had a rather mediocre meal surrounded by some of the local residents, bemused by my scribbling in a notebook. They seemed curious about me, but didn't actually ask.

By the time I decided to return to my Bournemouth hotel, where I was supposedly on holiday, the rail network was extremely busy and I was forced to change trains three times. Annoyed and by then very tired I was eventually compensated by the most magical ride through the New Forest. The colours of the trees, the wild ponies and deer and the flowers were just beautiful. I wondered whether any of the people living in those awful flats in Cove ever ventured as far as the forest.

GILLINGHAM

Our next home was in Gillingham, Kent, an area known now as Medway. The River Medway flows for seventy miles through a varied landscape across Kent and Sussex, from Ashdown Forest to the Chalk Downs. The river has seen a long and diverse span of human history. After the Stone, Bronze and Iron Ages, dwellers came from the Celtic tribes, the Saxons, Vikings and Romans. The Medway was seen as the gateway into Britain. Some invaders stayed in the lush green valley where fish were plentiful. Today, wildlife, plants, orchards, hop gardens and rich, waterside woods still flourish and in between there are still some picturesque villages, churches, castles and great houses.

The Romans withdrew after four centuries of law and a certain amount of order though the next few hundred years saw waves of teutonic marauders. At first there were hit and run raids and then larger armies came which eventually brought more peaceful settlements.

After the Norman Conquest in the 11th century the Medway became an ordered river, defended by great castles at Tonbridge and Rochester. The river was used for trade and the movement of Kentish stone to build the Tower of London.

From the Middle Ages to the 18th century the river was important for water power. The growth of the iron industry in Kent and Sussex meant that the Medway was used to transport cannon to the Royal Dockyards which had developed because of the closeness of London and the good depth and anchorage in and around Chatham. Ships of war were a part of Medway life and the long association that the river has had with the Royal Navy and Royal Marines.

The Medway region was inevitably caught up in war. In 1648 there was the Kentish Royalist uprising and in the 19th century Nelson foiled what might have been an invasion by Napoleon, who had planned to land at Deal and march along Watling Street to Rochester. Troops have always been stationed at Maidstone and Chatham and the army, although much reduced now, still has a presence in Chatham and Gillingham.

During the Second World War the River Medway was in the front line when German bombers used the line of the river to attack London and there were great aerial fights over the middle and upper valley.

Since the war tributary valleys have been flooded to provide reservoirs and a flood control scheme has been built near Tonbridge following the flood disaster of 1968.

Now the largest ships at the deepest water berths are oil tankers, car ferries, transporters and container ships. Warships are a rare sight since the Navy was reduced, although more sinister nuclear submarines have occasionally been seen slipping out of Chatham along with the odd frigate. There is still a dry dock at the Old Historic Dockyard where restoration work is in progress on historic ships such as HMS Gannet. This is a £3 million pound project to restore the 1878 warship which once policed the waters of the British Empire. Powered by both sail and steam the 1,130 ton ship is the last example of a Victorian naval sloop. Work on the Gannet can be seen taking place alongside the World War II destroyer HMS Cavalier and the Cold War Submarine Ocelot.

For more than 2,000 years the banks of the Medway and its tributary land has been cultivated for cereal crops, vines, orchards and hops. The vineyards still adorning the Eden Valley and elsewhere are a reminder of a far off Roman heritage.

By 1952 my mother had had enough of army life. The constant moving and the insecurity of it all had taken its toll on her both physically and emotionally. However, she remained a compliant wife because there was little else she could do. Women in those days were not expected to be independent single mothers and if they could find a way to escape their unhappy lives they were scorned by society in general, and usually very poor.

My father was a law unto himself. No one else's opinion mattered. We all had to be obedient and do as we were told. It didn't mean we had to like it. Our houses were always depressing though we children were never quite sure why. We always thought that it was something we had done. At every turn we were told that Dad wouldn't like this, or he wouldn't let us do that. No need to ask for anything. The answer was 'no' whatever the request. Money was always short, we were told. My mother would continue to make and mend or adapt clothes and we rarely had anything newly bought. Even after wartime rationing had ended we lived by the same frugal rules as before, though my mother was a good and resourceful cook. We were never aware of being hungry.

I think my brother and I felt hungry in a different way. We did not feel loved or valued. We were a nuisance. If we sometimes dared to venture opinions about anything, or if we asked about anything at all, we received a long lecture when a short explanation might have sufficed. My father's lectures were delivered in a very precise, deliberate and loud voice. They were delivered as appropriate for young army recruits and not children, so that even if we had asked something quite trivial and innocent, we felt that we had somehow transgressed.

Since my father's return from the Middle East there were many such loud lectures, followed by a lot of weird silences. My brother and I couldn't know and my mother didn't want to know the gory details of my father's time in the Middle East. I know now that for all his swagger he had been deeply traumatized by it and that may explain to some extent how his hard nature was further consolidated once he returned to civilian life. He found it difficult to adjust to a home environment again. It is worth describing a little about the life of the Sappers at this point.

The Royal Engineers or Sappers (named after the trenches or 'saps' they constructed) have always operated at the forefront of technology and in the most inhospitable conditions. Their commitment to ingenuity and the solving of practical problems means that these soldiers are usually highly skilled in more than one trade. They help armed troops to move. They deliver arms, supplies and troops to crucially important locations. Sometimes they have to overcome all sorts of obstacles in order to help armoured and mechanised troops to reach their targets. The Sappers build and employ a wide variety of equipment including tank-mounted and amphibious and girder bridges. They are trained to clear minefields, destroy enemy bridges and installations, roads and runways and to lay anti-tank minefields. Personal survival and that of his men was my father's main preoccupation. He had to build accommodation in 'the field' wherever that may be, produce drinkable water and food, distribute electricity supplies, fuel stores and field hospitals.

My father told us how he had bartered with Arabs in Libya for coffee and eggs, but also how his jaw had been smashed by an enemy rifle butt whilst attempting to rescue soldiers from a burning building. He lost all his teeth.

Nowadays soldiers who became traumatised or badly injured are given treatment or counselling and help to return to normal life. In my father's day they were given a few painkilling tablets and a short leave home and were then expected to carry on as before.

Following a rare train journey north to Sheffield, for my grandfather's funeral, my mother suffered a miscarriage whilst we were staying with her father and stepmother. That unsettled both my parents. Those unsettled feelings must have sown seeds of determination to escape army life and try to find what they perceived as a better future.

My father relinquished his life as a serving soldier, for the time being, to become employed in Chatham at the Officers' Mess. It became a kind of re-training period before fully returning to civilian life. He had been a great success looking after troops abroad, both from a practical, material point of view and also in terms of increasing their morale, so he was an ideal candidate to work in a more relaxed capacity in the Officers' Mess.

He learned everything there was to know about catering and corporate entertainment, managing staff and book-keeping.

For a short while we lived in a little rented house in Strover Street, Gillingham, part of a neat Victorian terrace.

It had an exquisite front porch with colourful tiles lining the walls. At the back of the house was a verandah with steps down into a small garden. There was a trellis fence, hollyhocks, delphiniums and wonder of wonders a plum tree laden with fruit. Our Aldershot garden had only borne vegetables so we thought this vastly superior. We soon learned to climb the tree to find edible fruit. Needless to say my brother and I suffered many stomach aches and had our legs smacked for either wrecking the tree or our clothes.

I remember very little about Arden Street School, probably because we were not there for long. My class teacher, dear Mrs. Harris, somehow discovered that I could play the piano and encouraged me to play for the other children. I managed partially to overcome my shyness and found some new friends

Strover Street house, Gillingham

Arden Street School,Gillingham

who enjoyed singing the few songs I could play. This was my fifth school in five years so there had been an appalling lack of continuity and I had missed several important parts of the curriculum especially in arithmetic. My reading skills were well developed because most of my home reading was from my father's socialist newspapers and my parent's books. I remember struggling to read Howard Spring's book 'Fame is the Spur'. I was almost eleven.

I failed the 11-plus exam along with everyone else in my class except for one girl, Hilary Phillips. She had lovely long red hair, plaited in two neat ribbons. She always smiled. I suspect that she will probably be a lawyer or doctor now . . . We did discover that children in other schools had been coached in exam technique but we were not. It all seemed irrelevant at the time as I knew that we would surely be moving again sometime. I tried to enjoy school. I loved writing stories and poems and I adored the library books which I didn't dare to take home. I made several interesting friends though none were ever allowed to visit our house. I once used to visit a girl who had TB and I took her daily milk from school until my parents found out. Then I wasn't allowed to go there any more. I'm not sure whether my parents acted out of fear because I had been desperately ill with Diphtheria when I was four years old, or whether it was some other reason. I learned never to question.

In view of all that had gone before I was very surprised one weekend to be allowed to go to The Strand, (Gillingham's seaside) with Beatrice

Moore (Beaty) together with her parents and granny. There was a beach and sea to paddle in. It was wonderful and exhilarating and a strange feeling to paddle at the water's edge feeling the sand fall away beneath your toes. I didn't want to go home. I wanted the day to last forever. I couldn't understand why we never did things like that as a family. It was just beginning to dawn on me that parents could be different to mine. Beaty's family laughed a lot and talked to each other without shouting. The experience of being with them was warm and happy. I treasured it and I remember it.

Some of my other schoolfriends went with their families every summer to pick hops. It was an annual tradition for many families and just after the war years provided a welcome boost to the family income. Everything they did during the year was either before or after hop-picking. Other children said they were going 'on holiday' but were actually fruit picking. I think the fruit picking must have been best because the hop pickers got very brown, sticky sore hands. The children seemed to enjoy the season whatever they helped to pick. They had fun and freedom and fresh air.

While the hop or fruit season lasted families would live in small wooden huts. After they had booked themselves in each year some families would travel down a week or two beforehand taking with them pots and pans, even wallpaper to make the places more comfortable. Everyone slept on wooden bunks and they bathed at the weekends. I used to long to go with them, but never did.

Sure enough after a few months we had to up sticks and move again. Still in Gillingham, but this time to the Rock Avenue Club where my father, temporarily free of the army, had become the club's manager. We lived in 'quarters' above the club building. There was no garden, just a small yard enclosed by a high brick wall. My bedroom looked out over a derelict bombed site, where houses once stood, and we were located on a road junction with Canterbury Road and Shakespeare Road, very near to Watling Street. I was fascinated by the names and I remembered their significance from things we had learned at school.

For the first time in her married life my mother was expected to do a job of work as well as running the household and looking after us. The hours were long and tiring. My brother and I spent many hours by ourselves. In those days we had no television, video or hi-fi. We listened to the radio and read my parents books until we were able to go to the public library. I spent a lot of time playing the piano and writing childish stories and poems. It was my escape into a better, happier world.

1953 was a momentous year. It was the year of the Queen's Coronation. Because of my father's political leanings the Royal Family

Rock Avenue, Gillingham

were not approved of or spoken about. I didn't know that King George had died the year before. Very little was mentioned at school in Aldershot about the King, which was rather surprising when one remembers marching around the school playground waving flags on Empire Day. At school in Gillingham we were given a commemorative Coronation mug which was disapproved of at home. Nearer to the actual event I remember finding a cut-out model of the golden coach. It was on the side of a Weetabix packet. I spent ages cutting and pasting it all together. It was a wonderful thing but no one admired my efforts because it represented the rich and privileged. I was urged instead to admire the conquest of Mount Everest by Hillary and Tensing, Stanley Matthews winning his first FA Cup and Gordon Richards first win at the Derby. To my father's disappointment I took little interest.

Coronation Day dawned and unbeknown to my father I was allowed to play with a friend nearby. In fact the front room at my friends house was packed with chairs and cushions as more than a dozen grown-ups and several children pressed around the tiny television set to watch the black and white pictures of the procession and service. The music was lovely and I was spellbound by the spectacle of the whole thing. Every so often when the children became restless we were shunted out into the yard with some cake and a drink of tizer pop.

When I reluctantly returned home I sat at the piano trying to work out some of the Coronation music, my little cardboard coach taking pride of place on top of the piano. It had been a very happy day, a secret day.

Soon after the Coronation my parents received my end of year school report urging them to find me a piano teacher. I suppose with a long summer holiday looming they thought it was a good idea to keep me occupied. My father persuaded a young man from the Royal Marines band to come to the house to teach me. He seemed incredibly tall and handsome and had a very shiny badge on his cap. Other than that I cannot remember much of what he taught me. He couldn't have been visiting us for long. In 1954 we were to move house again.

I'm afraid that my father's forthright manner and Marxist views upset people everywhere he went. It was a recurring pattern. His intolerance meant that he often lost his temper. He could never accept that there might be another point of view.

We would miss friends again as we had missed them several times before. We had only recently been allowed to go to the Saturday morning cinema for children and we loved it. We were miserable at the thought of possibly not being able to go to the cinema again.

OCTOBER 2002

It was a long, tiring and convoluted journey from Edinburgh to Chatham. After four hours of tolerating a noisy child, cramped seating and unworkable toilets on the train I wished that we had travelled by air to Heathrow. Security alerts and delayed trains on the London Underground system meant also a delayed final train to Chatham. We finally arrived late at our accommodation. It had taken a total of seven hours to reach our destination.

Undaunted we revived ourselves and found reserves of energy enough to take a taxi ride to 'The Honourable Pilot' – an eaterie named after an Elizabethan Chatham sailor, Will Adams, who intriguingly had been instrumental in founding the Japanese navy. There we spent a pleasant evening with Jackie and her family. Jackie and I had known each other fifty years ago when our fathers were stationed in Aldershot. In 1952 Jackie's family had been posted to Berlin and mine to Gillingham. Our mothers had continued to write to each other until one of them passed away. Jackie and I had an impossible task to cover fifty years of news and events, but we tried. I was conscious of our daughters listening in and wondered what on earth they would make of our alien world. Jackie's husband was retired from the navy so Gillingham was a natural place for them to stay while my family kept on moving.

In daylight I realized that our accommodation in the Officer's Terrace at the Old Historic Dockyard at Chatham was something very special. Built between 1722 and 1731, Officer's Terrace accommodated high ranking dockyard officers. No. 10 (the place we stayed) had been designated to The Master Caulker. The houses were built to large proportions to accommodate the many servants required at the time. The porches at the front of the houses would have been used for waiting chairmen with their sedan chairs. These would transport the officers around the dockyard.

Since 1986 the buildings had been gutted and left to go to rack and ruin until a building company bought them with the intention of restoring all twelve houses. The company went into receivership and sold off the houses to private buyers who appear to have lovingly restored them to their present glory. Many are used as guest house accommodation. Staying here was the best part of our visit to Medway.

The Historic Dockyard at Chatham is a place where legends were made. The flagship HMS Victory was built here and visitors can see the Loft where the sails were made and the warehouses where the timber was stored until it was ready for use. It is the most complete dockyard of the Age of Sail to survive anywhere in the world and was once the most important naval dockyard in Britain. The Historic Dockyard is now in the care of the Chatham Historic Dockyard Trust, an independent charity whose task it is to restore and preserve this important part of our national heritage. Visitors can discover four hundred years of maritime history through fascinating exhibits and inter-active features. The Wooden Walls gallery allows visitors to walk through the Royal Dockyard of 1758 and discover how Britain's wooden warships were built. The RNLI National Exhibition Hall 'LIFEBOAT', tells the heroic story of the RNLI with exciting displays of fifteen full size lifeboats, film and artefacts.

Chatham, Rochester and Gillingham are all very small towns in close proximity with each other, so it was just a short ride to find my former homes at Gillingham. Strover Street is still there but the porch at our house seems to have been replaced with a nasty PVC one, but the fruit tree seems to have survived. We took the photograph and pressed on to find Rock Avenue. The taxi driver told me that although many of the local pubs were closing the working men's club still thrives, in spite of a lack of working men, because the beer there is cheaper.

The Club was indeed still there, smaller than I remembered it and rather shabby looking. The derelict site had been built on but I remembered little else and felt nothing.

Visiting the Royal Engineers Museum at Brompton Barracks had to be the second most rewarding visit of our time researching Medway.

Although first established in 1912 in a smaller building the present Museum was opened in 1987 by the Queen. It has one of the finest collection of Victoria Cross medals and a map used by Wellington to deploy his Army on 18 June 1815 and marked with the blood of Sir William de Lancey, who carried it during the battle. The Museum offers much more to visitors of course since it displays the history of the Royal Engineers since the eighteenth century. For me of course the most interesting exhibits were those pertaining to the military situations which my father was involved in. It was good to read actual accounts of the Middle Eastern conflicts, Suez, Korea and so on. As a child I only knew the stories in my father's words and then only what he thought fit to retell. I certainly reached a better understanding of what he had endured.

We visited nearby Rochester which might have been a wonderful day had it not been raining heavily, thus curtailing our interest in the place. I remembered being in the Cathedral as a child at some military event. We didn't brave the Castle in the rain, but instead found the delightful Dickens Museum and the largest second hand book shop in Britain.

Since one of the aims of this 'pilgrimage' around former places I've lived in was to assess not only my feelings but also to discover what might have changed, I have to record that Gillingham and Chatham, apart from the two marvellous museums were really disappointing. One of the town's librarians told me that it was like two ghost towns. Only nearby Rochester retained some sense of its former history.

The decline of the army and navy has meant a severe unemployment problem. Without the forces and their families, many service industries have suffered. However, The Strand in Gillingham still exists and now has a Leisure Centre. Further out of town there is a skateboard and skating park and there are military re-enactments which interest summer visitors. Chatham's theatre has had to be demolished and may be replaced with amusement arcades and Bingo. Small amateur theatre and music groups struggle to interest young people and town centres at night are unsafe with many drug addicts, alcoholics and prostitutes in evidence. Street crime has increased as it has in many of our towns and cities. Life has changed drastically for the ordinary family. The tradition of hop picking has gone. Most hops are mechanically harvested and the casual fruit pickers are mostly students trying to eke out their student grants. In schools the country crafts, traditions and dancing are almost non existent. Everyone is aware of having to be politically correct in response to the other, modern problem, in the Medway Towns. That is an influx of refugees and asylum seekers from across the English Channel, either from the tunnel or the Kentish ports. Some arrive legitimately and have fled all kinds of real or perceived persecution. Others have arrived illegally.

It is not my place here to comment on the wisdom of having such a large concentration of refugees in one small town, simply to state the facts.

The arrival of so many homeless people into an already depressed area only serves to make the problems worse. If Gillingham and Chatham's already disconnected youth is to have any kind of prosperous future then more investment in the towns will be needed, and not just as a short term measure.

One small glimmer of hope might be provided by the promise of improved rail and road links to the Channel tunnel and the building of a controversial airport at Cliffe. Both of these possibilities are causing great concern to some rural residents who fear loss of houses and land, noise pollution and increased rates. However, at the time of my writing the population according to the local newspaper is about 50/50 in agreement with the new proposals. Only time will tell if Medway can become proud and prosperous again. It has lost its former sense of identity and purpose, and will never be the same again. A new identity and purpose needs to be developed.

GRAYS – ESSEX

When my brother and I saw Rook Hall, Dell Road for the first time we could hardly believe that it was true. It was just beautiful. A large, ivy covered mock Tudor, half timbered house set back from a winding drive and nestling at one corner of an area known as The Dell.

We could only think that somehow our parents must have come into a large amount of money. We had no idea that in fact the house always went with the job. We didn't own anything. However, we all instantly recognized this as the best place we had lived in, so far. I found it difficult to relax at first and constantly asked whether this time it was for ever. No one gave me an answer.

My room had a large bay window and overlooked the drive. For the first time I was to have a room newly papered and painted. The floorboards were painted black and I had a brand new pink rug to match the tiny pink rosebuds of the wallpaper. I was thrilled and spent many happy hours admiring my room, hiding 'treasures' under a loose

Rook Hall, Dell Road, Grays, Essex

floorboard and arranging my few books on a newly acquired white bookshelf. It was here that my creative imagination really began to flourish, helped in no small way by the proximity of The Dell. The stories and poems I scribbled on scraps of paper were all neatly folded and tied up and hidden in my floorboard treasure place.

Because we had moved just two weeks before the end of the school term, my last year in Junior School, I had to attend a new school for just two weeks before the long summer holiday. After the holidays I would go to Grays Park School for Girls. The new, temporary school, was in the end of year chaos and the teacher handed me over to the care of Maureen (Mo) who would show me what to do. She put a comforting arm round me and invited me to sit beside her at the old dual bench desk. The desk had a lift up lid with a writing slate, which thankfully we didn't have to use. Each person had their own inkwell which had to be washed out and re-filled every morning. I dreaded getting the job of cleaning inkwells. I was sure to make a mess. It was bad enough trying to write neatly with a metal pen. I always managed to dip it too far into the ink and left numerous messy splodges all over my work. I was greatly relieved when we were allowed to write in pencil. It would be another year or two before we were allowed to write with fountain pens. Girls whose parents had equipped them with fountain pens were allowed to fill them up with ink from the teacher's bottle, and in time some girls took their own small bottles of 'Quink' to school with them along with the vital sheets of thick blotting paper. I can't ever remember being allowed to use a biro pen at school. Biros were considered to encourage sloppy handwriting. It would be another three years before I owned my own fountain pen and ink.

That summer (1954) I felt the world was beginning to be a nicer place, except for the onset of menstruation, a monthly occurrence about which I knew nothing and was totally unprepared.

My parents seemed to be calmer and happier in their work. They even made music together occasionally, usually on a Sunday afternoon after some liquid refreshment! We had a family holiday for the first time. Butlin's at Clacton was the choice. In the 1950's holiday camps were regimented to the last detail so it suited my father. Keeping to a timetable and joining in every scheduled activity meant that you got your money's worth. We slept in a wooden chalet and woke every morning to a voice over the tannoy loudspeaker telling us to go for breakfast. We sat at a designated table in a designated row and ate everything we were given.

Free time was limited but we were allowed to venture out on the rowing boats. This was great fun until some older children decided to make it into a game of rowing boat dodgems. Since I couldn't swim and things became a bit precarious, I soon gave up on the rowing.

Back home at the Dell my new friend Maureen and I spent many hours in 'our' woods, sometimes just walking and taking sometimes collecting wild flowers which we could draw, press into little books and label. We would make our own secret 'den' and sometimes we would shin up the red brick wall at the top of the Dell which separated us from the convent of La Sainte Union on the other side. We giggled as we watched the nuns hanging out their washing. My brother and his friends made their dens too and most of the time were separately enjoying ourselves. Then the boys would spy on us or swing like Tarzan from the trees nearby. A big chase would ensue among the trees and undergrowth. Making 'our' territory seemed to be very important. This we might do using branches tied in a certain way, or with twigs, string, bits of cloth, even the illicit bonfire or two. Now and then a group of strangers, older boys mostly, would invade our woods so we became a collective with a common purpose of tracking the interlopers.

The Dell had evolved from a former chalk quarry and was an area of land which once belonged to Alfred Russel Wallace, a naturalist and joint discoverer with Charles Darwin of the theory of natural selection. In 1871 Wallace built a house called THE DELL above the overgrown quarry. He chose the location because it was not too far from London and what would become the Natural History Museum, where he hoped for an important post. Wallace's plans for the quarry and The Dell were ambitious.

"It is a bit of wilderness that can be made into a splendid imitation of a Welsh valley," he told Darwin, *"and will enable me to gather round me all the beauties of the temperate flora which I so admire . . . and the fixing on a residence for the rest of your life is an important event."*

Eventually, after a few years, Wallace discovered that the climate and the soil were not as productive as he had hoped and he sold his newly built house and the land. In 1979 the house was annexed to the convent where the sisters had opened a school.

The changing face of Grays throughout history has been more dramatic than anyone could imagine. Pleistocene gravels yielded amazing remains of mammals including wildcats, hyena, wolf, bear, bison, hippo, rhino and mammoth. Human remains from Palaeolithic to Roman times are well represented. By 1086 Grays had a small rural manor with a population of twenty eight and in Mediaeval times the town grew rapidly. Eventually Grays became a small Thames port with chalk quarries and brickworks, at its height in the eighteenth century shipping bricks to London in barges. A brewery utilized hops grown in the nearby countryside, and barges and small boats were built and repaired at Grays until the late twentieth century. The biggest escalation in population, as everywhere else, was with the coming of the railways. Traditional industries and farming declined after the First World War and have been replaced with light engineering, plastics and packaging companies. In the early part of the twentieth century the Council bought a hundred acres of the Grays Hall Estate and began a huge building programme of council housing.

I have made two return visits to Grays since we moved away, not counting the three or four occasions when I 'ran away' from home to find Mo again.

My first adult visit was in 1963, together with my first husband and on our return from three years living abroad with the army in Germany. I had half hoped we might be able to settle somewhere in the area where I had been most happy as a child. We stayed in a wonderful cottage in Orsett. It was a white-painted stone cottage complete with thatched roof and an orchard garden. It might have been the subject of a Victorian painting, so often used nowadays on boxes of chocolates. Our few days there were spent finding Mo and her family and Rook Hall. I was devastated to discover that Rook Hall, our lovely house, had been demolished and what appeared to be a block of flats now in its place. All I could think of was that underneath the rubble of that house would have been the scraps of childhood stories which I had hidden beneath the floorboards and had forgotten to retrieve when we moved to London. I was deeply disappointed. My second visit some ten years later was even more disappointing when I realized that most of The Dell had also disappeared.

The town has lost many of its old and historic buildings, replaced by new and unlovely glass and concrete structures. An out of town shopping centre called LAKESIDE has decimated many small businesses in the town. The cement factories, Thames Board Mills and other industries have closed along the riverside and have been replaced by various housing complexes. The docks at nearby Tilbury, historic site of many great Elizabethan vessels, now employ only a fraction of the 1950's workforce.

Before people had cars they were mostly content to live and work in one place but now, of necessity, and because travelling is easier, many people travel into London to work. London can now be reached in under an hour, unlike the long coach journeys undertaken by Alfred Russel Wallace.

Grays has become a dormitory town in every sense of the word.

TOTTENHAM (NORTH LONDON)

I have no idea why we had to leave Grays. I can only guess and now with the hindsight of adult reasoning. My brother and I had enjoyed living in Grays with the added freedom that The Dell had afforded us. For the first time we had allowed ourselves to develop personal friendships and we were deeply upset when we were told that another move was imminent. Once more we had to say our goodbyes.

Tottenham could not have been more different. The autumn day that we moved to Bruce Grove (Trades Club) was dark, damp and dreary. The piano had to be raised on ropes and lifted up the outside of the building and through a large window on the top floor.

We didn't have a garden, though there was an area of wild land to the back of the building. It was overgrown with weeds, nettles and twisted bushes, evidence or years of neglect. We were not supposed to play in the 'wilderness'. We were confined to our top floor rooms and an area of flat roof which was surrounded by a wire netting fence and overlooked the busy Bruce Grove. At night time we

Bruce Grove, London N17

could look down at the traffic and the lights gave it a different feeling. It was easy to imagine we were in one of those Hollywood movies where a lonely boy or girl would sit on the rooftops singing about their lost love.

My father hadn't bothered to inform his new employers that he had a son and a daughter. There were not enough rooms for us and at first we all had to sleep in the same bedroom.

My new school, on Parkhurst Road, was aptly named. I hated it from the first day. My arrival upset teachers, just as happened many times before. They had to find an extra place, extra books and they had to fill me in with missed work. Classes still numbered more than forty pupils and no attempt was made to assess my ability in anything. I have only scant memories of lessons. There was one kindly lady, whose name eludes me now. She taught needlework. Although it was not one of my talents I remember being awestruck by the exhibits when she took us to the Royal College of Needlework. The only other teacher who made any impression on me was Miss Buck, the music teacher. She was a fine pianist and whilst I was one of the few girls to respond in lessons, I was too afraid to admit that I could play the piano. My over-riding memories of Parkhurst School was the name-calling and bullying.

As before, my parents either couldn't or wouldn't find the correct school uniform. I had to wear their nearest version of it. In this case the uniform was a dark brown gymslip or skirt with a white shirt and dark brown cardigan and dark brown stockings or socks. I was sent to school wearing a light brown tweed skirt, home-knitted jumper and garters to hold up my brown stockings. By now I was developing a bust and without a bra was becoming more noticeable by the day. This alone gave the bullies plenty to go at. Then there was my accent. From Merseyside to rural Dorset, Hampshire and then Essex I had acquired a conglomeration of accents which became a source of great hilarity to North London working class schoolgirls. I retreated into myself. The main objective each day was to get to school and back again without being accosted. I couldn't tell anyone about it.

My father was unsympathetic and mother kept silent. My brother was only eleven and went to Lordship Lane Primary School, some distance away. He seemed to be fine. I was completely alone. My main source of comfort was the piano and my other escape was to the public library. If I happened to encounter anyone from school along the route to the library, I would cross the road to avoid them.

My brother seemed to spend most of his time climbing trees and playing in Bruce Castle Park. I must admit that until I decided to research this book I knew next to nothing about Bruce Castle and its history and even less about Tottenham. I might have warmed to the place had I known what an interesting and colourful history there had been. My time at Parkhurst was quite brief, but I do not remember Tottenham or its environs being mentioned in school at all. The daily struggle at school meant that my time away from it was spent in my own fantasy world of music and books. I felt no inclination to go exploring, even with my brother.

Bruce Castle Museum is now home to a huge collection of maps and history of the area which I now realize is truly fascinating.

Seven miles to the North East of Central London, Tottenham may have originated from Saxon times when it was known as Totta's village. Then it would just have been a clearing in the forest. By the seventeenth century all that remained was an area known as Wood Green. During the sixteenth century King Henry VIII hunted deer here and it was at 'Maister Comton's House by Totnam,' now Bruce Castle, that he met up with his sister Margaret, Queen of Scots in 1516, when she came to reside at her brother's court at Bayford Castle, having been exiled from Scotland.

By the turn of the seventeenth century Tottenham was said to be prosperous, with numerous almshouses, endowments and charities for the poor. Building increased greatly and Tottenham became famous for its greens and taverns. Some were named with historical significance, such as The Black Boy (referring to slavery). When Izaak Walton came to fish he stayed at The Swan Inn.

By 1800 the Wood had largely disappeared. In spite of the founding of rubber and crepe factories Tottenham was still largely rural. Market gardening had been a profitable trade for almost two hundred years, the gardeners easily able to sell their produce in Covent Garden. In 1843 shocking housing conditions prevailed and references have been made about 'Tottenham High Crosse' where they kept 'tippling houses without licenses' among tumbledown cottages.

Because of Tottenham's close proximity to the City of London, travellers, refugees and migrant workers throughout the centuries have found it a convenient staging post. With its growing population it was also a convenient place to hide from slave masters, landlords, police and so on. From the 1870's cheap rail tickets for workers meant that men could travel further to work. Great building activity resulted, light industry was developed, the Prince of Wales Hospital was built, and then the Tottenham Hotspurs Football Club. The Palace Theatre which once hosted Marie Lloyd was seen as another asset for the area. Sadly, it eventually closed and became a Bingo Hall.

During the twentieth century, perhaps as a result of the First World War and the emancipation of women, many of the fine, large, family houses ceased to be solely occupied by one family.

Many women found that they had to work during the war years and with the advent of birth control methods did not have to bring up such large families. Most of the larger houses have been converted for multiple occupation as flats and bed-sitting rooms. Some have been rebuilt or renovated for use as hotels and boarding houses.

It is easy to understand why the large properties were converted for use by several families.

During the Second World War thousands of men and women were recruited into the armed forces. The Empire Windrush ship stopped in Jamaica to pick up servicemen who were on leave from their units. Many of their former comrades decided to join the ship and young men with adventurous spirits thought it would be a good idea to see England, 'the mother country'.

Few of these early immigrants had intended to stay more than a few years. In 1948, Britain was recovering from the ravages of war. There was plenty of work but housing was a problem. Many of these young Caribbeans found themselves living in lodging houses in Tottenham.

Excluded from much of the social and economic life around them, they began to adjust the institutions they brought with them – the churches, and a co-operative method of saving known as the 'pardner' system. At the same time, Caribbeans began to participate in organisations to which they did have access, such as trade unions, local councils and professional associations. They fought many conflicts and issues of discrimination.

Throughout the nineteen seventies, the children of this first wave of post war migrants began to develop a 'black culture' which is now part of a black British style shared by Africans, Asians and white young people alike.

OCTOBER 2002

It was clear from the moment we arrived at Bruce Grove that the area is multi racial in every conceivable way. In the few short yards we walked to my 'home' we observed eight or nine different ethnic groups of people. It seems largely Afro-Caribbean but a quick glance at the churches in the area also gave an indication of many other groups.

There are Orthodox, Liberal and Reform Synagogues; Greek Orthodox; Russian; Bahai; Pentecostal; Mosques; Sikh Temples; Hispanic; Buddhist; Moravian; and several evangelical and Pentecostal churches as well as exotic sounding names. There is a Pillar of Fire Chapel; Beacon of Light; Faith Miracle Centre and a Mennonite Church.

We passed a Rastafarian with glazed eyes and a far away smile. He wore a large colourful hat of which we would see many more.

We found the Trades Club. It seemed to still function as a political club. It was much dirtier than I remembered it and the flat roof seemed smaller. As we took the required photographs we were aware of a fast car screeching to a halt in the middle of the road. The driver, a young black man shouted to a group of young girls waiting at the bus stop. We moved on, trying not to look like visitors, but taking in everything we could. There were groups of noisy youths on almost every street corner, some talking loudly on mobile 'phones to their friends.

Although the youths were not visibly breaking the law in any way it is quite understandable how people, especially the elderly, might feel threatened in their locality. The sheer size of groups, the volume of noise they emit, the fact that you have to walk round them on the pavement, and the obvious presence of some 'weed' gives the whole place an uneasy or aggressive feel.

Tottenham is no different to many other towns and cities these days in that residents are sick and tired of anti-social behaviour and lack of community facilities. But in Tottenham there is evidence of a more serious problem. That is the serious problem of gun crime.

Mothers marched with the Haringey Peace Alliance in September last (2002) in memory of their sons and brothers, killed in violent gun crimes. There is also evidence of some good community initiatives. A team of Neighbourhood Development Officers work with communities to ensure their concerns are raised and the Council listens to what they have to say.

The most encouraging thing one can observe is that there is a willingness to make things change for the better. The key to this would seem to be giving residents the knowledge, information, skills and expertise to help themselves.

PLUMSTEAD . . . ABBEY WOOD . . . WOOLWICH

In one sense it was a huge relief to be moving from North London to the South East corner of the city. We had no idea whether it would be any better or worse living there. We were to have two homes in South London, one at Plumstead, bordering on Abbey Wood. The second place was at Woolwich immediately opposite the Arsenal.

Plumstead is a community of considerable antiquity and surprising contrasts. Two burial mounds survive from Pre-Roman times, on Winns Common and on Shooter's Hill. Roman burials were discovered on Wickham Lane beside the old riverside highway. The southern edge of the parish has always been part of the great Roman road, Watling Street. It runs over the slopes of Shooter's Hill. The lower levels by the river have been dominated by industrial development and the building of the new town of Thamesmead. The higher ground to the south preserves some of its former rural character with its two commons and open land. By the time of the Domesday survey the village of Plumstead had been divided into two manors. It was a prosperous village with extensive well drained marshes for sheep grazing and fertile soil for fruit growing. Until the nineteenth century little was changed. However, Plumstead's close proximity to the Arsenal at Woolwich meant much development over the marshes. The industries created to serve the Arsenal would have included foundries, metal shops for making munitions and cannon of all kinds, rope-making, gun powder and supplies warehousing. The arrival of the railways in 1849 meant even further development on the Burrage Estate to the west of the village adjacent to Woolwich.

Developers had hoped to acquire some of the land on Plumstead Common, but attempts at enclosure were resisted with increasing militancy, until in the late nineteenth century soldiers from the Woolwich garrison began to use the common for drill and exercise. Riots ensued and local leader John de Morgan was imprisoned, but it provided the necessary stimulus for the Metropolitan Borough of Works to acquire Plumstead and Winns Common, to preserve them as public open spaces.

Woolwich owes most of its history to the Arsenal, the Royal Artillery and to King Henry VIII who established his Royal Dockyard there in 1512. 'The Great Harry' flagship of the king's new navy was built at Woolwich. The yard saw many royal visits and voyages of exploration began here. In 1581 Queen Elizabeth I welcomed Drake after his circumnavigation of the globe. She knighted him aboard the 'Golden Hind'.

Eventually the yard converted in order to build and repair steamships but eventually closed in 1869 causing great distress and unemployment in the town.

Eighty odd years after the Dockyard closed was our time in the area. In the intervening years there had been two world wars, the Depression era and the rise of the Co-operative movement, along with the strengthening of left-wing socialism. This suited my father as he became the steward of both a Radical Club and a Co-operative Club.

Our first house in Plumstead was on Ceres Road, surrounded by other roads with colonial sounding names. Benares Road, Kashgar Road, Amardeep Court, and then curiously, Bannockburn Road. Our house belonged to the Club. It was a late Victorian villa, like the Gillingham House. We had no bathroom and the toilet was outside. The Daily Worker newspaper was cut into neat 6" squares and wads of the paper

Ceres Road, Plumstead, South London

were skewered through and tied with string on the back of the toilet door to use as loo paper. As for bathing we made a weekly visit to the Public Baths on Plumstead High Street. A large, overalled lady ran the water for you and told you when to come out. We took our own towels and soap, but if you had enough money you could hire a white fluffy towel and buy a scented pine bath cube to crumble into the water.

Our garden was not much more than a yard, with little to commend it except for a high brick wall. At least our dog, Spot, could be safe there though it wasn't so much fun for him as being able to tear around The Dell, in Grays.

It was 1955. I was thirteen years of age, deeply shy and introverted. I was happy with my own company and dreaded the thought of meeting new people.

I was sent to my new school, in Abbey Wood, completely alone on the first day. I dawdled through St. Nicholas's churchyard and arrived late at school. I wonder how I ever made it to the Head Teacher's Study.

The Head Mistress was very stern looking, like a hospital matron. She wore a plain grey dress with a neat white collar. She never smiled. She articulated every word she spoke very precisely and clearly.

'Which form were you in at your last school?' she asked.

'Please Miss, I was in the 'A' Form,' I replied.

'Indeed! We'll see about that,' she said.

I felt deeply humiliated when I was introduced to the 'C' Form, where I spent a very frustrating couple of weeks before being upgraded to the 'B' Form temporarily. There I was tested in every possible way with teachers sending me on meaningless errands to other teachers. It felt like the army initiative tests. I must have proved satisfactory because I was at last allowed to 'graduate' to the 'A' Form. I did struggle desperately to understand maths. With every previous house move I had missed something important like long division, tables, fractions and so on. I loathed science lessons. I felt sick and faint every time we had to 'dispose of' a worm, snail or frog. We had to dissect them, pin them out and draw and label them. I had recurring nightmares for years afterwards, about frogs. I was so affected by it at the time that my writing-up of the task was full of mistakes and ink splodges, for which I was then punished.

I dreaded cookery lessons too. My father would grumble every time I had to take money for something we were cooking. He scorned the results of the lesson when I returned home with my effort. What earthly use was a tiny fillet of rolled plaice? We should be taught how to make proper family meals. And on it went . . . I was so lacking in confidence that

The Author and Church Manorway friend, Doreen

the cookery teacher described me as slow and lazy, in reports. She had no idea what repercussions that would bring at home.

P.E. was exactly the same, although in a way worse because my father could not tolerate weakness. I did try as hard as I could, but I just couldn't run fast, or catch balls. Tennis was a complete mystery to me. I seemed to be completely devoid of the co-ordination required. As if I didn't feel bad enough, some of my classmates and the teachers saw my inept nature a cause for great hilarity. However, all things being relative it was not nearly as bad as the bullying I received in Tottenham.

There were two saving graces in my life. My two guardian angels as I would come to regard Mrs. Devonshire and Mrs. Cakebread. They were both to make such an impact, such a difference to my miserable existence, and ultimately to my future, that I shall be eternally grateful for their presence, their vision and inspiration.

Mostly, the only real music we had in school, was singing. I loved it and always thought these lessons were too short. We sang folk songs, the odd anthem and classical songs and glorious hymns, the words of which for some unknown reason would bring a lump to my throat. 'Hills of the North Rejoice!' 'To be a Pilgrim', 'Jerusalem'. I often had to bite my lip in Assembly when we sang such beautiful words and tunes.

In Singing lessons mine was often the only hand up when we were asked which song we would like to do next. Mrs. D. must have deduced from my requests that I had more than a passing interest in music. Somehow I became brave enough to divulge that I could play the piano. However, it took another year and not a little prompting in school reports before my parents agreed that I could look for a piano teacher. After months of searching I could not find a teacher. Mrs. D. agreed to take me on herself. I was overjoyed. I felt the need to slip quietly out of school to piano lessons without telling any of my class mates. Mrs. D. lived at Blackheath in a basement apartment of a grand Georgian house. Sometimes I would deliberately arrive early for my lesson and I would sit on the top step listening to Mrs. D. playing Chopin or Mozart. When she stopped playing I would ring the bell.

Learning the music was wonderful of course, but more than that I really appreciated having someone to encourage me. She never belittled me. She had only constructive criticism, help and encouragement. After lessons with Mrs. D. I always came out feeling slightly taller, and generally more aware and alive. The fact that someone had any faith in me allowed me to cope with the wretched misery that I felt was the rest of my life.

Mrs. Cakebread, my form teacher and brilliant teacher of English Literature, became the second most influential person I've ever encountered. She was petite, poised and assured in her manner, strikingly good looking with immaculately coiffeured black hair and flawless make-up. She could have been a model or film star. That is how we all regarded her. Mrs. C. commanded respect and attention from the moment she walked into a room. She never seemed to lose her temper or raise her voice, but at the same time we always knew whether she was cross about something.

Mrs. C. brought poetry and classic books alive. I remember being very impressed that she could quote great chunks of literature to us and even knew the page number in 'Jane Eyre' where Rochester could hide his feelings for Jane no longer. Mrs. C. fed my imagination and nurtured it. She spoke to me as though I was an intelligent adult and I tried my best to respond to all the stimulation she provided. My attempts at creative writing prospered under her guidance. For 1956/7 Mrs. C. was amazingly progressive and open with her class of girls. She taught us so much more than just the school curriculum. She was discreet when necessary and discussing personal things such as hygiene, manners and even polite etiquette as understood in social circles way above us all. Together with our music and art teachers Mrs. C. opened us up in many ways and gave us many worthwhile experiences which we would carry with us all our lives. One would not think that a walk through Bostall Woods, pausing awhile with our reading books on a bright sunny day, would make the impression that it did. We were introduced to art galleries, museums, Hampton Court and architecture, and best of all concerts and ballet. We had some really exciting school visits including one to McCalls fashion business. We learned how designers worked and how dress patterns were made for the mass market. As a follow-up we made clothes for ourselves and held a fashion show in school. Girls with enough confidence and poise were chosen to 'model'. A class mate who was a great artist sketched the pictures and I 'reported' on the whole thing. We were just like the professionals in the big fashion houses.

Many girls in my class came from poor, working class backgrounds and only possessed one school shirt, which was usually laundered at the weekends.

Just for that afternoon we all felt important. The sense of pride and dignity we felt was truly life-enhancing and helped to sow a lot of seeds in fertile young minds.

Mrs. C. spent a great deal of time preparing us for adult life. We never actually discussed childbirth, or ways of preventing it, so this area of knowledge was a little vague, even for those of us who liked to think we were grown up. However, there was much talk about how to behave with the opposite sex, and how to dress properly for job interviews and the world of work. "When you have husbands . . . or a home . . . or children . . ." were frequently used phrases. No one ever mentioned unmarried mothers. At that time it was definitely considered a terrible shame and girls who found themselves in such an unfortunate position were usually ushered away from home and had their babies in mother and baby homes. The babies were almost all adopted and the girls returned to their previous lives if their families were prepared to have them back.

I just lived for my music and the English lessons. Home life was difficult and stressful. When I felt really low and anti-social I would skip days at school when I should have been in cookery lessons or P.E. and Games. If I had no money I would ride across the Free Woolwich Ferry to Victoria Park or to Silvertown. Sometimes I would look down at the Ferry paddles and wonder how deep the water was. I wondered, just out of curiosity, how long it would take someone to drown in the dark, smelly water. Across the river, away from people who might recognize me, I would read a book in the park on fine days, or just walk out. I'd skip over the cables by 'Standard Cables', watch the river traffic, even walk as far as Greenwich.

If I had any money I would take a bus or train to the City and go to wonderful lunchtime recitals in churches like St. Martin in the Fields, or to the Festival Hall. It was at the South Bank that I met two new friends, Anna and Dov, both violinists with the London Schools Symphony Orchestra. We shared sandwiches and cake by the river, or if it rained we had to find cover inside the hall. Anna's father worked in shipping insurance in Woolwich and knew my father, but they lived in a lovely house in Lewisham. Dov lived in Surrey, near Leatherhead and his father did something important for the government which he didn't talk about.

A certain amount of devious behaviour was employed on these illicit days out of school, although it wasn't every week. My school uniform was a giveaway and I dreaded what my father would do if he was to discover what I was doing. So, instead of taking my school satchel on those days out I would take my music case instead. Rolled up inside would be a green corduroy skirt and my mother's scarf which I would change into in the public toilets at the station. Carrying my music bag to concerts and rehearsals looked entirely appropriate. I would pretend that I was on my way to a piano lesson, which sometimes was true. Only Anna and Dov knew that my piano lesson could take me from South East London to Central London and might detour to Lewisham or Blackheath. I am not sure how much my teachers at school knew of my exploits. Nothing was ever discussed or reported to my parents, for which I was truly grateful.

In the event of there being no concerts or rehearsals to go to I would go to the cinema. I saw all the musicals of the 1950's and somehow felt more guilty in the cinema than in going to the concerts.

In 1956 my illicit trips came to an abrupt end. There was a crisis in the Middle East and my father was recalled to the army as a reservist solider. My mother became ill with worry. She had to continue looking after the political club, holding my father's job open for him. I had to take care of the household cleaning, cooking and shopping and supervise my twelve year old tearaway brother. I missed my piano lessons for a while, and I missed my music friends desperately. The only good thing was the calmness in the house without father. I felt wicked for even thinking of it. He might even be killed. I didn't wish for that.

The peace at home did not last for very long. The day my father returned from Suez we actually saw him striding purposefully down the road towards our house. He was wearing a red beret. Only paratroopers wore red berets, my father's was navy blue. We peered in disbelief through the window and my mother's face drained of colour. She opened the door, but instead of greeting each other, they started shouting. My father was not allowed, of course, to discuss the method or reasons for his 'escape' or why he had arrived home carrying a rifle, which presumably should have been handed in to stores. We were led to believe that he had left a dangerous situation in a hurry.

The atmosphere in the house became unbearable and we all felt that we had to take great care before opening our mouths.

One night, during the small hours, I heard a stranger's voice downstairs. Past experience taught me to be cautious so I remained where

I was, peeking through the banister rail on the upstairs landing. A policeman was talking in hushed tones with my father.

"Keep your daughter at home for a few days," he said, "we can't guarantee what the papers will say!"

Fear gripped me. I had no idea what they were talking about. Could it have anything to do with me? Had they discovered my days out of school? Surely not! It might have been a bit naughty but I couldn't believe it would mean a late night visit from the police. No! It must be something else. Something serious? I wondered if it might have anything to do with my father's cloak and dagger return from the Middle East. I crept back to my bed, but I tossed and turned all night, hardly sleeping.

The next morning I prepared for school as usual. Downstairs my father was sitting at the table leafing carefully through the newspaper. Unusually, he was not washed or ready for work and my mother was no where in sight. He looked up and quite coolly said,

"You aren't going to school today. Your mother isn't very well. She's been taken to the hospital. She'll be home in a few days. You've got to look after the house and your brother."

There was no explanation. I didn't know if it was serious, but I knew from the look on my father's face that I'd better not ask. He gave me a shilling and suggested I go to the corner shop to buy a couple of bananas for tea.

I wandered to the shop in a daze, bought the bananas and returned home to a tirade of abuse because I had spent too much. Bravely, I tried to defend myself, then dared to add that I was going to see my mother.

"They won't let you in," he shouted, "children aren't allowed".

I went to the hospital and demanded to see my mother.

"No children allowed! Sorry!" I was told.

I insisted that I needed to see my mother and refused to go until they let me in. I was shown in to my mother's single room by an anxious looking young nurse. Five minutes! That's all I could have.

"What are you doing here?" is how my mother greeted me.

I said that I was worried and wanted to know what the problem was and how long she would be in hospital.

"I was going to have a baby," she said. "It decided not to come."

She assured me that she would be home in a day or two and urged me to go home.

I was so innocent that I had no idea of what had really happened.

Did babies just not grow? Did it come out dead? We never spoke of it. Some weeks later I caught sight of a local newspaper and read about a doctor who had helped women who didn't want their babies. In 1956 abortion was illegal and there were heavy penalties for anyone who assisted women in this way.

During my final year at school we moved to Woolwich, just a mile or so along the road. My father was to manage the Co-operative Club. It was near a parade of shops where my friend Yvonne's parents kept a pet shop. Yvonne and I sat together at school and sometimes walked home together but she never came into 'the house'. No one did. I was ashamed of it and fearing friends might reject the invitation I didn't issue them. We were friends in school. Astonishingly, forty seven years later we are still friends and have been writing to each other all that time as we moved to the north of England and Yvonne's family emigrated to Canada. She did get the better deal, I thought!

Our rooms at Woolwich were again a hotch-potch of spaces. At first I was allocated a first floor room, away from the family. It was a former store room. There was no lock on the door. One night I was in my bed reading when the door opened and a slightly inebriated man stumbled in. I screamed and he made a much swifter exit than his entrance. I barricaded the door with furniture in case it should happen again. The next day I protested vehemently about being placed in an unsafe situation. Hasty moves were made to clear chairs from another store on the ground floor next to our kitchen and a lock was fitted to the door. My new room was dark and dingy. The only window looked directly out onto a high, dingy brick wall, part of the 'Matchless' motor cycle factory next door. I had at least got my own room. I didn't feel that I could complain about the heavy drop-stamping machine which thudded continuously day and night. When that noise stopped for a while I was aware of noise from the ballroom which was over my head. I learned the band repertoire from memory in a few weeks. They always played the same music in the same order and the drummer never varied his patterns. They played the hit songs of the day, (though not yet rock and roll) and music from the 1940's. They tried to play Glenn Miller songs but were not quite up to it. I recognized the last waltz every night and knew that after that things would quieten down and I could go to sleep.

The club cat, kept for mousing, produced an unexpected litter of kittens one day and I fed the tiniest white one with drops of milk from my finger. It wasn't expected to survive, but she did. I claimed Libby for my own and she slept in my room. She seemed to love my music and would sit on top of the piano, purring, as I played. I'm sure we were soul mates.

It was my last year at school. I had no idea what I could reasonably do after that. I worried about it and of course sometimes dreamed of being a pianist or a librarian. I knew that I would have no choice in the matter and would have to do as I was told. My music friends Anna and Dov would be remaining at school until it was time for them to try for scholarships to music colleges.

I would have no chance of joining them. I had no music exams and would have no school examinations either. Some of my classmates talked about work in a tea packing factory at Charlton. Others joked about working in Woolworths, but many did expect to work in shops. A few dreamed of being models or air-hostesses. Only my artist friend Carol and a girl called Natasha, whose father was a chemist, had any real aspirations to find rewarding careers. I wondered if my friend Yvonne would work with animals but eventually she emigrated with her family to a new life on a smallholding in Canada.

In what was described as a 'leaving' interview the Deputy Head of the school told my parents that I would probably make a very competent clerk. My heart sank. However, I was told some time later that there was another option. By some miracle I had managed to be top of the class in my final year, worthy enough to be offered a place at Kidbrooke a newly built comprehensive school, where I could stay on and study for 'O' level exams. That was a rare opportunity for a secondary modern pupil. Usually only grammar school pupils could follow this route.

My father had already begun to investigate possible positions for me at Woolwich Docks. He had associates in the shipping and insurance offices. I felt utterly wretched at the whole situation. Once again I was not consulted. I had no choice at all. What was the point of even telling them about Kidbrooke? They had decided. People like us didn't sit examinations to better ourselves. Music was never considered to be any kind of future for me. It had been a hobby, just to keep me occupied. No! I would be found an office job for a few years, then I would find a husband and leave home. I would no longer be anyone's responsibility. That was the parental logic of most working class parents at that time. It was no use a girl getting ideas 'above her station!' Conversations would go on around me, but never with me.

Eventually, to my initial relief, I was told that I didn't have to work in an office in Woolwich. We would be moving again. I'd work in an office in Sheffield, in the steelworks!

"Sheffield!" Mrs. C. said in disgust, "What on earth are you going to Sheffield for?"

"I don't know Miss," I said, "so I won't be able to go to Kidbrooke School. I have to get a job."

We had a final school Prize Day. The then Lady Summerskill was to present the prizes. I was to play the piano so that Mrs. D. could conduct the choir.

I was so pleased to be able to participate in this way I overcame my nervous anxiety and my disappointment that my parents were not there.

I wasn't too nervous playing the piano, but I was petrified with anxiety when I had to climb the steps onto the platform to receive my awards. I was given a beautiful copy of Charles Dickens' 'David Copperfield', a prize for Literature, and a book called 'The Young Eve' as a First in Class prize. The music prize was a descant recorder. Mrs. D. told me years later that it hadn't been her choice. However, she couldn't have known then that I would learn to play it, along with the Treble and Tenor versions and develop a huge interest in Renaissance and Baroque music.

I read 'David Copperfield' several times through and then sought out other books by Dickens. I was eager to read everything he had written.

My friend Dov gave me a copy of 'Great Expectations' and Anna gave me some writing paper and envelopes before we said our tearful goodbyes.

'You will write won't you?' Anna said.

'Every week,' I said.

Dov promised to send me concert details and reviews. We promised each other that we would try to meet in the holidays. At that stage we did not realize that I would have a world of work and no school holidays and that Sheffield was quite a long journey on a train and cost money.

I was a schoolgirl one day and an adult the next. That's how things were. My school uniform was put aside and I was taken to Woolwich market for my adult wardrobe. After that I would be responsible for buying my own clothes. I was glad that my clothes were to be ready made and not home made. I was allowed to choose a suit with two skirts, one straight and one pleated. It was a soft pink. I chose a white and green dress with a big flared skirt and a pair of black suede shoes which had a tiny heel. The other necessary addition was an adult suspender belt and stockings, not forgetting a bottle of clear nail varnish to 'stop' any ladders one might have in the stockings.

I was told that the money for this extravaganza had come from an insurance policy, designed to mature just as I was leaving school. I think I was more pleased to realize that for once they had considered me than I was to spend the money. The biggest surprise was to be taken to

Selfridges store on Oxford Street to choose a new coat. All my coats and most of my clothes until then had been second-hand or made at home, my mother having had the one dress pattern for many years, simply added a few inches all round as I grew.

The coat I chose was not to the approval of my father, but I persisted and he reluctantly paid for it. I loved it. It was a princess style coat with a shawl collar, pale green in colour. I wore it until it literally fell apart!

The family prepared to move to Sheffield. My mother, brother and the dog were made to travel in the removal van, to save money. My father and I travelled with Libby on the train. After my hysterical protests at being told she would have to be put down I was allowed to keep her.

This move would be the last we would make as a family. There were things in my parents' lives about which we knew nothing, but would soon come to realize. Things which had triggered the decision to move and things which would bring devastating circumstances to all of us. When my grandfather, who lived in Sheffield, had posted my mother a local newspaper showing houses for sale he had simply helped matters along.

VISIT SUMMER 2002

Meeting Doreen at Woolwich Station after forty-five years gap was quite lovely, if a little bizarre. We had lost touch after leaving school, and after we moved to Yorkshire. Doreen was the only person to respond to an appeal I made in the South London Mercury newspaper. I had described my aims in writing this book and hoped someone would remember me. Fearing she might not recognize me I had sent a photograph of myself and my daughter, but Doreen didn't send one to me. It was interesting to people spot and eventually Doreen found us first. When she touched me on the arm and said 'Have I got the right person?' we just hugged each other and giggled as though we were still fifteen. Of course we are both older, greyer and larger but the years rolled away. My friend had found an old photograph of us, taken by a teacher on a school trip, which I had forgotten about. It amused my daughter and it reminded me of how much she resembled me at the same age. As the afternoon wore on and we talked over the lunch Doreen had prepared for us, I found myself slightly envying her. She had never moved more than a few miles from her childhood home. She had been happily married to a kind man, for forty years. She had raised three beautiful daughters and was now enjoying her grandchildren. Doreen was just the same kind, gentle person I remembered. Looking around her home it was obvious that she possessed some artistic flair, and culinary skills. She liked to read and was planning to learn to play her newly acquired electric keyboard. She is a very solid citizen, a rounded person, interested in other people and comfortable to be with. I warmed to her and I regretted that we had lost touch for so much of our lives.

Doreen took us to my old school, now called Churchfields and now a school for special needs children. We walked through St. Nicholas' Churchyard to Ceres Road. It hardly seemed to have changed at all. It seemed to be a clean, quiet street, a gentler environment than Tottenham. The only observable difference from forty years or more past was the presence of many Asian faces. The house was exactly the same except for having new, plastic windows. In spite of it being a warm, sunny day, I shivered as I remembered looking through those windows as I looked for my father returning from Middle East conflict.

Our second home in the Borough of Greenwich, at Woolwich had been demolished. I was glad that the motor cycle factory had gone too. There is still a Free Ferry at Woolwich, but now there are attractive riverside gardens lining the walkway towards the Arsenal and further down river the Millennium Dome and village at Greenwich shows that the area is reviving. Where I once skipped over huge cables and boxes by 'Standard Cables' and crates at the other side of the river, people now drive to the City Airport, or to the new town of Thamesmead. Plumstead and Winns Commons still remain public places, though there is some infilling with houses.

Woolwich is still dominated by the huge complex of Royal Arsenal buildings down river from the site of the sixteenth century dockyard that helped Tudor England dominate the world's oceans. Now, the Great Harry is a pub nearby, in a town centre that is rapidly re-building itself as a new tourist attraction in this part of south east London. One of the chief attractions is the Thames Flood Barrier, one of the world's biggest moveable barriers. The largest of its ten gates weigh almost 4,000 tonnes and are five storeys high when raised from the river bed. Two tides sweep in each day towards the barrier at 100 metres a minute. The Polar Ice Caps are gradually tilting London towards Europe, causing the water levels to keep rising. So this amazing structure isn't just dramatic and beautiful, but also reassuring.

The sheer scale and grim elegance of the Royal Arsenal is awe-inspiring. At 1080 feet the Georgian façade of Woolwich's Royal Artillery Barracks is the largest in the country. However, it is the secrets of the weapon making that took place here for 300 years that are most intriguing. Today, FIREPOWER, the new Royal Arsenal Museum complex, spread over seven acres, reveals the history of artillery, from Roman catapults to modern missiles.

Greenwich Borough has more open space than any other London borough, including seven walking trails. A forty mile network links most of the area's green places, from Thamesmead through to Crystal Palace. The Riverside Walk follows the Thames virtually all the way from Woolwich to Deptford. Bostall Woods still exist as an atmospheric area of heath and sloping hills overlooking the Thames and not far away are the ruins of Lesnes Abbey, built as a penance by Richard de Lucy for his part in the murder of Thomas a Becket.

Oxleas Wood, eight thousand years old, is all that is left of London's mediaeval forests. It is an area of great scientific interest and was once famous for its highwaymen. South Londoners and others are watching with interest and not a little apprehension at proposals for a new Thames crossing, possibly linking Gallion's Reach with East London. The present Mayor of London, Ken Livingstone has given his promises that Oxleas Wood will remain untouched by the proposed new road though sceptics are remaining vigilant on the matter.

My return visit was interesting and worthy of a second visit, especially to Greenwich. There was no real emotional pull, it was just a place we had passed through.

TINSLEY, SHEFFIELD

Tinsley, a small hamlet in Sheffield's east end might have remained an insignificant place in history except for its geographical position by the River Don. Plenty of evidence has been unearthed to indicate previous civilizations. Iron and Stone Age dwellers, Romans, Angles and Vikings and then the Normans. All of them found the river to be a vital element in their survival and progress. Water was needed to cultivate crops, to navigate and move goods and people and also as a marker for routes north and south. The Romans had built two forts nearby at Templeborough and at Brinsworth, with dwelling houses for their families and baths not far from each fort. In Anglo Saxon times manors were created at Tinsley and Brinsworth but were given to Norman knights after William's victory in 1066.

Tinsley eventually became a dependency of Tickhill Castle, owned by the de Busli family. William de London held the tenure of Tinsley and held the post of sergeantry by being presented annually with hawks to care for and train up for falconry, sport of noblemen. Falconry was probably carried out in Tinsley park and woods, or in open fields. Goshawks and sparrow hawks would have been used in woodland but peregrine falcons, merlins and kestrels would be used for hunting in open fields.

The woodland around Tinsley was also frequented by outlaws and robbers, so the Bawtry Road was at one time a dangerous place. In time turnpikes and tollgates were erected and the money collected was used to improve the roads. Bawtry Road was mainly used by drivers of covered goods wagons.

Mail coaches eventually operated along the main Sheffield Road, calling at safe coaching inns and picking up passengers along the route.

Until the gradual development of industry Tinsley inhabitants either worked by the river, canals, locks or barges, or they were farmers. Tinsley became an important loading and unloading place for Sheffield. It was popularly known as the Port of Sheffield until the canal was cut to Sheffield, opening in 1819. Until 1762 the barge boats had been pulled by men, but the towpaths were widened and improved to allow horses to be used. A boy could lead a horse and do the work of several men.

By the mid-nineteenth century the railways had arrived, and so came a huge influx of workers, including both of my grandfathers, though both from very different backgrounds.

Coal, iron and stone had been worked at Tinsley for many years before the railways arrived, but this rapidly increased along with the cutlery and steelmaking industries.

Hurried building of back to back worker's cottages (one room deep) and two-up, two-down houses sprang up in long terraces. Bigger and better houses a short distance away were built for the managers and foremen. The burgeoning community needed schools, churches and sadly, large burial grounds, and in the course of time, shops. Until then fresh vegetables and eggs and other produce was bought from the local farms or from deliveries by the horse drawn purveyors of household goods of all kinds.

As Tinsley grew in population and wealth so too did the interest in cultural affairs. A library was endowed by the Scottish philanthropist Andrew Carnegie, and church-going was also a serious pursuit. One was either 'church' and slightly aloof, or 'chapel' and given to public displays such as dressing up at Whitsuntide for the huge gatherings in Sheffield Parks, for the Whit Sings. The Annual Sunday School Queens with attendants and masses of flowers provided much colour and excitement. The rhythm of the year and the church festivals provided most of the community involvement, except for the local public houses of course, which were looked upon as dens of iniquity by respectable people.

By the turn of the twentieth century Tinsley was among the first of Sheffield's outlying hamlets to use the new electric trams. They provided workers with the means to travel further to seek work and the general population with the means to explore the wider amenities of the city.

In 1914, the year my father was born in Carbrook, near Tinsley, nearly 17,000 Sheffield families still lived in back to back houses and another 8,000 families lived in sub-standard houses. Determined efforts were made by the Sheffield Corporation to replace privy middens with water closets. Tinsley people considered themselves well off when the new sewage treatment plant began in Blackburn Meadows. No one complained of the smell. With the steel factory chimneys belching out acrid smoke all day there were more things to worry about.

Traditional light crafts expanded rapidly. Cutlers, file cutters, edge tool makers and silversmiths manufactured a great variety of goods which required specialist skills. Much of this work was carried out in 'little mesters' workshops. These were independent men of skill but little money. They were gradually threatened by cheaper, foreign competition. At first they were reluctant to spend money on new expensive machinery but eventually realized they would have to do just that. Sixteen weeks of strikes against the installation of file-cutting machines in 1866 ended in defeat, but it was several more years before most of the 'little mesters' realized the benefits to themselves and workers, of the new mechanisation.

The early trade unions had a long struggle with bosses when they attempted to install machinery. Some took extreme measures to bully workers into membership. The 'Sheffield Outrages' became a national scandal and led to the passing of the 1871 Trade Union Act which allowed unions to meet openly rather than in secret. Twelve of the unions had been involved in violent assaults and in 'rattening' practices, whereby a non-union worker's tools and wheelbands were stolen, and gunpowder was placed in chimney stacks and grinding troughs.

Sometimes it was difficult for less educated workers to discriminate between well meaning socialist leaders and destructive anarchists. There were a number of other political factions in between, not to mention government spies and infiltrators.

The steelworks employed large labour forces in Tinsley from the First World War onwards. The works stretched all the way along Sheffield Road, through Templeborough, Tinsley, Carbrook and Attercliffe towards the city centre.

Mercifully, for Tinsley at least, Hitler's bombers during the Second World War had not yet developed reliable radar, and whilst they attempted to bomb the steelworks they were largely unsuccessful. The city centre however received a massive bombing blitz. One of my uncles had a lucky escape when he left the 'Marples' hotel. Moments later it was flattened by bombs.

Well into the 1950's Tinsley remained a heavily polluted area with chimneys belching out smoke and filth. Eventually a Clean Air Act was passed and the environment began to improve. Sadly, the future of steel-making, mining and cutlery-making would steadily decline along with their unique close communities.

THE MOVE TO TINSLEY

The train journey from St. Pancras to Sheffield seemed endless. My tiny kitten was fretful being in the box. My father read his newspaper and we spoke little. I was immersed in my own thoughts. I felt a deeper sense of injustice about this move than I had about any of the previous ones.

Instead of looking forward I could only think of what I was leaving behind. I had begun to grow in confidence and make friends. My music was at last showing some promise and I had begun to appreciate all the music and culture that London could offer. It seemed to me that we were taking a retrograde step. I spent much of the journey thinking of ways in which I could escape and return to London. During the next two years I would develop a level of resourcefulness which I had not thought possible.

We travelled by tram from Sheffield to Tinsley, a dismal journey of about five miles. My father pointed out and named all the steelworks buildings along the route. There were Tommy Ward's (Thos. W. Ward), Brown Bayley's, Firth Brown, George Cohen's 600 Works, Darwin's and Tozer's (Steel, Peech and Tozer).

Our house, on St. Lawrence Road, was at the top of a hill and we arrived exhausted. I was glad that I hadn't made the journey in the removal van, though my mother and brother seemed to have endured it quite well and were fairly comfortable when we arrived. After cups of tea all round and milk for Libby I was at least heartened to see both kitten and dog snuggling up together in the big basket, fast asleep.

Looking on the bright side we had at last a proper house, a bedroom each, an attic and a cellar. The cellar top had a heavy stone slab which was as cold as any fridge. This is where we kept milk and dairy things. The toilet was outside, but close to the house, and we had a decent garden with a lovely lilac tree. Between every two houses was a shared passage and each house had its own back gate. Entry to the house was by a side door in the covered passage, or from a back door.

The side door led into a tiny hall and the stairs beyond. To the right was the living room and kitchen, to the left was the sitting room. We had stopped using the term parlour when we stopped living in a proper house.

The bay-windowed sitting room looked out onto the 'Rec' (Recreation Ground) where men played cricket on Sundays and there was a children's playground. The public library was a short walk through the Rec.

Tinsley 'front' on the main Sheffield Road boasted a few shops, mainly food shops and a post office and also a betting shop where my Uncle Frank still worked 'on the books'.

Towards the bottom of the road where we lived was a row of terraced houses where my Grandad lived (my mother's father). I hadn't seen my Grandad and Nan (Grandad's second wife) since I was seven years old. Their house was permeated with the smell of years of St. Bruno tobacco smoke. My Grandad sat in a large Windsor chair most of the time. He

The first Sheffield house, 1958

suffered from angina. Once he had been a foreman on the new railways. It was quite difficult to imagine him doing hard, manual labour. He seemed such a quiet gently spoken man, keen on reading books and completing crossword puzzles. It was easier to imagine him belonging to his previous existence in rural Lincolnshire and Suffolk. He had journeyed to industrial Yorkshire with his young, first bride, my maternal grandmother, in search of work.

My Nan had been his friend and helpmeet following the early death of his first wife. Now they lived with their daughter, my step-aunt if you like, though I never called her aunt because she and I were so close in age.

It was a pleasant discovery to find that we had relations to visit. My brother and I would find aunties and uncles, though no cousins. The only uncle who had in fact had six daughters had argued with my father years before and all contact had been lost. I began to appreciate why my mother had been so keen to return to her childhood home. For my father it was quite a different story. For the time being we had a home.

My father detested having to work in the steelworks, though his engineering skills learned in the army had equipped him to take skilled work. Even though he was spared the toil of hot, dirty labouring, it was still a noisy and unhealthy workplace. He also had to work shifts, early mornings, daytime and night working. Most men sought their escape at the end of a shift in the way they had always done, in the local pubs and working men's clubs, familiar ground to my father. More familiar now were the pubs, clubs and sporting venues of his youth. Some people had never moved away. My father soon re-kindled old friendships, including that of a former girl friend and comrades in the communist party. Father had lost none of his Marxist fervour and extreme political views, but recognized that he still had to be covert in his activities if he wanted to keep his job. Industrial agitators and industrial espionage was a very serious matter in the steel business as I was to discover for myself in later employment.

As expected I was found an office job in a steel factory nearby. I had no choice in the matter and my opinions counted for nothing. My brother had to start a new school, again. His south London accent disappeared in the first few weeks. He was a survivor!

Work was worse than my worst school. The days were long, from 8.30 a.m. until 5.00 p.m. with just thirty five minutes for lunch. I couldn't afford to buy lunch in the canteen so I ran home, up the hill, ate a quick sandwich and ran back again. At least Saturdays and Sundays were free. I would be entitled to one week's holiday in my first year. The system was that the most senior members of my office were allowed to put their names on the holiday grid first, so that I was obliged to take my holiday in the week which no one else wanted. The office could not allow for all of us to be absent at the same time. I thought it rather strange that during 'works weeks' the entire steelworks closed down and except for a small skeleton staff who cleaned and serviced machinery, the entire workforce was obliged to take their holidays.

My wages, as a junior clerk, were £2.9s.0d paid weekly in cash, in a small brown envelope. I took it home to my parents. I was allowed to keep nineteen shillings for toiletries, stockings and clothes. There were many weeks when I painted ladders in my stockings with nail varnish to make them last longer. No one dared to go to work without stockings. I went without make-up and used my mother's talcum powder. I had few clothes. I needed to save for books, music and train fares to London whenever I could manage it.

My job was incredibly boring. It required little of me than the ability to climb up and down ladders to a wall full of files all day. I was in a purchasing office. Typists had prepared orders to various places for engineering supplies. Each order form had five duplicate copies of different colours. My afternoon job was to tear off the top copies and place them in envelopes for posting. The next day I separated the copies and some were arranged in alphabetical order, some in order of dates, others in number order and the last copy to the originator of the order.

All had to be filed correctly. There were piles and piles of them. Generally the other 'girls' in the office, whose ages ranged from sixteen to forty something, were good natured. Of course I was teased about my London accent and I was sent on various missions so that people in other offices could hear me speak. I learned about office cliques and soon sensed when gossip was rife about someone when voices were hushed. I could remain neutral because I didn't really know anyone personally. As a Junior I was unlikely to be a party to their whisperings. Again I was an outsider.

I didn't really care. However, I was extremely bored and frustrated with work. When the opportunity arose for me to try a bit of typing I urged one of the girls to show me what to do. As workloads increased when people were away on holiday I was allowed to take on some typing and stationery work. My confidence increased and I enrolled at evening classes to study shorthand, typing and English language. I realized that if I did well I could apply for a more interesting and better paid job. More money would mean that I could have longer trips to London.

Whilst I was in Sheffield I was very single-minded and focused on my objectives, but when I was in London I found it more and more painful to make the return journey.

Eventually Anna became a student at Goldsmith's College. Dov, a year younger was destined for the Royal College of Music. His parents saw my visits as an upsetting diversion. Although they were always polite and hospitable they never asked about my life and they never allowed their son to visit me. In one sense it was a blessing in disguise. I would have been too embarrassed to let him see our house and there was no where for him to sleep overnight. Dov felt just as suffocated by his parents as I did by mine. He liked me to visit because he could escape for a short while. He wanted to go to college and he didn't mind the hours of daily practising, but he resented his parents' interference in his life. I identified with that, though curiously I had begun to feel more in control of my life as my parents became engrossed in their own problems.

I desperately wanted to live in London again but couldn't see a way of achieving it quickly. For a while we had to be content with afternoons in Greenwich Park, or by the river. Sometimes a concert. These trips helped to strengthen my resolve. If I worked harder and gained some real qualifications perhaps I could get a job in London. I might even be able to study music again. Dov was enthusiastic and encouraging. Sometimes, when we were a threesome, Anna, Dov and myself dreamed aloud about us all living together, with no parents.

I continued to work hard at my classes and just went through the motions at my office job. I sought out my mother's childhood piano teacher, now a very aged, but kind, and more importantly, cheap music teacher. She gave my piano work more sense of purpose, for a while at least.

I discovered that it was possible to study for other exams at night school including 'O' and 'A' levels. People who for one reason or another had been unable to study at school could enter themselves. I pored over the exam syllabus for weeks and there were frantic phone calls to Dov to ask his opinion about subjects. He was excited for me and said I should most definitely study English Literature and History. I enrolled for several subjects, having excelled at R.S.A. English Language and Typing. I'm sorry to say that Shorthand proved to be a disaster.

My parents had little to say about my classes. There was certainly no encouragement or praise. I sensed that things were not right between them.

I tried to play the piano when my father was out of the house. There was such a stifling atmosphere when he was at home that it was impossible to concentrate.

One day a visitor arrived to see my father, but he was not at home. I recognized the stern looking woman as one of the evening school teachers, though not one of mine. She showed me a red card with CP emblazoned on it, but she quickly returned it to her purse when I explained that my father was not at home. She said she would call again for his 'contribution' but she didn't.

I became used to my father having visitors who were nothing to do with the family. They were usually let in through the side door so that we didn't actually see them. Every time one particular visitor left the house my parents seemed to argue and doors were slammed as my father left the house soon afterwards. I didn't ask anyone about it. I thought it prudent to remain quiet and neutral. That way I could try to get on with my own life without too much interference. I felt concerned for my mother but I didn't know what I could do. She wouldn't talk to me about anything.

My father was not the only one able to renew former friendships and interests. Amelie, was my mother's childhood friend and they had written to each other for all the years that my mother and we had been traipsed all around the country. Amelie was living nearby and was badly crippled with arthritis. She would soon be wheelchair bound and physically helpless. Of course we visited her often. I think the two of them had ideas that I might strike up a relationship with Simon, Amelie's middle son, who was the same age as me. However, I found him to be quite arrogant, loud and uncouth. Anton, who was four years older was much more interesting and completely different. It was difficult to accept that they were brothers. I would learn more about Anton as time passed. This was a family with secrets too. We lived in a time when family secrets were just that. Children were told nothing. By comparison to the youth of today we were naïve and unquestioning. The strange thing was that Anton seemed to know all about my parents and I knew nothing of his. Amelie's husband was very remote, but she kept Anton closest of her three sons. He did everything for her and he did it with a quiet dignity and no shred of resentment. Anton became an understanding and gentle friend, just like Dov, though slightly older. For some time my relationship with both of them was purely platonic. In time my loyalties would be severely tested and torn.

Anton was an apprenticed electrical engineer until he was twenty one years of age, after which the government would take him away for two years National Service in the Army. He planned one day to develop his own business and build his own house. He was cultured and read books of all kinds, including poetry. Encouraged by Amelie he was learning to play the trumpet and loved the dance music of the 1940's especially the music of Glenn Miller, Paul Whiteman and Woody Hermann. He took me to see the ballet and loved it as much as I did. We had much in common. His undemanding company and gentle nature was a pleasant relief from the tensions which existed at home. When we were together I felt protected.

It wasn't so much that Dov and I grew apart. We were like-minded souls. We had been forced apart by our parents and found it impossible to maintain a close relationship with so many miles between us. We would remain friends from a distance and I would, for a while at least, rely on his wisdom and advice when it really mattered.

Feeling totally frustrated with the lack of opportunity in my job, I spent six months in two different, but equally unfulfilling posts. The first was in a small family run engineering firm where I spent all day typing the same letter, individually, to potential customers in Africa and Asia. Each letter had to be pristine and perfect. This was long before the days of word processors and printers, and photocopying had yet to be invented. Undaunted, I used the situation to learn something else to add to my C.V. I befriended the telephonist who showed me how to operate the PBX switch board. I then worked in another job as a Receptionist/ Telephonist/Typist and general dogsbody, until one disastrous day when I felt compelled to walk out. This was very untypical of me. My parents were furious. Both of them refused to listen to my reasons. I tried to explain that the Managing Director had been extremely abusive towards me. He had a green carpet in his office around which he played golf. Unfortunately for me one afternoon I was taking in a tray of tea when inadvertently I hit the golf ball with the door. I was shocked to hear the torrent of swearing and verbal abuse which followed. Without thinking I flung the tea towards him and fled.

I was out of work and angry because it wasn't my fault. I spent the weekend in London being consoled by Dov before he finally started his college career. I didn't know it then, but I wouldn't see him again for several years.

Anton was patient and loving. I don't understand to this day how he had managed to cope with all of his life experiences without feeling bitter or depressed.

Shortly before his twenty first birthday the brown official envelope arrived. It was his National Service Call instructions. He was among the final group of young men to be called for army service. His father was unemotional but worried because now he would have to take on the role of major carer. Amelie was tearful. In private I was distraught.

Selfishly I was thinking only of myself. Why did everything disintegrate? Would my life never be stable and safe? It seemed that everyone I grew fond of would desert me.

Of course we all knew that National Service was compulsory but somehow we had hoped that it would be abolished before it was Anton's turn.

I couldn't bear the thoughts of losing Anton as well as Dov. I decided that I would try to work really hard and get myself into a college somewhere. Anywhere would be better than staying at home where I continued to feel belittled and of no consequence.

Anton had been thinking of the future too, but he was several stages ahead of me.

Anton had discovered that if he was prepared to sign on for an extra third year as a regular solider, he would be entitled to be accompanied by his wife.

I was almost eighteen when Anton asked my father if we could be married in two months time. I expected to encounter deep trouble, but instead it was quietly accepted, except for my father asking my mother how on earth she had let this happen.

I still did not realize that our wedding and my leaving home at last gave my father the opportunity to solve his own dilemma.

The Registry Office was booked. I bought a new dress (turquoise brocade) a tiny white petal hat and some white lace gloves. I thought that I looked like Grace Kelly. Anton borrowed his father's navy suit. The day arrived and so did a beautiful corsage of three pink carnations and white freesia, from Amelie. I still remember the smell of the flowers.

A small gathering had been hastily arranged at my parents' house and a neighbour had been persuaded to drive us to the Registry Office in his car. I was completely oblivious to the fracas which had ensued there. I was told some time later that my father's girl-friend had arrived to see the guests and me arriving at the Registry Office. Back at the house my father gave a short polite speech and wished us both well. We cut the cake and as soon as we could respectfully leave we were driven to Sheffield station en route for a few days honeymoon in Scarborough, paid for by my in laws.

Scarborough in early March was bracing to say the least, but it was a welcome escape. Afterwards I had to return home to my parents and Anton had to journey to Catterick to undergo his army basic training. Wives were not allowed to join their husbands for that period and the six weeks wait seemed a very long time. Like most new recruits Anton was homesick and worried that he wouldn't survive the physical training. But he did. I was worried about my parents. Aware that things were not right

Wedding Day with Anton, 1960

84

between them I felt helpless to do anything and guilty that before much longer I would be leaving home to join Anton wherever he might be posted.

After his initial training Anton was a regular solider with the Royal Corps of Signals. He was to be based in Germany with the British Army of the Rhine.

We were both young, very naïve and certainly uneducated about Germany and what had happened there during the war, fifteen years before. The government had suppressed much information about the war and the great and informative films and books were still being written. We knew some basic facts but had been shielded from the horrors of the war which had touched our families more than we knew at that time.

I was soon to experience the same feelings as my mother, as an army wife. The army at that time simply treated wives as excess baggage. There was no sense of dignity or consideration whatsoever. I couldn't travel with Anton. I followed later and flew in an aeroplane for the first time. I was terrified about the journey and very sick.

VERDEN, NORTH WESTERN GERMANY

Verden lies twenty eight kilometres south east of the port of Bremen. It is a former Episcopal seat of some importance and has a fairly mixed historic background. This area of north western Germany, once part of the Hapsburg Empire and once under the jurisdiction of the Swedes, lies in a strategically important position on the main Hanover rail line and within easy reach of the coast. To the south of the town is the River Aller. Before the Second World War Verden had been a garrison town for German soldiers. After the war the German garrison became a British one.

The British Army of the Rhine began with the end of the war. After German capitulation the Allied forces remained in the positions they found themselves at the end of hostilities. There followed a time of political reorientation and the division of Germany into occupied zones. After the end of the war the British army was greatly reduced in manpower, to such an extent that the newly formed British Rhine Army consisted of only two Brigade Divisions, the 7th Armoured Division and the 2nd Infantry Division, which were based in various former German Army barracks in Lower Saxony and North Rhine Westfalia. In 1950 and 1952 these were strengthened by two more divisions.

The Royal Signals, Anton's regiment, are responsible for all communications in BAOR, including radios, directional radios and telegraphy in war and the telephone system in peacetime. Each BAOR Division has a Signals regiment and each Brigade a Signals Squadron.

These are responsible for maintaining communications and the passage of information for units up to Battalion size. They maintain and carry out emergency repairs on the radio equipment of front line troops. Importantly the Electronic Warfare Signals Units jams enemy radio nets, intercepts and deciphers enemy signals.

In recent times the collapse of the Warsaw Pact and the Soviet Union has called into question the continued existence of BAOR. After the re-unification of Germany and the withdrawal of Soviet troops from the former DDR, the British Ministry of Defence has begun to reduce the numbers of its forces in Germany. The remaining troops are now a part of the new Allied Rapid Reaction Corps (ARRC) which is British led. There will be much fewer large scale field training exercises, since computer simulation at regimental level has been introduced and live firing exercises will only take place on ranges.

Because there are fewer troops stationed in Germany there are fewer families living there and many of the former homes occupied by the military units have either been sold, or in some cases demolished, to make way for new motorways or re-development schemes.

Verden is no exception. The Army has disappeared from the town. There is now no Forces Club or Naafi shop. The town has been transformed.

TO GERMANY

My mother found the confidence and the fare to accompany me to the airport in London. It was a strange feeling remembering three years before with my father, travelling in the other direction.

I promised to write home every week, then bit my lip as we briefly hugged each other. I didn't have the courage to tell my mother that I was expecting a baby. She might have prevented me from going. I would tell her in my first letter home.

The flight to Hanover was traumatic from start to finish. There was a fault with the engines and we were delayed. By the time the plane finally took off my imagination had run riot and I was firmly convinced that we would crash into the North Sea. I sat next to a charming Swedish gentleman, a representative of Electrolux, travelling on business. He attempted to involve me in polite conversation, sensing that I was terrified of flying. When I found it necessary to use the 'sick' bag he was very gallant and simply took the bag from me and buzzed the cabin attendant. We were over an hour late arriving at Hanover. I spotted Anton and his military driver immediately. They looked relieved.

It was dark outside and the long drive on fairly straight roads almost lulled me to sleep. When we arrived at Verden the driver left us and we were free to talk. It seemed that our names were on a waiting list for a military house. For the time being we had to live in a hotel room. Initially this seemed to be a satisfactory solution, especially as I discovered that there were a number of other young army couples, some with children, also living there.

As the weeks passed it became clear that the prospect of being allocated our own accommodation was remote. The problems of living at the hotel seemed to escalate daily and I grew increasingly anxious and ill. I tried to learn the German language but the opportunities to use it were limited. I had some brief conversations with the hotel maid who changed the bed linen weekly. The manager and the other staff were not keen to converse with us. They were in fact very un-cooperative, though they were quite happy to accept our money.

Our room was on the top, fourth floor. There was no lift. It was cold most of the time and hot water took a long time to find its way up the pipes to our washbasin. If we needed a bath we had to use the bathroom along the corridor. It had to be ordered and paid extra for. The long windows in our room overlooked the cobbled street, then named Richtofenstrasse, to the small parade of tiny shops and small Hansel and Gretel type houses beyond, with their orange tiled roofs.

From my very first day the army families were living under a night time curfew because of a serious incident in the town. A British solider had become embroiled in a fight with a German youth who had later died of stab wounds. This incident did nothing to help the existing coolness between the townspeople and our soldiers, who now occupied a former German barracks. We all had to live together. There was no option. However, in general the local population disliked us and some people made daily life as difficult as they possibly could. It was a small town of most elderly people. The younger families were sparse and mostly had one or both partners working for the army establishment in some way. Others travelled out to Bremen, the nearest port, to work, and some in the other direction, to Hanover.

We were unable to afford food in the hotel. We were forced to eat our meals at the Toc H Forces Club which was a few hundred yards away from the hotel. The food was mostly fried and very limited. The staff though were extremely kind and realized the limitations. Most of us shopped only at the Naafi stores, at the barracks, over a mile's walk away. Some of the town shops were unwilling to serve us, though we were received warmly by the farm people who came to sell their produce in the market square once a week. Many people relied heavily on parcels from home, or on supplies bought whilst they were on home leave.

History repeated itself when I realized how difficult it was to make and retain friendships with army people. Soldiers and their families were constantly being transferred to other units, or moving accommodation. It was a transient existence in a mostly unwelcoming and worrying environment. Husbands could be sent on missions or exercises at very short notice. We could not contact them or even know their whereabouts and we did not always know when they would return.

Apart from meals at the club, shopping trips to the Naafi and visits to the medical centre I occupied myself by writing and studying correspondence courses in Literature and Religious Studies, always conscious that I had better keep Jewish history books under lock and key when I left the room. Sometimes writing projects were unfinished because my attention and concentration waned. I felt frequently ill, lonely and depressed, especially when Anton was away. I tried to have a routine of daily walks around the town or down to the River Aller. On those days I was anxious because not having a front door key I had to ring the hotel doorbell and just hope that someone would answer it. Sometimes they didn't and I had to go walking round the town again until I could get back to the room. This was not very pleasant on cold, wet days. I felt uncomfortable too if the manager's wife answered the door. She did not speak any English and she never smiled. I made a point of smiling at her in any case and always said, 'Guten Tag!'

The manager, Herr Mahlmann was a huge, bespectacled man who spoke quite reasonable English when it suited him. He had formerly been a tank driver in Rommel's Desert Army. He always had a superior air about him as did his friend the Police Chief, who, armed with a pistol, frequented the hotel bar every night until closing time. Although I had no real reason to feel nervous I felt that I needed to be cautious and on my guard the whole time. It was only fifteen years since the war had ended and I was carrying a Jewish child whose grandparents had disappeared in 1939 en route from Vienna to Berlin where they thought they might be safer. They entrusted their baby to the Red Cross and eventual adoption in England. What happened to them afterwards remains pure speculation.

Anton and I tried to keep dark thoughts from our minds. The secret was our own. It was a difficult time for him too. He was ill and deeply distressed following an army visit to Bergen-Belsen and suffered injuries to his shoulder whilst firing a rocket launcher on Luneberg Heath during an army exercise. He too was at a low ebb. Worse was to follow.

When we should have been celebrating her birth we were mourning the loss of the baby. It was a wonder that we didn't all die of pneumonia. It was so devastatingly awful that even now, forty three years on I can't allow myself to dwell on it. At the time I was inconsolable and deranged. The pain, the sense of overwhelming sadness and loss and the feelings of guilt are with me still if I allow them to surface. Every birthday, anniversary, Christmas still creates painful remembrance. The hospital, doctors and nursing sisters did their best but I was not an easy patient. I spent months hoping the pills would kill me, or at least numb the reality. All I wanted was to curl up in a ball and never wake up. I felt the need to go home but was confused about where home was. I couldn't face my parents and I had nowhere else to go. My world had crumbled and even kind, loyal gentle Anton was at a loss to know how he could help me. I had let everyone down. I was so lethargic that I hadn't the energy to worry about anyone else. Being a depressive patient means that you become totally selfish without meaning to be. There were people who offered help which I was not ready to accept. I had bursts of activity and brief flashes of self-motivation. I busied myself with mundane things at the clinic and was eventually and reluctantly drawn into a different activity when I was persuaded to play the piano for an Inter-faith Sunday School, organized by a Salvationist soldier. I had a love-hate relationship with this activity. Some of the hymns were uplifting, but there were many times when I would end up in a crumpled heap hearing the words of others. I tried not to look at the children's faces for fear of losing my composure. I was glad to hide behind the piano. One day the children sang an old Sally Army chorus,

> *"Climb! Climb up sunshine mountain*
> *Heavenly breezes blow,*
> *Climb! Climb up sunshine mountain*
> *Faces all aglow,*
> *Climb! Climb up sunshine mountain*
> *Looking to the sky,*
> *Climb! Climb up sunshine mountain*
> *You and I."*

Back at the hotel I found myself humming the tune. I was shocked that I had allowed myself to sing. I had no right to be happy. How could I possibly sing when life was so awful?

Anton, sensible as usual, though no less sad, made me believe that it was a sign of hope for me. It must be a starting point. A key to my future.

> *"You can become a teacher, a music teacher,"* Anton said, *"When we get*
> *back to England we'll find out what you need to do."*

We both decided to continue studying Jewish History, together with Torah, and we would speak with the Rabbi in Sheffield when we were finally home. We wanted to properly understand those parts of our heritage denied to us. Both of our families had squashed any leanings towards religion. As far as my father was concerned God was a figment of imagination. He didn't exist. Religion had only caused hurt to the Jewish people and many other people across the globe. My father's view was that people who needed to rely on religion were weak.

We kept our aims to ourselves. It didn't matter what anyone else thought. We were trying to build our own lives in a way that suited us.

Sooner than expected we were on a flight back to England. Anton had been selected for special training in communications and we would spend time in beautiful Richmond, North Yorkshire, while he was engaged in work at Catterick. On his return to Germany he would be part of a unit responsible for patrolling the area around the newly built Berlin Wall.

Anton was promoted which meant there would be an increase in salary and hopefully we would have a house too. At least that was how the army wanted to portray the situation. In reality the promotion meant more responsibility, slightly more money, but no house. The promotion was meant to encourage him to sign on for longer service, which he had no intention of doing. He had been a model solider in the face of a great deal of personal anguish. He had done everything that was required of him, but he wanted his life back again. That didn't include Germany or the army.

It had been the worst three years of our lives. We returned from Richmond to Verden Garrison for another year. We accepted several kind offers, spending some time in the army house of a family who had returned temporarily to England and we spent the long summer and Christmas holidays in Officer's quarters, usually occupied by two school teachers and a nurse. It was a huge relief to be away from the hotel room. We were able to relax more and I was able to gather more strength.

At about this time something else happened which would have a lasting effect on my future. I was thrown another lifeline and I gladly grabbed hold of it. A Grand Piano had been uncovered in an upstairs room at the Forces Club. It hadn't been played for years. I was able to play the piano every day for as long as I wished and at first nobody knew I was there. Eventually, to my annoyance, I was discovered by the Head Teacher of the Garrison School who begged me to teach his son. I really didn't want to become involved and I was full of apprehension. However, he was a very bright, keen boy, and I was encouraged by his progress. Music was posted out from England, for both of us. My gloomy thoughts were lifted and it became a therapeutic process. My pupil's progress was rapid and his interest was gratifying. He was the only person I would miss when we finally returned home.

I had no desire to ever return to a place of hurt and disappointment.

Because Germany had been such a traumatic experience I have felt quite unable to make a return visit in the way I have for the other chapters of this book. Who knows? Maybe a return visit would help to allay a host of fears and ghosts? But what if it didn't? I haven't felt so far able to take the risk. However, I did want to try and discover what life in Verden is like now, so I have had to do this by remote control.

I have used material obtained from military sources, archives and museums. Verden's council now boasts a tourist information office and kindly sent me a number of useful leaflets, though all in German. I have talked with voluntary workers from the WRVS and the SSAFA Forces Help organisation, and consulted libraries, newspapers and friends and colleagues who have some knowledge and interest in German and military affairs.

It has not been possible for me to speak with present day residents of the town of Verden, but it is clear that there have been many changes since the 1960's.

The British Army has been withdrawn from the town, although there is a small unit at nearby Celle. The Forces Club and Naafi shop is no longer there and military houses have either been demolished or passed into private ownership. The barracks now houses a Museum devoted to all things equestrian, a Horse Museum reflecting the main interest of the town today. The road name for Baron Richtofen is now part of the re-named and widened Grosse Strasse which now has a new shopping centre and improved transport links. I am pleased to know that the hotel we lived in so miserably has been demolished. The town now has several new hotels, catering for the hundreds of visitors and tourists who come for the seven horse fairs and associated festivals and other events. Riding schools abound. The River Aller also provides new attractions in the form of riverboat trips and parties. There is a children's fun fair and circus, a new swimming pool and leisure centre.

Since many of the town's inhabitants had once depended on the army for their employment or livelihood it was vital that once the army had left the town new ways of re-generating business were found. It would appear to have been successful, though one can't help wondering that amid all the razzamatazz, beer festivals and leisure pursuits the ancient history might have been submerged. Apart from the Horse Museum the Domherrenhaus, an eighteenth century gentleman's residence, probably once connected with the Domkirche, and one or two historic houses, there is very little to interest the 'serious' visitor. The huge Dom (Church) is still there, but I have been unable to assess whether it now influences anything in the town, or whether it is just an historic, imposing building, to be photographed by the tourists.

Finally in this short assessment, and most pleasing to me, is that the partly wooded, but mainly uncultivated heathland (Luneberg Heath) between Luneberg and Celle is grazed by flocks of sheep. In the northwest of the region is a 200 square-kilometre nature reserve where motoring is forbidden. There are networks of footpaths and cycle tracks and horse-riding is also possible. In late August the heather erupts in deep purple swathes. Picturesque villages are dotted around, with some examples of old timber and brick houses and churches forming a pretty backdrop for festivals, the annual coronation of the Queen of the Heath, and the shepherds who still wear traditional green outfits.

It was here on May 4th 1945, that Field Marshal Montgomery accepted the unconditional German surrender. British soldiers still exercise on the heath, though in much fewer numbers. One can only be grateful that the British Rhine Army played its part in helping Germany to become a united, democratic country and will continue to help defend and secure peace, whether in Germany, or under a United Nations flag somewhere else in the world.

RICHMOND, NORTH YORKSHIRE

It was difficult to decide where to place this chapter, the plan of the book being to treat each location as a separate entity, describing its origins, a short personal history and a return visit. As Richmond was in effect sandwiched between two tours of duty in Germany it would have broken the flow of the narrative to have inserted it between the German pages.

Richmond was in any case a special place. It proved to be a place of some healing and calm, though I hardly recognized it as such whilst I was living there.

Richmond was founded after William the Conqueror's harrying of the North in 1069. The castle was built two years later by Alain of Brittany, to gain control over the devastated surroundings. Perched high above the River Swale the castle dominates the countryside around. The town grew around the castle. In 1137, the Earl gave a charter for a market on the outer bailey of his castle, and in 1329 the market received a Royal Charter. In the fourteenth century, because raids from the Scots became so intense, a wall was built, remains of which can still be seen in the steep, narrow wynds that lead from the market place.

Soldiers were garrisoned in the castle during the eighteenth and nineteenth centuries and during the First World War, in the twentieth century, it was to house conscientious objectors. During the Second World War it was used as an air raid lookout post.

Richmond grew more prosperous during the Mediaeval period and later was an important trading place for farmers selling grain and wool and also the lead production from Swaledale. In the eighteenth century Richmond became a fashionable resort and grew significantly. Many Georgian buildings can still be found around the market place, in Frenchgate and Newbiggin.

The appreciation of the picturesque landscape, aided by sketches of the artist JMW Turner and other artists has been helping to bring tourists to Richmond ever since.

During the eighteenth century period of expansion an actor called Samuel Butler built a theatre on Friar's Wynd. It fell into disuse by 1848 but has been re-discovered and restored a number of times during its history. Today it is of national importance as a Grade I listed building. It is a working theatre with a wide ranging programme of events and a museum. The Georgian Theatre is on the route from the market place to the Greyfriars Friary, which dates from 1258. Although the Friary was dissolved in 1539, the tower is still standing amid pretty, well kept gardens.

It was the beautiful gardens and riverside walks that I most appreciated during the Spring of 1961. For the short time we were there, during Anton's Catterick training, Richmond gave me a period of complete escape and rest. No one made demands of me. I cannot pinpoint any particular moment, day, or event which resulted in my developing a more positive frame of mind. I think it was a combination of things. Fresh air, a better diet and a total change of scene must have been major factors in my recovery, together with the feeling and recognition of being cared for, but not suffocated with kindness or being constantly criticised.

We were living well away from Catterick Garrison and all things military, except that Mrs. Flynn the elderly widow we were fortunate enough to find, was used to accommodating short and long term 'guests' who more often than not were connected to the army in some way. One of our fellow guests was a scientist who, like Anton, was not able to discuss his work, so the conversation at dinner was usually very general and polite. Efforts were made to see whether I had ventured far during the day and suggestions were made for other adventurous walks.

The house on Frenchgate appeared to be two Georgian cottages knocked through to form one long building with an uneven, dark corridor at the point of the former 'join'. The house was like a time capsule. Darkly furnished with green fabric covering the walls in the hallway I didn't linger here because the hall and corridor were also home to a rather gruesome collection of stuffed animals and birds in glass cases. The cases of butterflies were colourful and quite pretty and had obviously been collected over a period of time by a wildlife enthusiast. There were a number of fine paintings throughout the house, mostly scenes of Richmond and the surrounding countryside.

Our room looked out onto a long, rather wild meadow garden and from the garden looking back to the house the sun would cast brilliant rays on an intriguing arched window which seemed too large for the building and unusually was not original to the place. Our room was a treasure trove of antique furniture and paintings, and the biggest delight, a nineteenth century square piano which I was encouraged to play.

Mrs. Flynn was a wonderful cook. She took great delight in serving dinner from a sideboard in the dining room. Home made soup was ladled

The Frenchgate house, Richmond, North Yorkshire

from a willow patterned tureen which matched the tableware. She made proper rice pudding with grated nutmeg and old fashioned mutton stew which she assured me would stick to my bones and strengthen them! Breakfasts were served in the same manner as dinner, from the sideboard and from silver dishes with lids. Mrs. Flynn favoured a cooked breakfast rather than toast or cereals and I struggled with scrambled eggs, mushrooms and tomatoes. I'm afraid the mere sight of black pudding and sausages in the mornings would turn my stomach, and I was over-faced with home baked scones.

After breakfast I needed to have long walks and Mrs. F. would enquire gently as to whether I wished to walk alone or did I yearn for company? She was not offended if I went out alone. I soon found the library and several bookshops in the town, and although there didn't appear to be a music shop I was able to order sheet music from a catalogue held by one of the book shops. This meant that I could play the square piano and pretend that I was Jane Austen. Our time here was all too short. I remember it with some affection as a peaceful place where I was able to relax, to write, and to some extent to reclaim myself.

2003

The return visit to Richmond involved an easier journey than I had imagined. Of course this time I hadn't flown from Europe or had a lengthy train journey. I was travelling from Edinburgh. The train from Scotland to Darlington passes through some of the most beautiful Scottish, Northumbrian and North Yorkshire countryside. Richmond does not have a railway station these days, but the half hour bus journey to Richmond Market Square is also pleasant and through farmland mostly.

We lunched at the King's Head Hotel in the Square. Once described by the artist Turner as 'the finest hotel in Richmondshire' this former Georgian town house offers all the requirements of a twentieth century hotel, though I suspect in Turner's time things were genteel, less hurried and certainly quieter.

The town was extremely busy with market traders and visitors, mostly day trippers and a number of motor cyclists. The town square seems to be a regular meeting place for bikers much to the annoyance of the elderly residents.

I did vaguely remember the layout of the square but there were just as many changes here as in all the other 'homes' revisited.

In the early 1960's no one had heard of Chinese or Indian food, burgers, fries or pizzas. All these now abound in beautiful Richmond much to the detriment of the surroundings. Rubbish and smelly remnants of fast food were all over the place and although on the outskirts of the town one can still find a few good tea shops and eateries of quality the town centre looks tired and tatty. Many of the formerly beautiful Georgian buildings need repainting and repairing. Most of the shops have removed lovely facades and replaced them with ugly shop windows and hoardings, and often selling poor quality goods in grubby looking surroundings.

Our hotel, on Frenchgate had similarly once been a Georgian gentleman's residence. We found it adequate for our needs though it was yet another place much in need of a makeover. My daughter and I spent two noisy nights there because our rooms faced the cobbled street and its constant traffic. In 1961 there were hardly any cars and no midnight revellers.

We walked the length and breadth of Frenchgate several times, and although I had forgotten the house number of Mrs. Flynn's I felt certain that I would remember it. I saw several houses which resembled the one we were looking for but began to feel very frustrated and upset at my inability to be precise. Of course I had not reckoned with the fact that during the forty odd years since my stay there, houses had been altered, added to and new ones built.

Even on historic Frenchgate houses had been given new windows, doors and inappropriate porticos. Some had new steps or forecourts and on the other side of the street newer built houses slightly obscured the view over the church and across Swaledale and the river.

Disappointedly, and thinking that we might have to abandon our search my brilliant, resourceful daughter spotted a 'ginnel', a passage between the houses which I had forgotten. We ventured through the passage, not knowing whether we were trespassing. Slowly things began to fit into place and my memory became clearer. We interrupted two elderly ladies who were chatting nearby. They had lived there all of their lives and explained that the long, wild meadow garden we were seeking had long since vanished. It had been sold off along with other surrounding gardens, for building land. The wild meadow garden was now a modern housing complex, purpose built for elderly people. We were very close to the house we were looking for. My daughter jumped on top of a bin store at the back of the Georgian terrace and there it was. The cottage I remembered, the arched window and the paved yard. It had a new roof and at the front of the house it was clear that there were new steps and door framed with Georgian style pillars. The new windows, although in keeping with the period of the house, were wider and gave the house a much lighter, different look. Mrs. Flynn will have died many years ago and with her passing I suspect that all the antique furniture, the paintings and square piano will have found their way into auction houses.

Pleased to have found the house we walked past the back of the building and I immediately remembered the route I would have taken through the wild garden and into the town. No wonder I hadn't recognized the front of the house. In spite of the modern changes, I remembered that we never used the front door. I would not have walked the cobbled street. It wasn't until I had traced my steps again that it all came back to me.

Cheered by our successful pilgrimage we explored the castle and the narrow wynds down to the River Swale, the beautiful parts of Richmond. I felt that I had travelled a long personal journey since the 1960's and I remembered gratefully the part played by Mrs. Flynn.

Today, much as I like the place, I couldn't live again in Richmond. My arthritic knees would not cope with the hills and the cobbles and I fear that the facilities in the town will only deteriorate, or cater for the day trippers and bikers. The age of quiet elegance has gone.

I am glad that we found the house.

THE RETURN TO SHEFFIELD

Our all too brief time in Richmond had allowed me to regain some physical strength and the kindness of people on our return to Germany for the final year of Anton's posting steered me through the remaining time there. The prospect of returning to Britain occupied my thoughts on a daily basis. I felt apprehensive about facing my family again but I was at least daring to look ahead for the first time in years.

The journey back to Britain was tiring and tedious. The soldiers were separated from their families and I spoke to no one. First it was a train journey to the Hook of Holland, then a boat to Harwich where the families were herded together in a waiting room until the men arrived to help gather up the luggage and proceed through the Customs Hall. We had bought two sets of glassware as gifts but one set was confiscated because we were required to pay a tax on it and we had little money. We were cold and hungry as we faced another two train journeys. This was long before the days of fast food and Ixxy's bagels! However we did manage a cup of tea and a bun on St. Pancras station.

There had been much discussion about which relatives we would temporarily lodge with. No one was happy with the solution. The fraught situation in both 'homes' was our biggest incentive to seek a place of our own as quickly as possible. At Anton's home Amelie was now wheelchair bound and slept downstairs in the lounge. She was crippled with arthritis and racked with pain. Her gnarled hands were unable to hold anything. The lovely embroidery she used to do was impossible. Amelie also suffered from anaemia and bronchial asthma. The many drugs she had to take caused other problems, but our main concern was her extreme frustration, which sometimes led to her screaming and shouting fits which could last for hours. Sometimes there were bouts of real, deep depression. My heart went out to her. She was totally dependent on a daily nurse and home helps, who varied greatly in the quality of help given. The really good ones were a great support to Amelie. The slovenly and un-cooperative ones just added to the frustration. In truth, our problems didn't have any impact on Amelie, nor did we wish to burden her further. We offered whatever help we could.

At my parent's house there was an even bigger shock awaiting us. My father, who had until then kept his long term girl friend a secret, had finally left my mother. He had sold what we thought of as our family home and installed my mother in a tiny two-up, two-down nineteenth century former workers cottage. It had no bathroom and only an outside loo at the end of the garden. The cellar was permanently flooded and the only heating was a two-bar electric fire in the living room.

My father had in fact left home shortly after I had, leaving my brother then aged fifteen, to look after my mother. My brother had been denied the chance to join the Merchant Navy because under sixteens needed their father's signature.

'I'm leaving first,' he told my brother. It wouldn't have seemed so awful if he had given my brother some explanation of his behaviour. The emotional havoc my father wreaked is still felt today.

I knew very little about my family's lives after I had left home. We were never a family who talked over things anyway, and we all kept things from each other. Not so much lies, but certainly secrets. My mother and occasionally her step-sister were the only letter writers. My mother rarely mentioned personal things about my father. She wrote about the weather and dreadful storms of the 60's when the shed blew away. She told me of the books she was reading and about my Grandad's health just before he died. She wrote of her worries when my brother bought a motorbike. That was all.

So having arrived home expecting some expressions of warmth and welcome perhaps, we were disappointed. It was as though we hadn't been away at all. To my family we hadn't had a life of any account and our pain was ignored except for one fleeting comment that we would have other children. My brother was working in a steelworks foundry and hated it, and my mother, in a poor physical and emotional state was having to work as a cook. She was continually exhausted and came home every day with what she called a 'sick headache'.

There was really no room for us in either household and for the first couple of weeks we slept wherever we could find a space. We scoured the newspapers for jobs and for rented accommodation. Anton was able to resume working for Metropolitan-Vickers as an electrical engineer. I found temporary office work, first with Ferodo and then with Laycock Engineering in the Personnel Office. It was my first experience of meeting Asian people, most of whom were applying for labouring jobs and spoke little English. I had to learn to count up to ten in Urdu, so that I could ask how many children they had. I also had to familiarize myself with company policy regarding many aspects of the workforce and in particular relations with the Unions and also possible industrial agitators.

When we were not working we trawled around Sheffield looking at dozens of disgusting flats and bed-sits. Each time we desperately hoped to find somewhere half-decent and had frequent disappointments. Eventually we found a small flat which we convinced ourselves would do for a while. We were on the verge of accepting it when the lady who owned it as a rental property engaged us in conversation. Having ascertained that we were recently returned from three years with the Army she urged us to meet her brother Charles, a retired Army Major.

I was a little apprehensive. I didn't need any more reminders about military life. I thought we had escaped all of that.

I need not have worried. The Major was a charming man. He was a very tall, straight-backed man with greying hair and a hint of a military moustache. He was approaching his sixtieth birthday and worked as a Company Director. He lived alone after his wife had left him and most of his six children were grown up and also living elsewhere.

'I am rattling around in this house by myself,' he said, 'I need someone respectable to keep an eye on the place and keep it warm!'

We warmed to him and to the house.

NETHER EDGE

Nether Edge was where we found our first real home. It was in a leafy part of Sheffield, north of the city.

The early history of Sheffield and its suburbs had been largely obscured by continuous development and building. However, some former camp sites of early hunter gatherers and Anglo Saxon villages have been found. Sheffield, by the River Sheaf, and Little Sheffield were like many villages with paired names. One village would develop out of the other, perhaps by a shifting population, or as happened in the case of the Sheffields, by the setting up of a church, the building of a castle or a market place at one village to the detriment of the other.

From early mediaeval times until the late thirteenth century many new farms were created. This was probably when most of the farms in the Nether Edge and Sharrow regions were formed. Some might have been set up by families from Little Sheffield wishing to spread northwards of the city. Rural life remained unchanged except for some additional farm buildings, or divisions, for family reasons until the building of the suburbs during the nineteenth century.

The country residences of wealthy landowners began to appear in the eighteenth century, but a hundred years later at the advent of the Industrial Revolution many factories, foundries and cutlery works were developed. The owners of these businesses began to build their family villas in leafy suburbs around the edge of the city. Nether Edge was one of those suburbs.

By 1850 there were large scale developments such as Kenwood Park, the Nether Edge Estate, Brincliffe Towers and Chippinghouse. These included developments by George Wolstenholm, Thomas Steade, the Newbould family and other speculative builders along with a few private individuals.

In 1853 the Nether Edge Estate was purchased by the Reform Freehold Building Society, a land society who would buy land and divide it into measured plots. The Society members could buy these plots, paying by instalments instead of having to find a large sum. This enabled less wealthy artisans to buy their own homes and thus become eligible for the vote. In 1854 the plan for division was complete and the work of building carriage roads, footpaths and sewers and water pumps was finished. The Montgomery Land Society took over the estate in 1861 and the work of selling plots for building continued until 1883.

Obviously both land and property development was mainly profit-generated, but it wasn't the only motive. Some developers like George Wolstenholm, a cutlery magnate whose firm were famous for making the 'Bowie' knife, was anxious to control the character and populace of the neighbourhoods. Land deals often specified a certain quality or style of house, detailing the building materials to be used, or there might be a limit on their cost. They didn't want the lower classes to move in.

Thomas Steade, an ironfounder, became deeply involved in property development in the 1850's. In fact the setting up of his own foundry was probably established in order to specialise in iron work for his increasing building projects. In 1863 Steade bought land from George Wolstenholm to build houses on Crescent Road amongst others. Crescent Road would be my home exactly one hundred years later.

A feature special to Steade's houses was the use of cast iron fixtures. These might be ornamental features on a roof or window lintel. Cast iron was also used on banisters or railings and gates. These would have been made in Steade's foundry, but were also bought by other builders. Thomas Steade had many profit-making ideas but not all of them were successful. He borrowed heavily and was unable to repay his debts. He was eventually made bankrupt and the stresses of his business life led to a fatal heart attack in 1889.

With so many business interests Thomas Steade, unfortunately, seems not to have known what all of his building workmen or gardeners were doing. Inferior workmanship became apparent in some areas and trees were often planted too closely together. This caused trouble with pavements later on and even today residents have to take care when parking their cars near to the trees in case the doors cannot be opened safely. Of course Thomas Steade could not have known that in the twentieth century residents might comprise two and three car families.

As a young, twenty one year old coming to the house on Crescent Road for the first time I knew nothing of its history. I just marvelled at the beauty of the building and the calm, comforting feel of the well-established gardens. Our bay-windowed lounge at the front of the house overlooked a profusion of ferns and many shades of rhododendrons. The stepped garden at the back of the house seemed to go on forever. In fact the far end of the garden was piled high with rotting compost and rather

The Crescent Road house, Nether Edge, Sheffield

overgrown. The apple tree would provide us with an abundance of fruit and although the garden had been neglected there was a small lawn and any number of nooks and crannies providing places to sit and hide from the world. The Major, cognizant of his neglect of the garden said that we could do anything we liked, though he certainly didn't expect us to 'do' the whole garden. We spent time tidying the lawn and borders and I planted geraniums, marigolds and blue and white lobelia. Each plant was measured out with exactly six inches between them in a long straight row, as I remembered my father planting out vegetables in Aldershot. The Major, amused by my precision, marched up the lawn saluting the flowers as though they were a line of soldiers.

We were hardly aware of the Major's presence in the house. He spent most of his time elsewhere, either at his business or with his sisters who lived nearby. Certainly he appeared only to eat breakfast in the house. He was a wonderful landlord, aware of our needs. He had a quiet sense of humour and believe he appreciated our being there. Following all the trauma we had experienced we could hardly believe our good fortune.

We began to relax and in time felt able to do the things which normal couples did. We invited people for tea at the weekends, though my family were not frequent visitors and Anton's never came because Amelie couldn't be moved. We hadn't yet managed to buy a car. For the first time we began to collect small oddments of furniture and a treasured china tea service. We set out to buy one piece every week until we could respectably serve afternoon tea for six people.

We made tentative approaches to the Rabbi and found him to be very sympathetic and encouraging. He provided us with a book list and many ideas about the way ahead. It would be some time before we could contemplate joining a congregation. There were many things to consider and we were very uncertain. I realized that the orthodox way of life was inappropriate for us. There was no sense of urgency. Interested we were, I more than Anton, but the terms liberal and progressive Judaism meant little to us just then.

Anton worked long hours and planned one day to have his own business and build our own house. Weekends were also full and busy. We sometimes visited relatives and we worked together on a scale model of our ideal house, long before it was a financial possibility. Anton pored over professional building books and when we were not busy with the model or reading Anton would listen to me playing the piano. I was playing with more sense of purpose and planned a structured programme of learning for myself.

Although Anton was always encouraging I was aware that my studying and practising was of its very nature all consuming and selfish. There were times when he doubted himself and he would say that I should have married a teacher. He would have liked us to have a child, but somehow it just didn't happen. We tried to encourage and support each other and when one of us was down the other would do the supporting. We worked hard and saved hard for the future.

Then the most amazing opportunity came my way. It was to prove another great milestone and defining moment.

My new job was at City Hall with the Sheffield Philharmonic Concerts Department. I was to join the admin team responsible for organising professional concerts, working with orchestras, soloists and conductors of international repute. The job might have been designed exactly for me. The mundane weekday tasks involved typing letters, answering the telephone, liaising with concerts management and agents, orchestra managers and personnel, printers and town hall officials. Programme notes were prepared and records meticulously filed for future use, rooms booked, special requirements for artists appearing in the concerts were all taken care of and a myriad of domestic jobs which ensured the smooth running of the concerts season.

On concert days things moved into a higher gear. The orchestra would usually arrive at noon for an afternoon rehearsal. The regular Halle Orchestra members knew where everything was and made their own way to dressing rooms. Sometimes there might be a guest soloist appearing with the orchestra and they would need to be looked after. Although there were guest conductors and different orchestras from time to time, the Halle Orchestra gave the bulk of the concerts at that time and their chief conductor was Sir John Barbirolli. JB as he was commonly referred to commanded huge respect from the orchestra and soloists he worked with. The way that JB built the Halle Orchestra during the Second World War and afterwards is legendary. Many of the young musicians had been called up to serve in the forces and his first players consisted of housewives, students, elderly men and men who had been rejected by the forces for one reason or another. He had auditioned hundreds of unsuitable players in his attempts to get an orchestra of sorts together. They worked like Trojans and rehearsed day and night to be ready for concerts, all viewed at the time as part of the war effort in upholding people's morale.

Sir John Barbirolli

Sir John largely looked after himself on concert days. He didn't eat during the day and often chided the orchestra for eating too much.

'No wonder you are always tired!' he would say.

I took him a tea tray after rehearsals at 5.00 p.m. He took black tea with no lemon or milk.

Most of the orchestra members would disappear into town between rehearsal and concert. Some would remain in the orchestra room with a sandwich and catch up on some sleep.

There were a rare few musicians who used the time between rehearsal and concert to work on their scores. The most conscientious player who would rehearse by himself for hours was the Principal Bassoonist Charles Cracknell. He was a perfectionist. Charles had joined the orchestra shortly after being demobbed from the army after the war. He and JB had immense respect for each other.

This is not a book specifically about music history and it would be very indulgent to proceed at great length about the many wonderful concerts I heard and the dozens of marvellous soloists I was privileged to meet. However it is relevant to record some small snippets of recollection because it proved to be an inspirational time for me.

Observing conductors such as JB, Carlo Maria Giulini, Arvid Yansons, Walter Susskind and Sir Adrian Boult, to name a few, was fascinating. The ways in which conductors and soloists prepared themselves and worked together, how they dealt with anxieties and nerves provided me with a great deal of insight into the world of the performer.

Some musicians appeared to be quite calm and self-contained before a performance. John Ogdon was one, in fact he seemed to be rather morose and uncommunicative. Others would be on an excited high of emotion (like Abbado and Argerich). Gillian Weir, fresh from the London Proms with the Poulenc Organ Concerto was just delightful, down to earth, normal by comparison to many other players.

I shall never forget Jacqueline du Pre, young and bubbly, a vision in pink taffeta, a very serious Maxim Shostakovich, here to play his father's Second Piano Concerto and probably most treasured of all the memory of Paul Tortelier and his son Yan Pascal. They were to play the Brahms Double Concerto together. Before the concert, in the Artists' Room they were oblivious of other people. They sang fragments of the work to each other across the room. They were rehearsing their various entries and how they planned to play them. It was a fantastic work and a wonderful performance. I learned every note of it following the score and sitting in on orchestral rehearsals. Of course there were artists who would work themselves into a frenzy of activity or fits of temperament. One famous pianist threw a fit of temperament because we didn't have a stool low enough for him. Another, moments before the start of the concert announced that he couldn't go on because his hands were cold. Our suggestions that he could run them through warm water in the dressing room made him even crosser and he demanded a jug of hot water. This was duly found and then after cupping his hands around the jug for just a few seconds declared that he was ready to go on!

There were odd exasperating moments like this, but we admin staff, often perceived as mere pen-pushers, had to remain cool and totally unflappable throughout whatever rudeness or unreasonable behaviour we encountered. I was sometimes forced to remember a military phrase and realize the wisdom of evading the line of fire.

Conductors varied too in their interpersonal skills. They could actually make or break a performance by their handling of the orchestra and soloists. Orchestras were not averse to playing a little below par for conductors who were rude and unreasonable, but they were capable of giving their very best work to conductors who inspired and encouraged them. It became possible for me to detect the mood of an orchestra when I was able to listen to rehearsals. It taught me a lot about teaching.

The Halle Orchestra responded hugely for JB of course and also to Arvid Yansons and eventually Kent Nagano. Barbirolli was very proud of what he described as his Northern string tone.

Sir Adrian Boult was a less frequent visiting conductor, but highly respected. A very formal, Edwardian gentlemen, he was more than happy to meet autograph hunters following a performance, but he made a small charge and insisted that the money be sent to the local children's hospital. Lady Boult often accompanied her husband and was a gentle, unassuming lady who preferred to sit in the ordinary stalls seats rather than the V.I.P. seats in the Grand Circle.

Arvid Yansons the great Latvian conductor helped raise the Halle string playing to new levels, one orchestra member told me. He also had twinkling and mischievous blue eyes and knew how to charm the ladies.

However, it was Sir John Barbirolli whom I encountered most and from whom I learned such a great deal, though I doubt that he really knew that until I thanked him much later when I was leaving the job. The real value and thrill of the job wasn't merely being able to meet famous musicians, for that part of it was only transient. The lasting value has been learning such a lot of music, listening to rehearsals and knowing how orchestras mould a piece to the conductors and the composers requirements, proof reading the wonderful programme notes compiled by Dr. George Linstead and making myself look up all the reference points in the scores.

It was an opportunity to develop my knowledge and learn about music from the inside out.

I found myself a skilled piano teacher and was encouraged to pick up my theory of music study. I was often completing my theory or harmony 'homework' during the tea break on concert days. On one such occasion JB appeared in my office to telephone his mother and he took a look at my writing.

'Oh, lass!' he said, 'I wish my bloody band would learn some music theory. They might play better!'

He was very encouraging and continued to ask about my progress. He sometimes asked me to sit in the audience to report back to him about certain effects, particularly his use of Wagner Tubas, or musicians needed to play l'ontano (off stage).

FRIDAY 13TH NOVEMBER 1964

The date is indelibly marked in my mind. The pianist Tamas Vasary was arriving to rehearse a Chopin Concerto. I took a late lunch and walked into town to find something for my tea as I would be working through the evening concert. During the time that my office was closed a message had been taken by staff in the hall's general office. Anton had been involved in a road accident and was in the Northern General Hospital. It wasn't considered serious. My colleague Joyce drove me to the hospital where Anton had been sedated. He only managed a few words. I asked him what had happened.

'I'll tell you later,' he said, 'my head hurts.'

The nurse urged me to leave.

'Don't worry, he'll be all right,' the nurse assured me. 'Ring us later. He needs to sleep now.'

Anton had been crossing the main Sheffield Road. He had left Metro-Vickers factory to buy a lunchtime sandwich. He had been standing on a traffic island when he was hit by a lorry laden with heavy steel. He was hit with such speed and force that he was carried some distance on the front of the lorry before it crashed. I learned later that he had sustained extensive fractures to his skull.

Tamas Vasary played his Chopin and liked the Steinway piano so much that he wanted to stay after the concert to play Bach's Forty Eight Preludes and Fugues. I was very anxious to get back to the hospital but could not bring myself to spoil Tamas Vasary's night by telling him what had happened. Soon help arrived when the caretaker very diplomatically began to switch off the hall lights and lock the doors.

By the time I reached the hospital Anton had been moved. He had been taken to the Royal Hospital for emergency surgery. He had suffered severe bleeding and medullary failure due to extensive fracture of his skull. The surgeon accompanying Anton to the operating theatre in the lift was heard to remark that he didn't know why he was taking 'this boy' to theatre. I sat outside waiting for hours and was moved from one place to another. Nurses, even at that stage misguidedly tried to reassure me when they knew it was a hopeless case. I was exhausted and feeling somewhat numb. This couldn't be happening to me all over again. I remembered sitting outside another hospital ward in Germany. Dark thoughts came flooding back, and then the tears. I was distraught and had not slept for twenty four hours. I was taken home and given a mild sleeping tablet.

The next day I sat beside Anton. His head was swathed in bandages and he was surrounded by huge blocks of ice. They were trying to reduce the swelling to his brain and lower his temperature. I was engulfed with fear, but for his sake I tried to maintain my composure. I had no idea whether he could hear anything, but acted as though he could.

Anton died on Monday 16th November without regaining consciousness. Once again my world seemed to have disintegrated. The funeral was arranged by other people. Barely comprehending I just went through the motions of waking and sleeping and trying to keep myself together because I knew only too well what the alternative would be. Nevertheless the world seemed to be a very black place. During the funeral service I stood next to Major Lawrence. The sun streamed through the church window and the heat of the sun dried the tears coursing down my cheeks. I was aware of a voice telling me that things would be all right, but the Major heard nothing. My mother told me that the day had been dark and snowing, then sleeting and very cold. I was given brandy to warm me up. So the sun hadn't shone. I was the only one who knew that it had. Could it have been real or a trick of my disturbed mind? I wish someone could tell me.

For a while nothing seemed to matter and I suffered an all enveloping sense of inertia. I hardly recognized that I had been whisked away from our lovely house at Nether Edge. I found myself living at my mother's tiny terraced house again. People avoided me because they didn't know what to say or because they had been sent away. The sense of loneliness and isolation was total.

In time I returned to work a different person. I knew that I had to help myself then or I would be letting Anton down yet again. He'd had such high hopes for us both. It was so unfair.

My brother, then twenty, had been deeply upset about Anton's loss and displayed a caring side that I hadn't noticed before. My father of course was of the stiff upper lip type which was useful at the inquest and legal wrangling over a claim made against the lorry driver. For once my father was on my side, fighting my corner. Sad and confused my mother, sometimes tearful, and generally not knowing how to react was still trying to keep herself together. I felt that I was an added burden on her.

The only way that I could cope with the experience of grief and loss for a second time was to work morning, noon and night. I decided that I would give myself two years to work for 'O' and 'A' Levels and music grade exams. I bought a syllabus from Andrews Book Shop. Having ticked the subjects I thought I could most likely pass I bought a collection of study books, past papers and music. I enrolled at evening classes and with private tutors and music teachers. I resumed piano lessons with Margaret Long and began to learn the organ with Edward Marshall at Crookes Valley Church. I practised the organ daily, during my lunchtimes. I was encouraged to use the nearby Unitarian Chapel organ and sometimes found that I had an appreciative audience of office workers and shoppers who had wandered into the church.

Studying at home was difficult. The house was cold especially in the bedroom. It wasn't really practical to study in the only downstairs room since my mother would return from her work exhausted and needed to rest. Her only escape was the television. The house had no bathroom so I would take a bus journey to my brother's home in order to use their bathroom.

My brother had married soon after Anton's death and although my father had long since left home

The author, 1964

still felt he had the right to criticize my brother for marrying young and 'lumbering' himself with a mortgage.

When my father discovered that I planned to leave my job and go to college he called me a fool. Why would I want to give up a good job to live on a student grant at my age? I think that he thought I would never hack it. I became determined to show him that I could. My mother couldn't understand why I wasn't content with what I had. She, poor darling, had just had so much disruption and disappointment in her own life that anything that resulted in change was a worry to her. I expect they both thought that I would re-marry and settle for a domestic life. It was a class thing too. Nobody in our family had ever been educated to college level. It was a world they knew nothing about. The highest anyone had aspired in my father's family was the 'turf' business where his eldest brother, who had won money on the Derby, had then turned it to his and Uncle Frank's advantage.

Neither of my parents realized the damage caused by our disrupted, army years. They did not understand the lack of confidence, feelings of insecurity and low self esteem created by the constant moving and my father's bullying. We had grown up at a time when children didn't answer back, when they were mostly ruled by their parents and had little free will or voice. It was not uncommon during the 1940's and 50's that children's spirits were frequently squashed. Mine certainly were.

In 1966 at the age of twenty four I finally rebelled against my background. I knew that I had to forge ahead in spite of it, in spite of them.

Encouragement came from unexpected quarters. My work colleagues just treated me as they usually did, for which I was grateful. They knew the pain I was in but were sensible enough to realize that normality and routine would help me through it. Besides, I also needed to earn a living and save for the future. I was the only one who could help me do that.

Councillor Mrs. Enid Hattersley (mother of Roy Hattersley MP) was the Chairman of the Libraries and Arts Committee to whom the Philharmonic Concerts were answerable. Mrs. H. was a wonderfully supportive friend and continued to be concerned about my domestic arrangements. She asked about my studies and when the time came she was helpful in putting my name forward to an educational trust who awarded me a scholarship. Musician friends were wonderful too and helped to buoy me up when the going was tough. JB continued to ask about my music studies. Finding a real sense of purpose became the therapy I needed.

For the next two years (the time I had set myself) I struggled with the complexities of harmony and counterpoint, with Shakespeare and Milton and continuing religious studies. In addition to Jewish studies I had to immerse myself in St. Mark's gospel and Christian studies in order to pass my exams. I didn't reveal any of my course material to my parents. My mother didn't really care to understand and my father, still a confirmed Marxist, would have been strongly critical as usual. It was difficult to find two hours a day for piano practise but I persevered.

I left evening classes because progress in the group was too slow. I entered myself for all of the exams and embarrassingly found that I had to present myself at a school, joining sixteen year old pupils sitting the same exams. I remained single-minded and when I had accrued enough reasonable passes I considered the various college options.

Musician friends persuaded me to apply to the Northern College of Music (now known as the Royal Northern College of Music) in Manchester. I was not entirely convinced that it was the right place for me but I had a very interesting and enjoyable time playing the organ at St. Ann's Church for William Hardwick and I warmed to him. He congratulated me on my playing of Bach and said that he would welcome me as a student. Ida Carroll, the College Principal was a very different kettle of fish. She seemed satisfied with my piano playing and was impressed that I had worked at the theory of music mostly unaided. However she was as I suspected rather perplexed by my unorthodox route through education, so many schools and house moves and several unrelated occupations, that is until the City Hall and Sir John Barbirolli. Somehow she believed that such an erratic background was my fault. She wondered whether I would stay the course, whether I would integrate with eighteen year olds who had experienced a 'normal' route into music education. Instead of outright rejection the Principal set me a challenge which I am sure she did not expect me to fulfil. I was to learn an orchestral instrument, preferably oboe or percussion (shortage instruments at the time) up to about Grade Five level. Then I might be considered for a place the following year.

I was not deterred, but I decided not to humiliate myself further in Manchester. By the time I was offered a place at a teacher training college for mature students I had been playing the oboe for several months, had a working knowledge of stringed instruments and had learned the whole range of recorders with Walter Bergmann on various early music courses at Ripon and York. I was approaching Grade Eight on both Piano and Organ and had an elementary knowledge of composition. In short I had exceeded the challenge set for me. There have been many times since that experience in Manchester when I have wanted to offer 'them' a rude two fingered salute! Still, a sense of decorum was maintained and I care not whether Ida Carroll knew that I was once voted a National Music Teacher of the Year, and I would become an examiner for the Royal Schools of Music, of which the Royal Northern College of Music is a constituent member. It is a sad fact even today that the establishment does not quite know how to deal with students who have found an unusual or circuitous route through education. I am just forever thankful that my training college and Betty Kerr in particular were prepared to take a chance on me.

I remember only too well the feelings of being belittled at school, each new school throughout the army years presented me with the same kind of indifference from teachers. Having to 'catch up with the others' seemed to be a universal phrase. It made me and my brother feel that we were inferior even before we'd begun.

1966 was an extraordinary year. Sheffield had many and varied celebrations around the city, designed to celebrate the Football World Cup. City Hall, instead of the usual symphony concerts, hosted concerts by a wonderful Hungarian Gypsy Ensemble, Rajko, and a concert with the Massed Bands of the Brigade of Guards in their colourful, red uniforms. The most overwhelming surprise for me that summer was finding my lovely friend Dov, nine years on, grown up and graduated and playing first violin at one of the concerts elsewhere in the City. We talked and talked as we used to do when we were teenagers. There was a

The author with Guards bandsmen, 1966

lot of ground to cover in a very short time, but cover it we certainly did. We arranged to meet on a fairly regular basis and I was treated to wonderful meals in expensive restaurants. Dov had become quite affluent but also extravagant. He was pleased and excited that we had found each other after such a long time without any contact, but he was concerned and upset to hear about my life since leaving London.

Dov had just signed a short term contract to play with an orchestra in Canada. After that he was planning to live in Israel for a while, to please his family. He asked me to go to Canada with him and wondered if I would consider living in Israel too.

Although it was fantastic to be asked the dilemma only lasted for a few days. Had the opportunity presented itself another two or three years later I might have felt more comfortable with it. As things stood I had only just about pulled myself together after losing Anton and I had worked so hard for my college place that I wasn't going to be deflected from that. Dov said that he understood. We agreed to stay in touch and the next year we would have a holiday together in Israel and try to come to some kind of decision then. Of course we had no way of knowing then that 1967 would bring a serious war in Israel and we had no way of knowing how things would work out for me at college. Our relationship was warm but we would tread cautiously for at least the next year.

Towards the end of 1966 Dov had left for Toronto and I was preparing to leave my job. Sir John wrote an inscription on my 'Dream of Gerontius' record set . . . 'For Joan in remembrance of our association in Sheffield and with all my good wishes for the future' . . . He also presented me with some Coty Cosmetics. What a mensch!

College began in January 1967 and was temporarily housed in school buildings in Swinton, near Doncaster, until the new college was completed. I had accepted a place at a teacher training college for mature students. I realized after making the tedious bus journeys to and fro that when the new college moved to Doncaster, so would I.

OCTOBER 2003

I hadn't seen Crescent Road and our lovely house there for almost forty years. I had no idea what I would find. I knew that Sheffield University had expanded and the newer Hallam University created from the former Pond Street Polytechnic had enrolled hundreds more students. Many of the houses in the Broomhill, Crookesmoor and Chippinghouse areas are now occupied by students and most of the large Victorian and Edwardian houses there have been converted into flats or bed-sits. I hoped that 'our' house had remained intact and that the area had not deteriorated.

Strangely, my first attempts to photograph the house had been thwarted when my faulty camera had ruined the film by exposing it to daylight. In late October I was more successful. Accompanied by my friend Rosie and equipped with two new cameras we ventured towards Nether Edge. The tree-lined road was exactly as I remembered. The red, gold and brown leaves carpeting the road and pavements were glorious. We hesitated when the lady occupant of the house appeared at the window. I felt a little embarrassed and awkward, but having set my heart on having a photograph I decided that the only thing to do was to knock on the door and ask permission. The rough drive I remembered had been neatly re-surfaced and now has a new pair of iron gates. The garden at the front of the house revealed the familiar profusion of ferns and rhododendrons. It had hardly changed. To my surprise and great joy we were invited in to look around the house.

I explained my mission to Jill, the owner of the house, and she was genuinely more than happy to show us around. I stroked the oak banister which I used to polish until it shone and I remembered the stained glass window above the staircase. The stone flags in the re-furbished kitchen are now covered with modern flooring. I felt completely at home, warm and welcomed. It had been a happy house when I lived there with Anton and I sensed that it was a happy home now. It didn't feel the least bit sad. The only sadness was that I ever had to leave it. Jill explained that following the Major's death the house had for a time been given over to multiple occupation and was in a poor state when eventually it was made available for sale on the open market. History repeated itself when thankfully a group of concerned neighbours banded together to buy the house and renovate it. The house was then sold on to a single, independent buyer who the group felt sure would care for it and restore tranquillity to the area once more. Just like Wolstenholm and Steade, I thought.

Walking through the rear garden felt like a time capsule. I was back in the 1960's. It was as though all that had happened since had not happened at all. I know that Anton would have been pleased to know that I had made the pilgrimage without creasing up emotionally. It really did seem uncanny that I hadn't been able to take the photographs on my first visit when the house was unoccupied, but on a second visit was received with such warmth and interest. The garden is still a treasured oasis of calm.

Spurred on by my findings I decided that this was probably a good time to re-visit Tinsley, Anton's childhood home where we stayed very briefly on our return from Germany, and the two other Tinsley houses. There was the house we lived in as a family after leaving London in 1957 and my mother's tiny terraced house where I was taken following Anton's death in 1964.

Tinsley is now a sad shadow of its former self. Like so many of the other places I have re-visited its character has completely changed but in some ways not for the better.

It is true that there are no black belching chimneys or works whistles to be heard, and the trams have gone. The present Tinsley children do not suffer from malnutrition or severe bronchitis diseases as once used to be the case. People can now safely hang out their washing and retrieve it from the line looking clean. All of this would seem to indicate a huge improvement. Certainly the Clean Air Act has been really beneficial to the population. However, there is another side to consider.

The steelworks, small factories and workshops and the small farm and dairy which once sustained the 'village' as my mother used to refer to it are all gone. There used to be a smart parade of tiny shops on Tinsley Front, as it was known. They were quality shops and included a master baker, a pork butcher, a greengrocery and draper's store. The Post Office remains but most of the other shops have disappeared.

Thee used to be a 'Spirella' lady who measured her customers for bespoke corsetry. Even the Co-op store has vanished. Now Tinsley can only offer a few grubby, graffiti-covered shops, motor spares and a launderette and chemist. There are a couple of uninteresting pubs and a few Asian general stores.

The Tinsley Free Library endowed in 1905 by Andrew Carnegie, which was my mother's lifeline, has now closed as a library. It has re-emerged as the Roundabout Community Centre. The present library is a tiny establishment squeezed between the grubby shops on Bawtry Road.

Tinsley's decline has been caused directly by the closure of industry and the building of the Meadowhall Shopping Centre a couple of miles away and also by the building of the roundabout and traffic access roads on to the motorway. The building of the roundabout has effectively separated one half of Tinsley from the other. Once upon a time sheep used to be herded along these roads, past the original Plumper's Hotel, and on to market in Sheffield. The Plumper's Hotel is also a victim of this development and has suffered such a loss in trade that it too will close shortly.

Many of today's Tinsley residents are Asian or young families looking to buy inexpensive housing. The old families of my mother's generation are dying out and along with them the last vestiges of large extended families where often aunts, uncles and cousins all lived near to one relation or the other. They would have helped in a crisis and usually had an aged grandparent to care for as well.

Both Anglican and Methodist churches still exist in Tinsley but with dwindling congregations. The festivals and parades with the bands and colourful floats and processions are a thing of the past. Families are smaller and rely less on each other for support or for entertainment. Most families have a car and seek their pleasure elsewhere. Huge cinema complexes, sports centres and bowling alleys are not far away for drivers. Meadowhall is a focal point for young people with money to spend or just a place to hang out!

A Rotherham newspaper still reports Tinsley births, marriages and deaths, the lunch club activities and the bingo winners.

I visited the churchyard to plant a small shrub for Anton. I sat beside the grave and told him about my visit to Crescent Road. It was good to observe that the former wilderness of a churchyard was much tidier than it used to be. I guess this is because the church wardens have the benefit of electric mowers and strimmers.

My parent's house was near the church so I used the opportunity to photograph it. The Edwardian villa would have originally belonged to a works manager or foreman. It is now home to an Asian family who have colourful wall hangings in the room where I used to practice my piano. The iron railings removed during the war, supposedly to be melted down for munitions, have been replaced by the council. The new railings are slimmer, more elegant than the old ones. I peered into the passageway between the houses towards the central door. In my mind's eye I remembered quite clearly seeing my father's mysterious young male visitor whom nobody would talk about. The place looked cared for though it is evident that the council have been forced to build traffic humps in the roads around Tinsley to curb the enthusiasm of boy car racers. When we moved there in 1957 only two families owned a car on our terrace. Now there are two or even three cars parked outside every house.

The Rec (Recreation Ground) is still intact though now Asian cricketers use the pitch and sometimes play friendly matches with white teams.

My mother's little terraced house on Dundas Road looked cleaner and neater. The council have spent 're-generation' money here too allowing residents to upgrade their surroundings. My mother's former house now has a new roof and windows as well as a bathroom and indoor toilet. There is an ivy growing up the wall. The only eyesore was the bright blue pin placed by the front door, a new move to encourage people to recycle paper. My maternal grandfather's house was on my route. I can still

118

imagine him sitting on the outside wall, catching the sun, watching the world go by and smoking his St. Bruno pipe. He was a quiet gentle man and I suddenly felt sad that I had really only known him for a period of three years. I had grown up away from Tinsley and I had escaped from the place only three years after moving there. I had similarly only known my Uncle and Aunt (Frank and Ada) for the same period of time and there were a number of other relatives that I had never met, but only heard about fleetingly from my mother. I realize that my parents moving away and my father enlisting in the army must have been the major reasons why we had little contact with our extended family. My father had been the youngest of eight children. All his siblings, except for Uncle Jim's twin who died, had married and there were at least eight cousins somewhere. Sadly all of my mother's siblings had died in early infancy except for little five year old Arthur who had drowned in Tinsley Canal. By the time my mother's step sister was born my parents had moved to Liverpool so there was little early contact there. So although there were family roots in Tinsley and Sheffield I have not spent enough time there myself to think of it as home. There are no emotional leanings towards the place except for unhappy remembrances of having to leave London, my parent's arguing, a job I had been forced into and the discovery that my father's teenage girlfriend had re-appeared on the scene to wreck my parent's marriage, and the secret visits her son had made to our house when he was quickly and quietly smuggled in and out of the side door.

Amelie's post-war, pebble-dashed little house is still there, freshly painted when I visited and home now to a young family with small children who were playing happily in the garden with their bicycles and other toys. It seemed a lifetime away when I used to walk past this house on my way to work in my first job at the steel factory at the bottom of the road. I used to have to take care crossing the road. It was easy to get one's heels caught in the tram tracks.

The trams finally stopped running in 1959 and the bus routes were increased. Ironically, the newly built Supertram which now operates runs from the city centre to Meadowhall Shopping Centre. People who have no reason to go to Tinsley do not even know that it exists. Likewise people travelling in the other direction from Rotherham to Meadowhall or Sheffield either drive their cars on the congested roads past Tinsley or they use the train which reaches Meadowhall after two stops. Tinsley is a forgotten wilderness of sorts.

DONCASTER . . . (SUNNYFIELDS, TOWN FIELDS AND SCAWSBY)

My student years were spent in Doncaster with just the occasional visits 'home' to visit my mother. She struggled with the menopause and work as a cook. My father, now living with the woman he left my mother for visited my mother fairly regularly with a small amount of maintenance money. The visits upset her and it would have been better if he had stayed away to let her get on with her life. My brother lived nearby and kept an eye on her, for which I was grateful and relieved.

Doncaster has a long history as a market town and there were settlements here long before the Romans built their fort (DANUM) here. The Romans built many roads in the area but the main route (ERMINE STREET) ran from Lincoln (LINDUM) via Bawtry to Doncaster and from there via Tadcaster to the major fortress at York (EBORACUM). Roman camps were built about fifteen miles apart, a days march for a soldier in full kit. By the eleventh century Danum had the Anglo Saxon ending CAESTRE (a camp) added. So Danum became DONCAESTRE. The Vikings, Saxons, Angles, Jutes and Danes, all from north European tribe settled in Doncaster. Many local names derive from Danish settlers.

SCAWSBY is believed to originate from a Danish name (SKALDS a poet) BY (a farm) and lies about two miles north of the town centre. As far back as Celtic times Scawsby was recognized as good farm land with easily ploughed soil, well drained and with a good natural water supply. These Celtic Fields were also found at High Melton, Sprotborough and between Hickleton and Marr. By 1086 the Domesday Book recorded Scawsby as part of the Manor of Tickhill (Roger de Busli) but was later granted to the Manor of Maltby to support Roche Abbey (1147). During the thirteenth and fourteenth centuries there were weekly markets and an annual fair until the charter expired.

In the Middle Ages the Black Death decimated almost a quarter of the population. This together with a time of recession is thought to be the main cause of the loss of many small villages. Scawsby may have been such a casualty. By 1397 Scawsby had passed to the monks of Bretton

Priory which lay between Barnsley and Huddersfield. At that time there were just seven married couples and thirteen single people in Scawsby. Surprisingly, in the census of 1871 there were only six married couples and nineteen single people living in Scawsby. Almost all were house or farm servants at Scawsby Hall.

However sparse the population of Scawsby the village was in a significant location and was for centuries the main salt route through the Pennines. Remnants of this history can be found in the names of Salter's Brook (at Goldthorpe) and the Saltersgate Schools. The eighteenth century tollgate at the end of the Scawsby turnpike is still known as York Bar (the first tollgate on the road to York). This was at the Sun Inn which straddled the Roman Bridge and had in its yard space for mail coaches and cattle drovers.

Doncaster owes its importance and survival to its position on the Great North Road. It was a major coaching centre throughout the eighteenth and nineteenth centuries. Because of its position, almost in the centre of the country, and with good access to roads, waterways and later the railways, Doncaster has been able to sustain its manufacturing and, until the late twentieth century, the mining trades. Undoubtedly the building of the railways and engineering workshops has been the mainstay of the town which is now mainly an inland leisure town based on the world famous racecourse.

The expansion of the engineering and railway industries and coal mining necessitated the building of affordable housing for workers. In the town itself streets of privately built terraced villas, council built estates on the outskirts and rows of collier's terraced cottages in the pit villages. For the sake of this quick comparison of history there were 6,000 residents in Scawsby in 1971, due to a Pre and Post War building programme. My student houses were in one of the pre-war type near the Roman Ridge, off Barnsley Road, a post war house off the Great North Road and a town villa built in the late nineteenth century.

The day I moved out of my mother's house to go to college was not at all how I imagined it would be. My mother had left for work as usual. I promised to return home in a couple of weeks time for a weekend visit. No one waved me off or wished me luck. There were no 'New Home' or 'Congratulation' cards. Not even a hug. I just had to get on with it. Nothing new there then.

My brother, then twenty three and married, against my father's forceful advice, arrived with his motorbike and sidecar. It was fortunate that I didn't yet know anyone in Doncaster to impress. Arriving in a motorbike sidecar would certainly have ruined my smart image. My piano stool was strapped to the rear seat of my bike and some of my clothes and other belongings were squeezed into the sidecar beneath my feet. I had never ridden on a motorbike, or sidecar before and it was not an experience I wanted to repeat. Still, it was kind of my brother to help. I'm certain that he didn't understand my decision to go to college any more than my parents, but he was not in the least critical. I am sure that if he could have escaped his hard physical work in a steel furnace he would have done so. Just then he had little choice.

The house I was to share with three other girls was at Sunnyfields, just off the Great North Road. It was part of a 1950's housing development and stood back from the main road at the end of a long, neat garden. The back garden was a sun-trap during the summer though I rarely found time to take advantage of it. The main advantage of the house was that it was within a few minutes walk to the college on Barnsley Road.

My first experience of living with other girls took every ounce of patience and tolerance that I could muster. I have no idea whether they felt the same way. Two of my housemates were teenage sisters who were trying to overcome their grief at the loss of their mother who had died from cancer a few months before. They had left the family home when their father had acquired a new girl friend in what the girls perceived as indecent haste. They were two very different girls but were very

First student house, Sunnyfields, Doncaster, 1967

supportive of each other and generally fairly responsible beings around the house.

The elder sister worked as a secretary. The younger girl was an art student who filled the place with bizarre paintings. She was also a talented folk singer. Listening to her was a new experience for me, though listening to soulful Dylan, Jansch, Paxton and Baez songs well into the small hours when we were all trying to sleep was sometimes very trying. More often than not it was her sister who yelled at her to stop. Our third housemate was a devout catholic girl from Southern Ireland. She was very quiet, reserved and self-sufficient. If anything she may have had more adjusting to do than I had. Youth culture in the mid 1960's was very alien to both of us but with teaching practice in schools looming before very long we had to learn fast.

Some weeks our timetables meant that we could go for several days without meeting up so we rarely ate meals together. I spent a great deal of time in college because it was generally easier to work there in the library and certainly it was easier to find a piano to practice on after daily lectures.

I had enrolled at a college for mature students, opened in response to a teacher shortage. Students came from various backgrounds. Some were retired from the armed forces, the police or prison service. Others had escaped from industry or commerce perhaps feeling they were not valued or doing worthwhile jobs. Some students were housewives whose children were grown enough to accept a working mother and there were those who like myself were trying to make up for lost time or opportunities in education. The majority of my fellow students had been educated in Grammar schools and I reasoned that because of that they must have been more academically able than myself. I felt more confident in my practical musicianship and seemed to be amongst the more advanced pianists. However that didn't mean that I would be any good in the classroom. I struggled to understand the Religious Studies Course and I felt that I worked disproportionately hard on essays for Education and Sociology.

I spent many hours reading and re-reading in college and felt impelled to work harder and longer than my colleagues just in order to keep up with them. I made copious notes which were read and revised several times before I dared to commit an essay to paper. It was very time-consuming. I had to understand things thoroughly and couldn't just re-gurgitate passages from a book, copycat fashion. I was driven to succeed. For one thing it helped me to cope with the loss of Anton but equally important to me was that I shouldn't flag. At the first signs of loss of motivation I could remember my father raising his voice to me as he did when I was a child struggling with arithmetic. I had very little social life during my first college year but I wasn't worried about it. I liked it that way. I didn't want to be drawn into the usual round of student activities, parties, pubs, men. That wasn't why I was there. I wasn't completely anti-social. I did talk to people and developed some lasting friendships with some maturer people. Obviously as a music student I had to work with other people and group music making was one of the great delights of being a musician. I just didn't want to be involved in male/female intimate relationships and I didn't want to be distracted from my goal.

Before my college career I had spent years clawing my way back into education and the previous four years steeped in the rarefied world of professional classical music. Going to work at a smart job in the early 1960's meant being groomed from head to toe. I went to the office in Chanel-type suits, gloves and sometimes a smart hat, silk blouses and cashmere were the norm and with upswept hair and Italian white leather shoes I fancied my style resembled Audrey Hepburn or Jackie Kennedy. Throughout my childhood I had always been described as 'serious', 'reserved', 'shy', 'bookish' and 'plain'!

Imagine then how the emerging flower-power, hippy era of the 'swinging' sixties came as something of a shock to my natural inclinations of reservedness?

It would be some time before I jettisoned all of my wardrobe in order to fit in. It was another year on before I risked wearing a mini-skirt and even then I never quite felt that it looked 'decent'. Needless to say the afghan coats, the loon pants and flowered shirts and headbands were never quite me either but we all wore modified versions of the current fashion. I suppose my most dramatic contribution to being a sixties student was to take down my long, upswept hair and cut a fringe! Because it was such a huge transformation it created much gentle joking but generally approval from my fellow students.

Of course the swinging sixties embraced much more than flamboyant clothes and even in a mature teacher's training college there was evidence of free love, drug use, debauchery just as there was in the 'outside' world. The advent of the contraceptive pill meant that women were freer to experiment with more than one partner and many students did just that, both with other students and lecturers. There were divorces, breakdowns, even a suicide and attempted suicides whilst I was a college student. There were students who knew where to obtain drugs but any hint of drug use in college would have meant instant dismissal. This as well as promiscuous behaviour either hetero or homosexual was deeply frowned upon. Homosexuality had only recently been accepted by the law. Previously people were imprisoned for such behaviour. We didn't know the word 'gay' though we knew that such relationships did exist. In college they were kept very much a secret.

College was a microcosm of society and although students were screened in interviews to assess their suitability as teachers there were inevitably a minority of students who held extreme views of one kind or another. The most disturbing examples of unsavoury or anarchic behaviour seemed to emanate from the arts and drama departments, but even the Student Christian Movement had its dark secrets and defectors!

There were also some students who quite successfully conned others out of money, meals or lecture notes. I was approached several times by the same girl who made a daily habit of 'borrowing' money for a cup of tea, or more if she could get it. I learned to develop a thicker skin. None of us had a great deal of money and we all had to survive.

Teaching practice in local schools proved to be a variable experience. For me it meant not a few crises of confidence. If it had not been for the continued encouragement, cajoling and occasional straight talking of my music tutors I may have given up. Education and Psychology tutors had little to offer in the way of help. They simply observed and wrote reports about voice projection or the state of one's dress. The music tutors were totally brilliant because, although one might not always have agreed with them, they were at least prepared to pitch in and have a go themselves. We were well prepared with lesson ideas and material from which to develop lesson schemes. Practical suggestions were freely given enabling students to modify or develop ideas in their own way.

I was blessed with music tutors who had the ability and wisdom to draw out of students whatever they had to give and then stood back to watch the development.

Sometimes we were placed in small groups of four or five for odd days or a week at a time. We were in schools to observe or to be involved in short-term projects. Eventually the periods of time spent in schools became longer and the types of school we experienced varied greatly. We all agreed that Primary age children were on the whole a delight to teach because they were curious and amenable. Something awful seemed to happen when they reached the time to progress to their Secondary schools. We learned about the features of adolescence and teenagers testing themselves in an adult world. We learned a great deal about environment, unemployed parents, poverty, limited aspirations and so on. But knowing of all these sociological explanations for how children develop and behave doesn't always equip one to deal with the reality in the classroom. Most of our problems were due to poor discipline within the school. Even experienced teachers struggled with this on a daily basis and listening to the conversations in the staff rooms was revealing and sometimes helpful. We counted ourselves very lucky if we were sent to a well ordered school where we could actually get on with the job of teaching and not just act as childminders until the bell rang. Schools with clear rules on behaviour and supportive Heads and Senior Teachers were really satisfying to work in, but not all schools were like this.

Poorly run schools made life very difficult for student teachers and did little to increase our confidence and stamina. We observed this in the pupils too. These were not always the schools in impoverished areas. One of my worst school experiences was in a middle-class area with a high proportion of able pupils. I found the arrogance and unwillingness of some pupils very difficult to deal with, and comments such as 'She's trying to keep us interested,' very galling. Trying to look objectively at the situation and talking with students and teachers at the school it was obvious that no one respected the Head or the Senior Management team who, cocooned in their offices for most of the day hardly ever spoke with pupils on an individual level. Student teachers were regarded as a disruption to the smooth running of the timetable and there was little support from Senior staff. Classroom teachers were delighted to have a student teacher because it meant they could have a break. They mostly allowed us to do whatever we liked. College tutors were regarded with suspicion when they made their fleeting, obligatory visits to their students. It was as though the school did not wish to be seen as in any way deficient.

Somehow I managed to survive the first year. This was in no small part because I was urged to learn to play the guitar, for use in the classroom. It took me three weeks during a vacation. I plugged away for hours on end playing half a dozen easy chords until I had the moves and shapes right on the fretboard. Then different kinds of strumming and finger picking of the chords until I could adequately sing and play at the same time. Goodness knows what my friend Dov, Anton or Sir John would have thought if they could have seen me in action in the classroom with a guitar!

During my second year, not totally happy at the way my piano playing had been neglected and thinking that I should work for an external diploma I sought out a professional pianist, a wonderful teacher, Molly-Ann Smith, who did a great deal to boost my confidence and piano technique. This would prove to be a very useful and necessary thing to do for the future.

The long vacations were useful for extra practising and for taking part in workshops and courses in Recorder playing, Choral music and Early Music seminars. I tried to spend time at home with my mother, but she of course was not privileged in the same way with lengthy holidays and she certainly could never afford to pay for a holiday away. I did manage to take her to London a couple of times which I think she enjoyed, though she fell asleep during the Festival Ballet's performance of 'Swan Lake'! We both enjoyed the parks and the river. I'm afraid museums and architecture meant little to my mother and she was quite relieved to return home to the world she knew about.

I felt a little sad and disappointed that once again, as was the case during my schooldays, that neither of my parents ever came to hear me play in concerts. Following each event there would be a sinking feeling of disappointment and anti-climax. That is until one of my music student colleagues decided that it was high time that she tried to fix me up with a boyfriend. Sadly, for him, this was very short-lived because I wasn't really very keen on him. He took my acceptance of a meal one night in a restaurant after a very stressful teaching practice as a signal of something more permanent. He followed me around and came to every concert making me feel very uncomfortable. He took my gentle rejection rather badly.

During the summer of my second year my friend Dov was busy touring with orchestras in the United States of America and Canada. Our plans to visit Israel the year before had been scuppered by the 1967 War. A year on and Dov was committed to contracts and couldn't travel to Israel when I was free to do so. I decided to go alone.

The least expensive way to travel was overland but it took too long so I decided a cruise ship was probably the next best way to go. The plan was to take a boat from Marseille, but because of a major rail strike in France I had to take a Belgian train from Ostende, a sleeper, which took me on a very long journey through Europe, and some beautiful and surprising scenery, all the way to Genoa in Italy. I was exhausted by the time I boarded the boat and quite unable to eat the wonderful supper which had been prepared.

Torrential storms at sea, a bout of awful seasickness and then a tummy bug contracted as a result of drinking the ship's water meant that I was in no fit state to enjoy the brief stop at Kusadaci (Turkey). I'd recovered somewhat as we docked in Piraeus (Greece). Accompanied by two newly-found friends we ventured into the seedy backstreets in search of a guitar maker who we were told would sell us a hand crafted instrument for a fraction of the price we would pay in England. It was a scary expedition and we were lost more than once, but we did eventually find the whitewashed house and guitar workshop. I wasn't prepared for the bartering and I didn't understand the language, but I think we probably did get a bargain instrument. I had to carry the guitar around with me for the remainder of the day as we made a short excursion to Athens, site of the Parthenon and the Acropolis. The summer storms had settled and the views across the city from the Acropolis were breathtaking. It was a pity we couldn't stay long enough to see the ancient sites in the evening when they were floodlit. Another outstanding experience, back on the boat was when we were to progress through the Corinth Canal. The boat's engines had to be slowed right down and with only a couple of feet between the boat and the steep sides of the canal we progressed inch by inch, slowly, slowly, gliding through to safety.

We sailed into Haifa on my twenty sixth birthday. The view of Mount Carmel rising above the city was amazing. In spite of all the activity on the harbour and the hustle and bustle of Herzl Street, the trams and so on, it was perfectly possible to imagine oneself back in biblical times and pondering on the significance of the great mountain in our midst. (Malcolm Williamson has composed a charming set of piano pieces called 'Haifa Watercolors' describing his responses to the city).

The whole point of going to Israel was to discover whether I might be able to live there, with or without Dov. So in a sense this portion of 'the search for home' is truly that, but not in the way that I have examined and re-visited former homes, in order to see if there was any affinity, any sense of belonging or lasting feelings of having roots.

Lower Galilee must be Israel's lushest landscape, with grassy slopes, fertile valleys, and to the north, rolling hills and imposing mountains. The Sea of Galilee, thirty six miles in circumference is the place associated with Jesus, who based his ministry there. Pilgrims flock there from all over the world, and to Nazareth with its enormous, ornate churches which are a far cry from the simple biblical sites of the imagination. The pace of life is gentler in Lower Galilee than in the busy coastal or historic towns that most tourists want to see.

Tiberius, named after the Roman Emperor, was founded as a spa in A.D. 18. It is the only settlement of any size on the lake, still famous for its curative hot springs it is now a rather characterless resort town with high class hotels and night life to attract visitors.

Of course I did briefly visit the tourist sites, but I was more impressed with the natural scenery and places like Capernaum which are relatively unspoilt, than I was with all the tourist tat and places riddled with commercialism and seedy bars.

The place I had really gone to visit was Kibbutz Lavi, ten minutes drive west of Tiberius. Lavi was founded in 1949 by members of 'British Bachad – the Organization of Religious Pioneers'. Today it is one of seventeen religious kibbutzim in Israel. There were about five to six hundred people living in Lavi when I visited. They live and eat communally and as well as settling the land and tending orchards and growing vegetables they are still world famous as manufacturers of fine synagogue furniture and are also pioneers in kibbutz hospitality.

The kibbutz Hotel Lavi hosts thousands of guests every year. An education centre provides seminars on educational tourism for those interested in enriching their knowledge of Judaism, the kibbutz way of life, and the Galilee religion. The kibbutz has developed a large dairy, a poultry farm and huge fields of crops. Young people from all over the world visit Lavi. Some stay for several weeks, months or up to a year living the life and sharing the work. Everyone shares in work in the kitchens, or in the fields, atop a tractor picking lemons, or harvesting other fruit.

At first glance the children of the kibbutz seemed to have an idyllic, wonderfully healthy way of life. They eat organic, fresh food, have much sunshine and an outdoors existence for much of the time. All this and a loving, extended family. Evenings are spent relaxing, dancing, singing, watching films, hearing talks or learning new hobbies. Sports are encouraged and the children of the kibbutz are taught to be kind and hospitable to their visitors. Visitors are told not to give the children anything (sweets, money, etc.). They have everything they need.

That is what we were told. The serious realization was, and still is that security is a major problem. Visitors were acquainted with regular drills, warnings, reminders in the case of an attack from terrorists, and although discreet, we were also aware of armed soldiers and ammunition and rifle stores. The need for vigilance and common sense and security checks is even more acute now than it was in 1968, the year after the Six Day War.

All the kibbutz dwellers that I met were peace-loving and generous people. They wanted nothing more than a quiet life. Many of them had friends in Arab villages, and at that time some Arabs even worked for the kibbutz, transporting goods to market etc.

In spite of the underlying worries about security I loved the place. I felt happy and comfortable amongst the people there. I did struggle with the heat at times, but I supposed that one would become used to it. The knack seemed to be the wearing of loose, cotton clothing and hats on heads. Trying to do manual work when the air was coolest also helped. I hoped that I would return one day. I didn't think about college or essays or anything else until I was on the journey back to England.

Suddenly, having re-joined the boat for the journey back to Marseille, the French rail strike now over, I realized with some horror that I had to perform Beethoven's 'Waldstein Sonata' in a concert soon after my arrival home. Panic set in and instead of strumming the guitar and singing up on deck with new found friends, I was forced to study my piano score, and when the ship's orchestra were still asleep in their bunks I was allowed to practice in the ballroom. It was very bizarre!

Second student house, Doncaster, 1968

Back in Doncaster the landlady of my first student house decided that she wanted to live in the house herself so we were hurriedly searching for new accommodation. The Irish girl teamed up with a student friend from her Geography group in a nearby house. For some reason the two sisters decided that they would still like to share a house with me and we found a town villa, a nineteenth century house with huge rooms. This may have been one of the houses built for the early railway managers. Although the house was much more comfortable than the cramped semi-detached house at Sunnyfields it was a couple of miles away from college necessitating bus journeys and expense we hadn't expected. It was good to have a proper lounge and dining room and somewhere to put my piano. It felt more like home. However, the more comfortable and relaxed surroundings eventually attracted a new housemate who was to wreak havoc.

I was about half way through my teaching course and feeling healthier and invigorated by my visit to Israel. The realization was slowly dawning on me that my relationship with Dov would never be anything more than friendship from afar. Although we had much in common there were too

130

many obstacles in the way of a permanent settled existence. His parents had won. Although I was the one who decided not to go to Canada with him (so that I could finish my course) I knew that his parents were relieved at my decision. Letters between us became fewer and fewer until Dov began to work in America. Then they stopped altogether. I always lived in hope that he would surface again as he had before. The life of a touring musician is very arduous and maintaining any kind of normal life is virtually impossible.

Following my exciting summer I approached college work with renewed energy and enthusiasm. I even ventured forth to organize Student Music Society recitals and listening groups. The Student Christian Movement invited me to talk about my visit to Israel and a slide show of my photographs was much appreciated. However, I was never a very confident public speaker. I was always conscious of my cosmopolitan accent. I had grown up listening to 'scouse' accents in Merseyside, country accents in Dorset and Hampshire, almost-London tones in Essex, sloppy south east London and Yorkshire accents in the north of England. An army childhood had meant growing up amongst people from all corners of the globe. Children always pick up the accents of their school friends and my brother and I were as adaptable as most. Once we had moved to Sheffield, my brother had the accent sorted within a matter of weeks.

All of this explains why I had to have an articulate, erudite and elegant frontman to introduce our student events. He was of course an actor possessed of all the self confidence and charm one would expect of a middle class, privately educated man who hailed from the south coast of England. Think of a Nigel Havers character called 'The Charmer'. That would be an apt description of Theo who was the boyfriend of my new housemate Julia (not her real name).

Naively, at first, I had failed to realize that Julia liked a good time and that meant having several men in her life at the same time. Her behaviour was really none of my business and I tried to remain impartial, but eventually it did have a devastating impact on my life. Julia spent little time in the house and communicated rarely with the younger girls. We went our own ways mostly. She criticized me for working so hard and for having so little social life. It wasn't very long before Julia was juggling her time and excuses between her various men friends, including Theo. We were drawn into making excuses for her or at least employing evasion tactics. The collusion made me feel really bad and when I couldn't stand any more of it I gave honest answers when pressed.

Theo appeared distraught and humiliated. He would appear at the house when it was least convenient for me and I would fall behind with my work. In short, he became somewhat of a nuisance. I once feared for his safety, and mine, since I was the one who had blown Julia's cover. In order to de-fuse the situation I persuaded Theo to accompany me to the nearest pub, something I wouldn't normally have done. I didn't even know where the nearest pub was. 'I can only spare an hour,' I told him. 'I've got such a lot of work to finish.' He seemed to understand and was grateful for the opportunity to let off steam. He said I was a good listener. Hoping that would have dealt with the situation I returned to the house alone. But that wasn't quite the end of the affair. It was a week or two before Theo and Julia finally parted company. Theo came to rely on me.

The remainder of the summer vacation meant a separation for all of us and a time to take stock. Afterwards I moved again, to my own flat. Theo came too.

The flat was the lower half of a 1950's semi-detached house in Scawsby very near to the college. The landlady lived upstairs and had a separate entrance. We hardly ever saw her. She was a travelling display window dresser for Boots the Chemist and she was frequently away. She was glad to have someone living in the flat to keep an eye on the property.

We saw little of the neighbours, so for once we had a quiet place to live and work. The flat was furnished by the landlady with old fashioned but comfortable furniture and we had a small black and white television set.

Third student house, Scawsby, Doncaster, 1969

Otherwise we had little to call our own but still managed to make it a sort of home. I was approaching my final year and continued to work as diligently as I could, except that now I was also being drawn into drama productions whenever they required a pianist or composer. It was fun participating in the background without the pressure of being the soloist.

Theo and I tried to keep our relationship as discreet as possible but without meaning to, we still caused a stir. Well-meaning people warned me to be careful and my religious friends took a dim view of my living in sin with a man not yet divorced from his estranged wife and who had two children to care for. I did have knowledge of two of Theo's former, short-lived relationships. I didn't know whether our relationship would last and I felt quite ambivalent about it. All I knew was that we had both escaped from difficult situations and perhaps a period of calm would be beneficial for both of us. We worked hard and had a kind of domestic stability. He seemed kind, charming and supportive, as I tried to be for him. I was aware that he might become bored with domesticity and could just disappear one day. All that I asked of him was that he would be honest.

It must have been during a short stay at my mother's house that first Christmas we were together that Theo came face to face with my father for the first time. Never known for his tact and diplomacy I read in my father's face what his mouth would eventually utter. He took stock of Theo's corduroy jacket, the bow tie, the cultured accent and as he moved Theo's 'Sunday Times' newspaper, in order to sit down, he said mockingly, 'I suppose this is yours?'

I introduced them, 'Dad, this is Theo. He's an actor!' Well that did it. My father held the common perception that actors were likely to be gay. In the 1960's more derogatory terms were used to describe such men in the arts, actors, dancers and musicians. Dov would have been viewed in the same way. It wouldn't have been so bad had Dov played a brass instrument, a real man's instrument. There was no way on earth that my father and Theo would ever be able to agree about anything. They would always be worlds apart. My mother on the other hand fell for Theo's charm and she fully expected that he would turn out to be a decent chap. My father was never convinced that he would be.

The year passed quickly. Theo was busy with drama productions and teaching practice. I was busy with concerts, teaching practice, a few private pupils and then final exams. It was a hectic time. There wasn't much time for frivolity or relaxation. The Drama department caused a storm of criticism when they organized a trip to London to see the controversial musical 'Hair'. Apparently towards the end of the show the cast members, and then some of the audience members divested themselves of their clothes in public. I wasn't there so I couldn't possibly comment on the show's artistic merits!

The event proved to be a catalyst for the College Principal. She denounced the licentious behaviour of students both in and out of college. The Principal was so disgusted that various sanctions were employed in the hope of curbing further displays of poor behaviour which might reflect upon the good name of the college.

Theo was a popular student and liked to be at the centre of things. He was in line to become Student President during his final year. But this was another event which wasn't allowed to happen.

To our great astonishment I discovered that I was going to have a baby. After previous history I'd thought that this would be impossible, but there it was, a fact. After I had recovered from the shock I became secretly ecstatic. I say secretly because although I felt I had been blessed with a second chance at motherhood there were huge repercussions at college. We kept the news to ourselves until we could no longer hide it.

Theo and I were individually summoned to see the Principal. We were 'carpeted' like naughty schoolchildren, at the ages of twenty seven and thirty two! Phrases such as 'How could you be so irresponsible?' and 'What were you thinking of . . . you are a respectable widow?' floated past me and all that I felt at that moment was thrilled to be expecting a child. I didn't care two figs just then if I was dismissed and I was surprised at my own feelings. Of course that may well have been the presence of hormones associated with my condition.

There were real problems and I was terrified in case I lost this baby. I would be six months pregnant when I had to sit my final exams in December. I was allowed to stay and finish the course but I was prevented from staying on to complete an Honours Degree. Theo received the sharpest of rebukes and the Principal made it known that she would not approve of his being Student President and refused to open the College Ball by dancing with him, as was the tradition. The final 'sanction' was aimed at the student body as a whole. As a result of much outrageous behaviour throughout the year there would be no official presentations of certificates to graduating students. Instead we would all assemble in College Hall, no guests allowed, where a list of names of graduating students would be sombrely read out. Fortunately I did receive excellent results and 'Highly Commended' more than once.

It is worth reporting here, as a matter of social history, that a girl friend of mine who attended a 'normal' college for training as a Domestic Science teacher was severely reprimanded at the age of twenty one for having become engaged to marry! The Principal at her college told her that she should have asked permission! In fact my friend taught for ten years before she had a break to have her first baby.

College came to an end. Friends kindly passed on a cot and stand for a baby bath. We bought a new bath but had little else for the baby until then. With an expected three months to go we thought we had plenty of time. I carried on teaching my private pupils and saved very hard. We knew that we would have to move out of the Scawsby flat but delayed a decision because we thought that we had plenty of time.

Suddenly, without any warning signs, I became very ill with very high blood pressure, a kidney infection and pre-eclampsia. I was admitted to hospital without delay and thought that maybe I would be released after a few days rest. In fact I was incarcerated in bed, with the foot of the bed raised, and filled with an assortment of drugs, for the next month. Potentially fatal my condition did not improve. By the end of January the staff nurse casually informed me just before lights out and having ensured that I had swallowed a sleeping pill that the doctors would be inducing the birth the following day, in order to save the baby and myself. I became so distressed that labour began spontaneously and immediately. I was given a further sedative and I have little remembrance of the twelve hour labour. I have a hazy recollection of the moment of birth and then I lapsed into a near coma.

It was much later in the day that I was allowed to briefly see my precious child. She was premature, tiny, unable to suck, but she was perfectly beautiful, just like a little china doll. The nurse whisked her away to an incubator in the special care baby unit where she had to be tube-fed, and where she remained until she had reached the five pounds weight deemed acceptable.

Theo brought my mother at the usual visiting time, not knowing that I had given birth. Nobody had a telephone so it had not been possible to send a message and anyway I had mostly been out of everything. Understandably, both Theo and my mother were very shocked and concerned. The following morning when I was feeling much improved and more aware, I woke to find a huge bouquet of flowers from my music student friends, and a little white quilted sleeping bag for the baby. It would be some time before the baby would be big enough to use it.

We both progressed steadily and were released from hospital. I was extremely weak but blissfully happy and overcome with joy at the birth. Theo was proud and adoring, but anxious for us and concerned that we had to move out of our flat the same day I was released from hospital. We reluctantly returned to my mother's tiny house at Tinsley.

DONCASTER – THE RETURN APRIL 2004

I needed to make two return journeys to Doncaster. Because the three houses I had lived in as a student were not close to each other I had to enlist the help of Swinton friends who graciously offered to chauffeur me around in order to take the photographs. I had no photos from the 1960's with which to compare them forty years on but it didn't really matter. The first house, the set back from the road flat-roofed house is still there at the end of the neat, long garden, but now the house is covered in ghastly vari-coloured stone cladding. It looks all the more incongruous because the adjoining house is unclad! The traffic, much heavier than I remember still roars up the Great North Road. I am certain that present occupants appreciate the long garden affording them some measure of peace.

The second house, near to Town Fields, where horse riding began during the seventeenth century, still looks much the same. It remains a house of multiple occupation. Many more of these old family houses appear to have been converted into flats or bedsitters. It is obvious that many of these newer residents are temporary and they care little for keeping the gardens clean and tidy. Some of them will be students and others are young, unemployed and lately there appear to be more people from Eastern Europe, Bangladesh, Pakistan and elsewhere. Some Asian and Chinese communities have been established in the town for some time and mostly live harmoniously together.

However, the arrival of the latest round of refugees from Eastern Europe and a smaller number from Yemen and other Middle Eastern countries has caused further frustration in the town. It is difficult to assess whether this is because of perceived housing and job shortages or because of the increase generally in drugs, prostitution, money laundering and an increase in illegal gangs of workers finding their way on to the surrounding farms in Lincolnshire and on the edge of Doncaster. Without knowing exact crime figures or the causes of criminal activity it would be irresponsible to hazard guesses why Doncaster is a more violent and seedy place to live. What is certain is that Doncaster is not unique in experiencing a rise in crime or in its moral decadence. Interestingly it is this very moral decline which worries many rural communities in Poland and other Eastern European countries. Now the European Union has opened its doors even wider some small, rural villages and particularly the older generations are afraid for their young people's future and a possible erosion of their former way of life and traditions.

Out of the town centre again and a visit to my third student house at Scawsby provided me with a pleasant surprise. What used to be an ordinary red-brick suburban semi-detached house in need of some attention had been tastefully transformed by the young family now living there. The house has been extended and a garage added where the car space used to be. White, gleaming beautiful wrought iron gates, fencing and an ornate grill hiding the garage, a new driveway, windows and door have given the place much more character, almost continental. Car parking in the cul-de-sac is a new problem since more people now drive and often have two cars to a household.

A short walk away I found the old college buildings. The college is now a school for disabled children and a resource centre. As it wasn't term time I was not able to get inside the college to see if the lovely octagonal music room is still there. When the college ceased to train teachers it was for a time used as a police training college. For several minutes whilst wandering around the college buildings I experienced a multitude of flashbacks and in spite of the passage of thirty four years it felt like yesterday.

A lucky visit to the only Doncaster friends I could locate found Joyce and Philip, now in their seventies, surrounded by packing boxes, ready for a move to Southampton to be nearer their daughter Ruth, whom I taught when she was a little girl. Doncaster held nothing for them any more.

I decided to visit the town centre on my own. It was a depressing experience. The taxi driver warned me that there was no where decent to eat lunch. He was right. Even the once grandest hotel in the town centre is a shabby ghost of its former self, and advertising 'Morning Coffee' on a faded piece of A4 paper in a front window!

The quality shops have all but disappeared though there still seems to be a thriving market in Goose Hill. The fish market is fantastic and has a wide array of inexpensive fare. People with money shop mainly in Sheffield at the huge Meadowhall Centre, just twenty minutes away by car.

The poor are limited to whatever Doncaster market, cheap shops and charity shops can offer. Shoplifting is rife, even in the market. I observed more than a few pale-faced young people, mostly girls of about sixteen or seventeen, stealing. Round the corner their equally pale-faced young boyfriends would be waiting, often with a baby in a pushchair. The number of similar young couples wandering through the streets of Doncaster on a wet Tuesday afternoon, was remarkable and sad. Once they might have lived with parents and had a job of sorts until they could be independent. Now they choose to struggle on state benefits and live in poor accommodation. They have children too young because it gives them some sense of self-esteem and achievement, and status among their peers.

Many of these young people will have come from former mining families. Although it is now twenty years since the Miners' strike, when Arthur Scargill tried to bring down the Thatcher government as Ted Heath's government had been ousted in 1974, the devastation and consequences of pit closures and the prolonged strike are still apparent. Many families suffered extreme poverty during the strike. The communities helped each other as best they could. Children were sent to scavenge for coal from the coal heaps. They survived materially through the generosity of supporters countrywide, but the strike and would be strike-breakers set brother against brother, fathers against sons and wives and sisters confused about who to support. Some men wanted to break the strike because they were so poor and needed to work. Arthur Scargill's political agenda didn't matter to many who were hungry and in debt.

There were violent clashes and running battles with the police who tried to restrain the striking miners and the flying pickets. Some of those policemen were sons and brothers of the miners. Whole communities became bitter and families divided. The time when a man's dignity, self-sacrifice, and solidarity were considered good working class values had gone. The future would prove to be one of anger, drug addiction, alcoholism, social deprivation and part-time temporary, non unionised jobs. The women of the old pit villages have adapted, as women always do. They are mainly the ones who go out to work at two or three jobs, caring, cleaning, or in service industry jobs. The older men have never really recovered. They can't accept what they consider to be women's work. Some find it difficult to drag themselves away from the old views and way of life.

Doncaster Council and the South Yorkshire County Council, with help from various sources of funding from Europe, have been making attempts to re-generate the area. Sadly, many of the initiatives have come too late for the miners who were unable or unwilling to adapt their lives. The new 'Earth Centre' at Denaby, the 'Leisure Dome', the war games and horse racing activities which help to sustain the town are expensive pastimes and employ a relatively small number of people. The proposed new airport at what used to be R.A.F. Finningley may offer jobs to younger men in time.

It is a tragedy, often repeated throughout Britain, that the government could not have been more prepared and honest about the inevitable decline in mining, and in the cutlery and steel industries across South Yorkshire.

By comparison, in Spain, the government there warned about seven years ahead of time that certain industries would diminish. Plans were made to re-train workers for other jobs before they became unemployed, demoralised and a drain on the state, and new industries were created.

We on the other hand seem to have eliminated jobs and destroyed some communities, then considered the process of re-generation. Much of it has been too late for certain sectors of the community and many new initiatives have proved to be short-lived or irrelevant to many, one example being the Centre for Popular Music in Sheffield.

Doncaster has fared better than some towns because it is still an important railway town and travel Interchange. The racing business has expanded attracting more visitors to the town, though opportunities have so far been missed to add quality hotels and facilities to further induce tourists to linger. Although mining and many manufacturing industries have gone there is work in the distributive and allied trades, warehousing, call centres, farm machinery and small tools, and in the service industries. However, I would venture to suggest that young people have to make a really determined and sustained effort to do well at school and college in order to escape what is essentially a drab and uninspiring place. I felt nothing but a poverty of spirit in the town.

SHEFFIELD AGAIN – THE NOOK, CROOKESMOOR

Living conditions in my mother's two-up, two-down terraced house were cramped to say the least. I recovered steadily from the trauma and birth of my daughter, and Theo and I were married.

We married in a ten minute ceremony in Doncaster, on a weekday, deliberately chosen so that no one else would be able to be at the ceremony. We had two witnesses, my music tutor Betty and Theo's drama tutor Stanley. I didn't choose to have flowers or photographs but Betty brought me a small posy. We couldn't even afford a proper ring. We had lunch afterwards with Joyce and Philip who had looked after the baby whilst we were being married in a ceremony which made us legal in the eyes of the law and thus respectable in the eyes of the world. In 1970 it still mattered.

Theo had to complete his studies in Drama with a year at Sheffield University so it was sensible to find a house near to the University.

I found a temporary part-time teaching post and my mother took time away from her job to look after the baby. She didn't approve of us looking for a nanny, and I upset at the prospect of leaving my newborn with anyone would only leave her with my mother, who adored her. She was a placid, beautiful child and much loved. She had my mother's undivided attention on the days when she was there. My mother sang to her, read to her, played with her and took her to the park.

The 1880's house we lived in for three years was at 'The Nook', off Barber Road at Crookesmoor, overlooking Crookes Valley. It was a hilly area which until Victorian times had been known only as a small hill village to the west of Sheffield, with wide open spaces and some woodland and was used for grazing cattle and sheep. Barber 'Nook' was named after the man who built Barber Cottage in the 1720's. Although situated only about a mile from the city the original dwellers here would have had no public transport and indeed little reason to go to the city. The villagers would have lived very self-sufficient lives. The gentry would have negotiated the hills on horseback or in a horse-drawn cab or trap.

When tram lines were laid at the turn of the twentieth century people doubted that the tram would get up the hill. Horse drawn buses had always needed extra horses in bad weather to pull them up. Extra horses were waiting at the corner of Harcourt Road in case they were required.

The Nook houses we know now numbered about twenty five and were built in a short cul-de-sac. They were short terraces with passages between to that the 'midden men' or night soil men could come and carry away waste from the primitive earth or bucket toilets. Disinfectant could be bought from the corporation for a few pence if people could afford it. The directories of the time when the houses were first built recorded occupations of householders. It makes fascinating reading. There were grocers, bakers, farmers, cow keepers, dressmakers and drapers. There was a blacksmith, horse keepers, a wheelwright and several grooms. Alongside these necessary and traditional occupations there were also silversmiths, cutters and grinders, file cutters, silverfinishers and an ivory carver. In the Barber Road area and on towards Commonside there were also a number of pawnbrokers and beer houses!

As industry developed in Sheffield at an ever increasing pace many workers found their way to the dozens of small tool, cutlery and engineering workshops which emerged nearer the city and eventually stretched the full length of the River Don.

During this period unmarried girls from lower class families would mostly have worked in domestic service, sometimes from as young as fourteen. Indeed until the Education Act of 1870 girls began to work in service at a much younger age. Records show that the majority of servants would have lived out. Only a relatively small number of wealthy families had live-in servants and even fewer considered themselves grand enough to have a butler. Most Upper and Middle class employers would have had a housekeeper, a maid and possibly two or three additional laundry maids. If horses were kept there would most likely have been a groom and a stable boy and almost certainly a gardener or two. Governesses or high class nannies or nurse-maids would have needed some kind of education or social attributes not common in working class homes.

When we moved to the Nook house I thought that life was pretty grim and difficult but it was nothing compared to life in Victorian times. I didn't have to stoke a fire or black-lead an iron grate. However the previous occupant had removed the existing over sink water heater which we had to replace immediately. With no bathroom and only an outside toilet (thankfully with modern plumbing!) and nappies to wash every day I spent two hours every day washing in the kitchen sink. We did eventually acquire a grant from the council so that we could install a proper bathroom. We had no central heating though, just gas fires downstairs. Upstairs the house was always cold. The sun never seemed to reach any of the windows in the house. At the front of the house the windows in the bay were rotting and there was rising damp below the sills. I spent a lot of time chipping off the decaying plaster inside the room to expose the bricks to the air. I brushed several layers of sealant on the bricks before lining the wall with foil and polystyrene sheets. When it was all done and hopefully dry for some time I covered it all with thick, very 70's, flowery blue paper. It didn't seem to matter how many tins of white paint I used throughout the house, it still felt a gloomy place.

The back garden sloped down towards Crookesmoor Road. It was full of rocks and weeds. I only managed to tame a small portion of it. I couldn't really drum up any real enthusiasm for it. I suppose at the back of my mind I recognized that we would not be living there for any length of time. I was also slightly resentful that the division of labour between us was just unfair.

The experience of my first teaching post very nearly made me abandon teaching altogether. Following a very short interview, of about ten or fifteen minutes, with the Head of a large comprehensive school I never saw the man again. I was to be a temporary, part-time teacher, recruited to fill the gap created by the hurried departure of the previous teacher. There were a total of seven full and part time staff in the Music Department. They were spread between two campuses a mile apart from each other. Movement between the two buildings, for me anyway took place during lunchtime. Having eaten breakfast at about 7.30 a.m. and often missing lunch because of the moving about I would go home exhausted and hungry, but often too tired to be bothered to eat a proper meal.

The Head of Music spent most of his time cocooned in a very nice study with a few very able sixth form students. The rest of his staff had to work out their own survival methods. He offered no syllabus, or guidance.

'Do whatever you like,' he said. 'I know you have been ill and have a young baby at home. It must be difficult for you. It's a stressful timetable but if things get tough just take a day off. There are plenty of staff to cover. Just don't bring me any problems to sort out!'

He laughed as he showed me out of the door. Like the Head Teacher that was the last I saw of him also.

My cupboard in the Lower School music room had very little in the way of resources. I was shown some old copies of the National Song Book, and that was about it. I really was on my own, but thankfully had plenty of interesting material collected whilst I was at college. This was supposed to be a flagship comprehensive school and community college.

The classes were still streamed by ability, but instead of 'A', 'B', and 'C' forms etc., the classes were named Alpha, Beta, Gamma, Delta and in spite of their classic names the pupils were only too well aware of the connotations of each. I never saw any Alpha forms at all and only a couple of Beta forms appeared on my timetable, along with some third year 'Remedial' boys. Not a term we now use, and not a group anyone else wished to teach. It soon became clear to me that the constant movement of teachers in and out of the job was as a direct result of the abysmal timetable, not just the lower ability level classes but also the anti-social time-plan and moving of rooms and buildings, but mostly through a total lack of support and expectation, and even interest. Consequently there seemed to be little respect for teachers in the classroom and certainly no continuity of work.

I had looked forward to my starting my first job and I didn't mind that it was to be for just one term. On reflection it was a blessing in disguise.

I spent many hours preparing interesting lesson materials, copying project sheets, arranging songs, copying music, recording music and listening topics. College tutors had always stressed to us that if we had plenty of good material and were adaptable to the children's needs we would be well on the way to being successful teachers. I am afraid that at that point in time and under the prevailing conditions those children were almost impossible to motivate. The girls alone might sing, if they felt like it. Percussion work, even simple clapping produced a great deal of hilarity, fooling about and non-co-operation. They said that they felt silly, though I know at the Youth Disco's they did just that, clapping and moving to music! In the classroom, listening to music, or to me, or writing down anything at all required much more effort than they were prepared to expend. The only thing they listened attentively for was the end of lesson bell. Mixed classes were far worse, since most of the time the girls were trying to provoke the boys and the boys wanted to talk amongst themselves, completely ignoring anything that I had planned to do. A few pupils would refuse to sit in their chairs, the chairs often being pushed around the room. Discipline was non existent before I came to the school, and it was nigh on impossible to impose it knowing that I had no back up at all from other members of staff.

My first lesson with the third year 'remedial' boys wasn't even scheduled in a proper music room. I had to use a first floor science laboratory. Determined not to be beaten I located the science block and walked up the stairs carrying my guitar. The boys had arrived before me and were hanging over the iron balcony yelling, 'Show us your legs!'

Once inside the lab I found about fifteen boys charging around turning gas taps and water taps on. One boy was trying to climb out of the window. I just couldn't believe that I wasn't on some horror film set. Throwing protocol to the wind I decided that I had had enough so I marched into the adjoining science room and insisted that the male teacher who was teaching a class there came to my immediate assistance. The boys were rounded up and the lab restored to normal. The lab door was locked and the boys were lined up outside the room where we all waited until the bell rang. I refused to teach in there again.

I worked out that from a possible twelve weeks in school with that group I could escape five of them through various short holidays, Sports Day, Exam weeks and mercifully, end of year trips out with other teachers. The remaining sessions with them were a nightmare. We had no music. I talked, they shouted, but at least by the end of my time with them they had learned to stop shouting and spoke in a more acceptable manner and tone level. Success of a sort!

My worst behaved class were actually a group of supposedly intelligent mixed, fourth year pupils, aged fifteen to sixteen. One boy was so rude and disruptive that I mistakenly asked for his name and told him to remain at the end of the lesson. I thought that if I spoke to him on his own, without his pals for an audience he might just apologise. Not a bit of it! He did wait outside the door after the class had gone, together with an older, bully friend. They threatened me and one of them showed that he had possession of a knife. I yelled at the pair of them as loud as I could and they fled. It took staff three weeks to locate the boys concerned. One had given me a false name and the friend wasn't a pupil at the school at all. The boy was suspended and I didn't see him again. During my time at this first school I had been sworn at, punched, kicked, threatened, ignored and undermined. If that was teaching, I thought, then I didn't want any more of it. I felt that I was a total failure.

Thinking of the future and realizing that I needed to be better qualified I investigated the possibility of studying again, for an Open University Degree. The course didn't begin until January but I began to buy books and start some preliminary reading. It took my mind off the awful term I had spent at the school.

We were desperately short of money so I decided to take on a few private piano pupils during the summer holidays. Theo took on a few students for lessons in public speaking and English as a foreign language, the latter were two lovely Chinese young men whose family kept a local takeaway shop. We took in a student lodger who was prepared to live in the attic and didn't complain about having to use the outside loo. She was a postgraduate social work student called Greta, a very sweet-natured and tolerant girl who has remained a good friend for over thirty years.

By the start of the Autumn school term it was clear that we were in a big financial mess. I summoned up the courage to take another short-term teaching post at a former city grammar school, newly comprehensive since government changes in education policy and the raised school leaving age to sixteen. I was dreading the new job and lay awake at nights worrying about it. However, the difference between this and my first school convinced me that I wasn't a total failure. These children, who were from very similar socio-economic backgrounds as those in the first school but were better behaved throughout the ability ranges were more responsive and generally keen. Again I was allotted classes from mixed ability ranges but never the really clever ones. New teachers rarely taught exam groups until they had proved themselves. It didn't matter this time. No one threatened me and most pupils were interested enough to complete work set for them. They were co-operative and polite. The greatest difference and it was immediately apparent was that in this school the Head was interested in all aspects of school life, and he was visible. The pupils knew who he was. The Head of Music Department was liked and respected by pupils and staff alike. He worked very hard with pupils of all ages and abilities and he had formulated a workable syllabus for class work and out of class there were choirs, bands, orchestras and smaller groups. I was especially impressed that sometimes during breaks and lunchtimes and after school pupils would wander into the Music rooms either to practice by themselves or with others and to work on their own compositions or arrangements. This was how it should have been in every school. A music community of interested and confident young people. Whilst I was at this second school dozens of pupils, ex-pupils and staff were rehearsing for a mammoth Old Time Music Hall performance. It was a fantastic success and ran for several nights to a packed hall every time.

My only negative experience in this school was an ugly and totally unexpected encounter in the staffroom with a truly obnoxious and snobbish young teacher who, observing me with my Open University books, attacked me verbally and poured scorn on the O.U. and on my attempts to improve my professional status.

'You should have worked harder at school,' she said, 'It's really getting a degree by the back door!' etc., etc., and on she went into a long tirade about working class people who hadn't made it to grammar school. I was so upset and cross with her that I didn't dignify this attack with an answer. I doubt she would have cared to understand that I had been to so many schools because of my disrupted childhood that I had been denied the chance to work harder. It certainly wasn't due to any lack of will on my part, and I had certainly made up for it later. I am still trying to make up for it. I wondered if the obnoxious one would recognize my efforts to study for 'O' and 'A' levels, RSA and music exams whilst doing a responsible full time job at Sheffield City Hall as hard work. In the early days of the Open University this was a common attitude in the teaching profession. O.U. students were often ridiculed or thought of as second class citizens.

Now, over thirty years on O.U. textbooks and research are highly regarded and are often used in conventional universities and sixth forms across the country. We go on learning. Education doesn't stop when we leave school. In fact it has been shown that older people are perfectly able to study to degree level and beyond and may even show a commitment and persistence that isn't always there in eighteen year olds. In this high-tech computer age many businesses expect employees of all ages to keep their skills up to date and Business degrees and Management Diplomas are not the sole province of the young. Surely it must also be the case that learning, scholarship and research added to the body of knowledge in all subject areas for the benefit of future generations ought to be valued for its own sake.

In spite of my run-in with the obnoxious one I left my temporary job feeling much more confident. I was continually tired. It had been exhausting leaving home early in the morning, teaching all day and then returning home to private pupils, housework, studying and spending time with my child. All had to be very carefully timetabled so that my child didn't suffer.

Theo finished his degree and I feared that he might take off and live the actor's life, but he didn't at least not then.

Theo's wife, that is his first wife dropped a great bombshell of a shock on us just when I anticipated things would improve for us. She took Theo to court for non-payment of child maintenance. I felt really ashamed since I thought we had been paying it. Theo pleaded with the judge and explained that he was not yet in employment and we had no money. The judge was not impressed at all and ordered Theo to sell the car (by then we had a second hand mini) and the money was to be paid to his first wife as soon as the car was sold. This meant that when Theo did obtain a Drama teaching post in Doncaster he was reliant on lifts from people. I was totally dependent on public transport.

When she was old enough we enrolled our daughter in the Jewish Kindergarten which necessitated a bus journey there and back and took most of the morning. It was well worth the trek and the time spent travelling. She developed in confidence and had a happy experience there. The Kindergarten was a calm, well ordered happy environment in the capable hands of Mrs. Bergmann, who had two degrees, and several other very competent helpers.

There were few small children where we lived so it was good for my child to have the company of others. Sometimes a little boy called Mark, the adopted son of a mature pupil and friend called Angela would come to our house to play. Tragically for all of us Angela developed anorexia and we did not have her friendship for very long before she died. We have treasured memories of Angela but also feelings of inadequacy as we wonder whether we could have noticed sooner, done more, helped her. It was another sad thing to come to terms with.

The best thing about living at Crookesmoor was that we were only a short walk away from Weston Park and Crookes Valley Park, which joined each other. The Crookes Valley Park had a children's playground, a boating lake and fishing on the Dam reservoir. A short distance away was Weston Park with a lake, and the ducks, and the wonderful Mappin Art Gallery and Museum. The Park, where generations of Sunday School children used to gather every Whitsuntide in their newly bought clothes to attend the Whit Sings had magnificent gardens. Banks and banks of rhododendrons and azaleas would remind me of reading Daphne du Maurier's book 'Rebecca'. Sometimes on a warm, sunny afternoon we would go to listen to the band playing in the bandstand, or just laze around with an ice-cream, people watching. Because it was close to the Children's Hospital there would sometimes be nurses sun-bathing in their brief time out, or parents with children in wheelchairs, brought out to take the sun for a while. It was a lovely place for old folk to come and read their newspapers or weekend fathers to play with their offspring.

While I was waiting for a suitable teaching post to arise, and conscious that I had to earn some money I explored the local church halls and the Community Centre at the newly finished and huge Kelvin Flats complex, built so that the council could re-house families from slum clearance housing estates. I took a real chance that I could develop some music classes for young children. It was trail-blazing in those days. I was inundated with children wanting to sign up. It proved to be a great success, real fun and very rewarding to see the children's enthusiasm and progress. The local radio and newspapers came to take photographs and featured us on several occasions. Soon other teachers were contemplating working with young children too.

My then two year old 'tagged along' and helped me to pack and unpack the boxes of instruments (rhythm sticks, chime bars, tambourines, glockenspiels etc). The children sang, danced, played

Music class at Kelvin, Sheffield ... author and daughter, 1972

rhythm backings to things, listened to music and stories, and even tried a few tunes on the piano, recorders, and guitar. Some of them made such progress that I had to begin proper instrumental lessons. At the end of the year we held a charity concert and invited all the parents along. I learned much later that many of these children have careers in the theatre or in teaching music. They include a theatre manager, several professional musicians, and dancers, a church organist and choirmaster, a Doctor of music and a number of teachers.

My little daughter, who I had allowed just to be there has surprised me beyond anything I could have imagined. Without my realizing it she had been carefully watching everything, listening intently and absorbing melody, rhythm and harmony without being taught. Sometime between her second and third birthday she was able to sing in tune, hold a steady beat and recognize bass parts. She had learned all by herself to pick out major and minor scale patterns on the piano. She would give a little giggle each time she found the pattern again on a different starting note. She was fascinated by musical sounds and totally absorbed when she was 'busy' making music and having fun. Watching her develop was a complete joy. Everything else came second. There was a little corner in my heart for her lost baby sister and I have always found it safer to keep that little corner tucked away, but never forgotten. I still can't talk about it. I hoped there might be other children one day. I didn't want my daughter to grow up feeling lonely, but more than anything I wanted to create a happy family life for all of us. I was ambitious only to capture a sense of security and stability. Something I had lacked as a child, and still lacked.

Though still living in Sheffield and still relying on public transport or lifts from colleagues, I obtained my first full-time teaching post in Rotherham, about ten miles away.

The school used to be a Boys and separate Girls Technical High School. With the advent of comprehensive re-organisation the two schools had merged. One building was the Upper School, the other was the Lower School where I would be mostly based, though I taught across the entire age range.

There were about nine hundred children at the school who lived either on the neat and green Broom Valley council estate or on the Duke of Norfolk's more affluent estate on the other side of Moorgate. A few children also came from Whiston and Broom.

The Head Mistress was a tall, straight-backed rather old-fashioned spinster lady. She appeared serious and unsmiling but she was a dedicated, caring teacher, interested in pupils and staff alike. She had a deeply compassionate nature, but was by no means soft. She regularly reminded the entire school that having high or low intelligence was not so important as being a good and decent human being, mindful of the effect we had on others. I liked her immediately and thought we would work well together. My interview was hilarious.

'You've had a lot of schools, homes and jobs!' she exclaimed incredulous at the list on my C.V. 'Will you stay put if I give you the job?' I assured her that I would try my best.

'I see you've studied Religious Education as well as music,' she said.

'Then you won't mind teaching a bit of history. Same thing really isn't it?' She thrust two books in my hands.

'You teach this in the first year. The Stone Age to 1066, and you teach the other one in the second year. Off you go!'

I had no chance to argue or ask questions. I'd got the job.

The Head of Music and I agreed to differ on many things. He had been used to teaching in the Girls Technical High School and was in his life out of school a brilliant church organist and choir trainer. A traditionalist he found the merging of the two schools difficult and having to prepare a syllabus for the first time had been a challenge for him. But having developed the syllabus he had no wish to deviate from it. There was no doubt that he was a brilliant choirmaster and his Boys Choir were so good that they were permitted to sing in many of the greatest cathedrals in Britain on occasions when the regular choristers took their vacations. It was a great honour for the school, and a great experience for the boys. However, my new 'superior' had such high standards and expectations that sadly, faced with ordinary children, who though willing were not all super talented or enthusiastic he frequently lost his temper and alienated pupils and staff time and time again.

I often found myself playing the role of mediator or being the calming influence in situations where tears of frustration were shed not only by girls. With one or two exceptions the pupils in this school were just wonderful. They were amenable and interested and we bounced ideas off each other. I think on reflection they were so pleased to be involved in a different kind of music making. I was the first teacher they had ever seen with a guitar. I suppose in today's parlance I was considered 'cool'. That isn't to say that we only sang folk songs in music lessons, but I have to admit that the rich tradition of 'old', traditional folk songs lent themselves to a guitar accompaniment.

Spirituals, newer industrial ballads about coal miners, weavers and the railways, and the protest songs of Bob Dylan, Tom Paxton and Joan Baez were eagerly received. The pupils even wrote their own songs. Thanks to my training college I had learned how to take a song, or a piece of instrumental music and arrange it every which way to suit any kind of pupil and any group of instruments. Who would have thought that a song with only one word, AMEN, could enthral and occupy a class of thirty-odd teenagers for a whole lesson and leave them wanting for more? I was so relieved and even grateful to them for not walking all over me as the wretched pupils in my first school had done. In time I developed a good rapport with most of the school and my pupils were willing participants in many performance projects. They even bucked up some enthusiasm for morning assembly. I would 'play in' our gowned Head Teacher as she swept through the middle of the assembly hall to 'Good Morning Starshine,' or 'Day by Day' or something similar. Then to make the pupils wake up with a smirk I sometimes changed the traditional tune for the hymn to a different and very unexpected tune. The staff, usually seated reverently down each side of the hall also appreciated my attempts to brighten up the mornings and even the most demure teacher might be found swaying to the music, and smiling. Sometimes I received requests for a particular piece of music. When the request came from pupils I was thrilled.

On the home front Theo had a full time Drama post in a Doncaster school, developed an interest in Liberal politics and disappeared to 'play golf' most weekends. Sometimes he played squash with my brother at a leisure centre in Rotherham. I was pleased that he seemed to be making an effort to get on with my brother but they were two very different men and I wondered whether it would last. It did make me think that Theo valued family connections and as we were a very fragmented family I thought it worth encouraging.

Theo signed over his ex-wife's house to her in total. She had re-married and was quite happy about that. I felt we had done the right thing.

We felt more confident about moving house again, to be nearer both our jobs. We were still without a car and relied on people for lifts. We didn't afford proper holidays until much later. We hired a car for a visit to Theo's aged parents. Nothing could have prepared me for the reception we received in Brighton. My new mother-in-law was clearly deeply upset at our appearance and couldn't bring herself to talk to me at all. In fact when I entered a room, she would leave it. She was very cold towards her son. We did manage to sit together in the lounge eating cucumber and salmon paste sandwiches from the tea trolley. Theo spoke mostly with his father though it was rather more formal than I had heard of Theo before. His father was a gentle and kind man who was obviously struggling to care for his wife and to contain a difficult situation. It was deemed that Theo had behaved so badly that he had let down the good name of this middle class, socialite, respectable family. Theo's mother could not face neighbours, friends and their prestigious golf club circle. Theo had disgraced them. It wasn't just that he had relinquished a secure banking job to become a travelling salesman, selling chocolate for Fry's. It wasn't that he had taken his wife and children to live hundreds of miles away while he embarked on a Drama course at college. It was that he had left the marital home and was now married to me. I was perceived as 'the cause' of his mother's feelings of shame. The truth was something quite different. Theo had destroyed the marriage long before I appeared in his life, but it was quite impossible to talk with his parents about that. In fact they probably knew far more than I did about his life.

On a subsequent visit I still received the silent treatment from Theo's mother although I did try to have some polite, gentle words with her. I had to have something to occupy myself with while we were there. Theo's father watched me carefully unpick an old red velvet dress of mine. I re-made it, stitching everything twice, by hand into a party dress for my daughter. The following morning Theo's father took me to inspect his garden and the glorious fruit-laden vine growing at the back of the house. It was a sun trap and the fruit growing there tasted delicious.

Theo's father asked me how much I knew about his son's previous history. Of course I only knew what Theo had chosen to tell me about the past before college. He thought that he would try to fill me in, just in case! He apologised for 'mother' being the way she was.

'I wish you had known us when we were younger,' he said, 'she wasn't always this way.' My heart went out to him. I gave him a brief hug and he puffed away earnestly at his pipe and pausing half way up the sloping garden he placed his hand on my arm and said, 'I would like to buy you a sewing machine.'

SHEFFIELD, THE NOOK HOUSE, 2004

When I returned to the Nook house, thirty one years later to take new photographs I was relieved that we hadn't stayed there. I felt no emotional pull at all, just relief. The house looked neater than I remember it. Perhaps because it now has new doors and windows and a proper damp course! A young family live there now and the children's bunk beds are visible through the upstairs window. I was glad about that at least. Some years ago I had read a disturbing news report about the police raiding that house, looking for drugs, which they found in the attic bedroom. There had been a drug dealer living in our house. The cars outside were parked bumper to bumper on both sides of the road. There was litter everywhere I walked and remnants of discarded food. Some of the houses are shabbier than I remember and one of them is a flats letting agency with an Asian name, so this has become a more multi-cultural area and a wider student residence area as the University has expanded.

Thank goodness the parks, museum and gallery are still there but the once vibrant Whit Sings don't happen any more and there are fewer band concerts at the park. Parents are more wary of allowing children to wander the parks on their own and there is marginally more apparent vandalism and unruly groups of youths who seem determined to spoil the environment for others. It is not the peaceful place it once was.

Lower down the valley and towards the city the small artisan workshops and some of the smaller cutlery and engineering firms have disappeared along with the old, insanitary 'courts' of sub-standing housing. The massive Kelvin flats complex, so proudly built in the 1960's to house slum clearance families has also been demolished. In fact the flats created even more problems for some of those poor, unfortunate families. Many of them had been taken away from their friends from the 'other' communities and the smaller and more claustrophobic nature of individual flats within the complex caused many problems for the elderly who should never have been located there in the first place. Young mothers, possibly feeling isolated and unable to cope, boisterous older children and teenagers, some with drug habits and other problems were all there in a concentrated microcosm of society. There was a myriad of problems for the authorities to deal with. This is where I taught dozens of Saturday children in their music classes but I have to admit that the majority of those children didn't live in Kelvin flats. I often wonder what happened to all of those children. I still remember most of their names. Some of them remember mine.

I tried to find the few friends we had known at the 'Nook' house but failed to locate any of them. Most of them have moved away and some have died. The children we knew have all grown up of course and are leading their adult lives somewhere else. It was just another place that I had passed through.

My brother and his family never visited the Nook, and my father only came once.

ROTHERHAM - BROOM ROAD

If you say 'Rotherham' to most people these days they think either of Rotherham Football Club or Junction 34 on the M1 and its easy access to the giant Meadowhall Shopping Centre on the edge of Sheffield.

Once in its history Rotherham was thought to be of greater significance than Sheffield. Because of Rotherham's situation at the confluence of the Rivers Don and Rother it was an important trade and through route from the time of the Romans onwards. The Roman fort at Templeborough was one of many military posts flanking the route to York. Rotherham retained its importance as a trading centre until the extension of the canal system all the way to Sheffield in the nineteenth century, and afterwards the development of the railways.

In Domesday Book (1086) Rotherham was described as an established town with a church, priest and a mill. The Earl of Mortain, William the Conqueror's half-brother, to whom he gave the town, in turn gave Rotherham to Nigel Fossard, one of his retainers. At Kimberworth there was a separate Manor held by Roger de Busli. During the fifteenth century the town passed to the monks at Rufford Abbey who judging by the records seem to have been good and conscientious landlords. The Parish Church was rebuilt, the ford was replaced with a bridge and in the 1480's a bridge chapel was added. Thomas Rotherham, Archbishop of York, founded the red-brick College of Jesus and he also added the beautiful Chapel of Jesus to the church. Erected on the site of his birthplace the college provided for a provost and three fellows who were required to attend the Parish Church every Sunday and at all festivals. They were to instruct the choristers and to teach grammar, poetry and public speaking. The foundation of Rotherham Grammar School required that the college accept 'six poorer boys of these parts' to be maintained and instructed until the age of eighteen.

During the sixteenth century following Henry VIII's suppression of the monasteries Rotherham along with other Rufford Abbey estates, passed to the Crown. The Church and Manor passed to the Earl of Shrewsbury. More property was seized when an act for suppression of chantries led to the closure of the College of Jesus and the Bridge Chapel. The Grammar School continued and the Feoffees of the Common Lands of Rotherham continued the charitable work which had until then been managed by the mediaeval gilds. The Feoffees were responsible for the next three hundred years for the Grammar School, the Chapel on the Bridge, the water supply and other amenities.

In the seventeenth century the manor passed to the Duke of Norfolk, and later in that century the church began to lose its influence as other religious groups emerged. The Vicar, Luke Clayton was ejected from his living and imprisoned for refusing to observe the Act of Uniformity. After his release from prison he helped to found a Unitarian congregation. Later groups of Non-Conformists included Methodists and Baptists.

Rotherham continued as a fairly prosperous market town. Following the Inclosure Award of 1764 many acres of open fields and common land were enclosed and shared out among the freeholders, a large portion of which went to the Earl of Effingham, then Lord of the Manor.

Turnpike trusts were formed and there was a great improvement in the local roads. Money collected at the tollgates (one of which was at the corner of Broom Road) was used to cover the costs of road maintenance.

In this brief outline sketch of Rotherham's history it is impossible to include every development of the late eighteenth and nineteenth centuries. Probably the single most important factor in the industrial development of the town was the use of canal transport. By 1857 canal transport carried over 400,000 tons of coal a year, but in time the new railways would move much more.

The economy of Rotherham during the nineteenth century was very diverse. Goods manufactured in iron foundries included war weaponry, kitchen ranges and stoves, fireplaces, railings, taps, valves, meters, railway wheels, axles, tools and so on. Glassware was manufactured at Beatson Clark's and there were a few potteries. All these industries needed coal to fire furnaces, and the coal was mined in local pits.

Industrial expansion led to a ten-fold increase in the population. Rows of terraced houses were built on the west side of the River Don and in the town itself there were courts of badly lit and poorly ventilated houses. Poor sanitary arrangements led to an outbreak of cholera in 1832.

There were a few doctors in the town, but they had to be paid for. The Workhouse Infirmary was the last resort of the poor. Eventually, in 1872 the Rotherham Hospital was built near the workhouse site on Doncaster Gate. This is where my maternal grandmother died.

The burgeoning steel industry at the end of the nineteenth century came to dominate much of the life of the town but the exciting developments at the turn of the century included electric light and power, improved roads and public transport and not least the 1902 Education Act allowing for the establishment of more schools.

The First World War proved to be the catalyst of the biggest social upheaval in Rotherham's history. Factories were used to provide munitions and as more and more men were called for military service women replaced them on factory floors. The same situation occurred in the Second World War except that in 1939 women were also able to join the forces, or were eligible to work in the Land Army, replacing farmers who had to go to war.

Between the wars the council demolished many of the old, insanitary houses and began to build housing estates. This was paralleled by widespread building of private housing on the outskirts of the town.

Our Edwardian semi-detached villa on Broom Road would have originally been owned by a wealthy businessman or factory manager. This row of houses built high above the level of the road would have been far away from the stench of the poorer housing in the town courts. These were built by a speculative builder, one of a group of builders allowed to buy small areas of land for building middle-class housing. They were large houses, roomy cellars and four bedrooms and a walk in landing wardrobe. Our house would have had a long back garden leading out towards the fields at Herringthorpe, but at some time in its history half the garden had been sold off to the Preparatory School two houses down the road, now known as Rudston School.

In 1973 the house cost us £12,500. I loved the sunny, bay-windowed lounge which became my music room. The light and spaciousness of the other rooms was a relief after the gloominess of the Nook house. Little by little I enjoyed decorating the house and we installed central heating. What a luxury! Theo, for once in domestic mode sensibly chipped off all the plaster underdrawing in the cellar below the music room so that we could check for ourselves the state of the timbers and whether it was safe for the piano's weight.

It was a lovely house and garden for children to grow up in. The time seemed right to think about a little brother or sister for our daughter and we made enquiries about adoption.

I have to admit that I felt more than anxious, in view of Theo's previous marital history and the fact that I was working. However, we filled in the appropriate forms, gave reliable references and crossed our fingers. We waited and waited and waited. It was a very long time before we received a letter telling us we were considered 'suitable'.

Rotherham house, Broom Road

We were interviewed separately and together and enjoyed several visits from the Adoptions Officer, a charming, very thorough but unhurried and very helpful lady. She discussed with us all the possible scenarios we might face. We were asked if we would be prepared to take an older child, or one with difficulties. We agreed that it didn't matter to us if the child was not newborn. We didn't want a child who was older than our daughter. We felt it better to take a child whose age would be as a natural gap between our own child. From a practical point of view, i.e. my part-time teaching and the fact that I didn't drive would preclude the adoption of a handicapped child. It was a revelation to us to learn how much care was taken in trying to match an adoptive child with its potential new parents. Where at all possible things like eye and hair colour, even physique and disposition, likes and dislikes, all were carefully noted to make a whole picture of the parties involved. Our four year old was asked if she would like to have a brother or sister. Without hesitation she said she would like a brother. We don't quite know why she said that. It certainly wasn't prompted by anyone.

I remember watching old movies where a couple would visit an orphanage to 'choose' a child, and I wondered if it was ever like that. Our experience was very different. The whole procedure seemed to take a very long time but we realized that it was all done with the greatest care and sensitivity with regards to the feelings of child, foster parents, new parents and of course the birth mother. Nevertheless we did worry about the protracted time it took and the effects of the delay on the child.

Eventually it was suggested that we might like to meet a baby boy who was almost a year old. His very young teenage mum had placed him in care from his birth. There was no chance that her family were prepared to keep him. The boy reported to be his father denied that he was responsible. Even so, every chance was given to the boy to accept his responsibility should he wish to do so. In fact the courts dealing with the formal adoption have to go to great lengths to seek the father's permission for the child to be adopted.

We were surprised that the baby, who had been born with a small port wine mark on his face, had never been properly investigated. The hospital had reported that sometimes there could be some underlying cell damage beneath these marks. This had alarmed the family and prospective adopters. We raised the issue and felt that he should be investigated for his own sake, whether we adopted him or not. It was obvious to us that he was a normal little boy.

The Social Services did go ahead with an investigation. At that time Sheffield did not have the latest scanners so the baby had to be taken by his foster parents to Great Ormond Street Hospital in London. It was a big ordeal for all of them, but we were all relieved to be told that no abnormalities had been detected.

Weeks and months passed. We bought a new car, and were able to take 'Andy' out in the car for short trips. We took him to a toy store in the city and usually came back with a toy train or animal. We took the children to the park and in time we took him to our house where the children could play together in more relaxed surroundings. They seemed to get on well together though we were a little concerned that Andy didn't seem to know how to play with toys. He had to be shown what to do with toy cars, trains and building bricks. Books, even baby books seemed to be totally new to him and almost everything he was introduced to was thrown up in the air or across the room. He had been in a kind and loving foster home and he had been taught how to hold a spoon and feed himself properly but otherwise he had few physical skills. Playing with a ball in our garden was very revealing. The lawn was divided by a concrete path about two feet across and a couple of inches in depth, a tiny step off the grass, but if the ball was on one side of the path and Andy on the other he wouldn't step onto the path to cross it, he would walk the full length of the garden to the end of the path and round the end of it then back up the other side. It was just a small thing but this and other things we noticed as the weeks passed convinced us that although Andy had been well cared for, was well fed and loved, he had lacked any kind of stimulation. His speech was indistinct and we realized that he had probably spent a great deal of time being bounced on someone's knee and eating biscuits while the adults around him talked among themselves or watched television. Lack of space in the foster parent's council house must have been a factor in the lack of opportunity for Andy to move around.

By the time the adoption was finalised and Andy came to live with us permanently he was nearly two years old. The day he moved in we had a special tea and all seemed well until bedtime. Both children were bathed, changed, had stories read, songs sung, hugs and kissed and were then tucked into their beds. Obviously a different routine to the one Andy was used to and he couldn't settle in his cot. He had been with us happily all day long with no tears or signs of distress but when bedtime came he cried and cried. The solution was simple however, and once I had discovered it the whole thing worked like a dream. I found that I couldn't put Andy in his cot while he was still awake. I had to rock him in my arms and after a few minutes he fell fast asleep. He was a real heavy weight so I was relieved when he learned to go to bed without being rocked every night. We had a few problems for a while when he woke in the mornings. He would stand in his cot and reach out to the wallpaper which he pulled off the wall in great chunks. Apart from these incidents he didn't seem to be exhibiting any obvious signs of distress. In retrospect I believe that emotionally he had to begin again. Although he was almost two years old he was learning day by day as though he was a new baby. He had new surroundings, people with different voices and people who greeted him and treated him differently. He was not unhappy. He took in all new experiences well. He enjoyed being the centre of attention.

As he became acclimatised and his language was developing he began to play more creatively with his sister, and importantly, by himself. He was reluctant to use his legs and we found various toys to try and encourage him. He loved his sit-upon dog, but he preferred to push it along rather than ride it, and when we introduced a little tricycle he would push himself along with his feet on the ground, never the pedals. We watched over him carefully and when he showed the slightest interest in anything we tried to build on it. The first signs of 'liking' anything, other than food, was his attraction to birds and animals. So, we drew animals and birds. We had story books, puzzles and toy animals to play with and we visited the donkeys in the park. We put food out in the garden to attract wild birds.

The ladies who looked after his play group adored Andy. He developed quite a fan base and enjoyed being the focus of attention.

Unfortunately when he was old enough to be enrolled at school, a private school run on more formal, disciplined lines, he found it very difficult to conform. His playful clowning around wasn't considered 'cute' any more, just disruptive. The private school had suited my daughter in the early years because the classes were small. She had liked her first two teachers who made her feel secure. Following a lengthy and debilitating period of illness with repeated throat and ear infections she had to have an operation to remove tonsils and adenoids and to clear badly infected sinuses. The operation was a great success and we discovered accidentally that the poor child had been steadily going deaf. How had we not noticed? I felt very guilty for not realizing sooner that something was wrong. On her return to school she was afraid to go into the playground and wanted to know why people were shouting all the time.

Andy loved being in the playground and in fact had to be chased back into the classroom where he found concentrating very difficult.

After we adopted Andy I decided to work only part-time at school. I would supplement our income by teaching at home. The idea was that I would be at home when the children came home from school and Theo would be there when I was teaching pupils. At least that was the theory.

School teaching continued to be challenging, but rewarding and mostly fun. There was however one incident which marred everyone's time there and was a shocking experience which we are unlikely to forget. I arrived one morning ready to take my first class of the day, a fourth year class of fifteen year olds. The staff room was unusually quiet and sombre. It seemed that one of the boys from the class I was about to teach had been taken away by police the previous evening. He had suffered some kind of brainstorm and had stabbed his piano teacher to death. He then called the police himself. I dreaded seeing my class. There was no way we could have had the planned lesson. When I entered the room the class were silent except for a few pupils who were trying to stifle their sobs. The boys were stony-faced and deep in thought.

Only seconds had elapsed when the Head Mistress and two policemen appeared at the classroom door. One by one the boy's friends were escorted out of the room to be interviewed by the police who were trying to establish what had taken place the night before. As each boy left the room, and didn't return, I was looking after a smaller and smaller group of traumatized teenagers until the lesson bell. We talked a little, not about the boy and what he had done, but how we could help each other get through the day, and all the harrowing days to come. There were a lot of hugs as the remaining pupils left the room.

Referring back to my description of the Head Mistress it is worth recording here that a mark of her compassionate nature was evident when she spent years visiting the boy in his detention. She visited him regularly and continued to take an interest in his education.

I was glad that for a while at least I had something good to take my mind off the awful event of that year. I was very aware that I had neglected my own music-making and keen to improve on the wonderful work I had participated in with Walter Bergmann (world renowned Recorder player and teacher) whilst at college, I decided to form an Early Music Group. We were a group of Recorders, a Spinet and a Cello, used in the absence of a more authentic Viol instrument. We were not experts but we made a good sound, respectable enough to perform in galleries, churches, arts venues, even in the ballroom at Sandbeck Park, home of the Earl of Scarborough. We had been invited to play throughout the day as visitors to the 'Red Cross' Open Day (charity of Lady Scarborough) walked around the house.

My daughter listened intently to everything we played as she had to my earlier music groups for children. This resulted in us buying a tiny violin, which she didn't care for. She wanted a cello like the one she had heard Tim playing in our group. So we bought a quarter size cello and at age six years she sat on her teacher's coffee table for her lessons until she grew into a proper stool and a larger cello. She continued her piano lessons at home with me. She wanted to be treated just the same as the other children and when lessons were over she would giggle and say, 'Will you be Mummy now?'

Theo wasn't ignored in all of our musical pursuits. He chauffeured our daughter to her lessons and orchestra rehearsals. He acted as roadie for the Recorder Consort when we had concerts where we used the spinet, or had equipment to carry. He acted as Front of House and Lighting Manager when necessary, and together we devised some programmes of music, poetry and readings where his talents as an actor could be employed. It was good for him to be able to develop artistically away from purely school productions.

Teaching, especially in Music, Drama and other performing arts is a very tiring, stressful and time consuming occupation and teachers in these disciplines often lose their own performance skills, not through laziness, but simply because their timetables are so intense that they lack the time to rehearse. This can work in the reverse way too. Highly skilled and busy performers often work at such a pace and exacting level of excellence that they have little time to pass on their skills to others and if they do manage it they can become very frustrated because students are not always at a sufficiently high level, or committed enough to satisfy their teachers.

College recital, Rotherham, 1982

Our Recorder Consort was dealt a severe and tragic blow when Helen, one of our lead players was killed in a road accident. We were so shocked and of course we missed her lovely playing. We missed her sunny and gracious nature too. I don't think we ever recovered from the loss of Helen though for a time we tried to carry on. It wasn't ever the same again.

My new work challenge was at an Arts college, part-time again, and teaching sixth form students, some of whom were aiming at careers in music. Alongside their 'A' level studies they were also learning to play the piano. Some of them were complete beginners at sixteen but were first study students on other instruments. They needed some facility at the piano if they were to gain a college place. So I had two years on average to get those students into shape.

When I taught in Rotherham pupils needed a couple or more 'O' levels to gain a place at the Sixth Form College, the further education colleges would accept pupils who may not have yet gained 'O' levels. It wasn't that one was superior to the other establishment, it was just that the two colleges provided a different learning environment. Many students felt happier in a more relaxed 'Arts college' where mature students also studied. Academic and vocational courses were available. Sean Bean, the actor was a Drama student at the college and other talented actors and musicians began there. Many of the music students graduated to universities in Hull, Leeds, Manchester, Cardiff and York as well as the specialist music colleges around the country.

My weakest student, and the least willing, was a punk with green hair and nose studs. In spite of doing little work he managed to have a short-lived career as a rock musician. I still hear from some of my former music students, thirty years on. Some are professional musicians, teachers, arts administrators, therapists or instrument makers.

The saddest, but by far the most rewarding and inspiring student that I never hear from, and probably never will, was Issam, a student from Iraq.

When he first arrived at the college Issam had to bring an interpreter. He spoke very little English. He was aiming to study guitar, piano and 'A' level music. In less than two years he had mastered the language and the instruments. His piano playing had progressed from being a Beginner to approximately Grade Six and his Guitar playing was nearer to Grade Eight. He had been back and visited his family in Iraq once or twice and he brought me a beautiful black and gold lace shawl as a gift one time. Then one fateful vacation he travelled home never to return. He had been refused permission to return to Britain and was forced to enlist in the army. We never heard from him again. I often remember Issam.

Mature students were encouraged to study music at the college and I had a few pre-retirement, redundant workers, early retired students on my books. No one realistically believed that these students would achieve great standards but their enthusiasm, their presence provided a beacon to the younger students who integrated with them well. It may well be that these students were being used for political ends. I do not know. I do know from personal experience that studying music and participating in choirs and in ensemble groups gave them a huge amount of pleasure and a new lease of life.

Colleges underwent a huge re-organisation during the 1970's and 80's. Part-time lecturers received a poor employment deal. At one stage I had been working for about sixteen to nineteen hours a week when a new 'rule' meant that lecturers working for more than twelve hours a week could be offered a permanent contract and holiday pay.

Fantastic, I thought! It would mean a bit more security. But no, what followed was further 're-organisation' of hours so that many part-time lecturers had their hours reduced to below the level required to give them that security of tenure. The college of course saved money in the process. Most infuriatingly for me my 'excess' hours were then given to a younger and less experienced teacher, and an ex-student of the college! I realized that I would at some stage have to leave the college job and I set about expanding my private work, little by little. I figured that if I became self-employed I would be in charge of my own destiny. The success or otherwise of it would depend only on my own efforts and ability and not on the whims of senior lecturers or mini-dictators. I refused to be manipulated any longer.

I wasn't the only part-time lecturer to be affected. Disgruntled teachers in many colleges, universities and school sixth forms were angry and disillusioned about the shoddy treatment they received at the hands of managers and authorities. Unions did become involved in negotiations and still fight the cause, but seem to have achieved little as far as I can tell. This was one time when I did feel drawn to the militant left. However I left the college before pursuing any real action. Colleges have always relied on part-time teachers in order to function and it is well known that part-time teachers often give time well over and above that for which they are paid. Many do it gladly, or with a sense of resignation.

I spent many extra hours with students who needed help, or in rehearsals for concerts, auditions and competitions. If I had calculated the actual hours spent working the hourly rate would have been a pittance.

I left the college with bad feelings about a number of things, and a very heavy heart. My Union representative was concerned that I would suffer a loss of status. I told him that he needn't worry.

However, I was deserting my loyal students after eight and a half years in the job. The students little knew how much their presence, normality and good naturedness had helped to sustain me through another very dark time.

By 1979 it was inevitable that Theo and I would part. Amid overwhelming feelings of frustration, anger, disappointment and failure I asked him to leave us. I didn't want it to happen but I couldn't live with the anxiety, the humiliation or trying to keep up a pretence any longer. I tried my hardest to provide a secure and loving home and family life, which he said that he appreciated. We were each involved in enough of our separate, but often overlapping interests to provide the freedom to grow and not feel stifled by too much domesticity. We were both involved in the children's activities, and we had lovely holidays in Devon and Cornwall, and a disastrous one in Belgium. When Theo was at home he played the keen caring father, and appeared to the outside world to be a charming and respectable pillar of society. It took me a while to realize that it was a total sham. He was an actor par excellence. Throughout the eleven years we were together there had been other women. He treated all his wives in the same way, though I haven't spoken with wife number four. The other two wives have confirmed what happened in their marriages. None of us deserved to be treated as we were. I should have listened to the well-meaning busy bodies who tried to warn me. It would have been better if I had walked away, but to have foresight would be a wonderful thing.

Of course at first I blamed myself for telling Theo to leave us. The pain of having to tell the children that their Daddy would not be living with us any more was excruciating. I was overcome with feelings of guilt. I had ruined the children's happy lives by showing Theo the door. I didn't eat properly for weeks and I lost a lot of weight. I slept fitfully and when I realized the enormity of what I had done I became very low and have fought battles with depression on and off ever since.

Strangely, it wasn't so much the deception which hurt the most, it was being made to feel worthless, yet again, and unloved.

My self-esteem and confidence received a severe blow.

It was a reminder, harking back to childhood, when I felt continually belittled and criticized about everything I attempted. It was the same feeling of loss of worth. I think now that to make someone else feel those feelings is sinful. I pondered whether in my adult life I have tried too hard to please people, because I had to please my father. I had to be perfect, compliant, to get things right because 'If you do it right the first time you only have to do it once.' To have to do a thing more than once meant you had somehow failed. You didn't measure up!

I tried to find reasons for the collapse of the marriage. What had I done? What hadn't I done? Could I have tried harder? It has taken me a very long time to come up with acceptable enough reasons to explain it to myself, to be able to bear it.

Rather than dwell on a catalogue of Theo's 'misdemeanours', which would serve little purpose, and out of respect for his other, now adult children, I will simply try to condense what I now feel about his behaviour. This is by no means a statement of forgiveness, as to forgive means you have wiped the slate clean and acknowledged that it is of no consequence any more. I don't feel that. The real, lasting consequences of what occurred has dominated and damaged not just my life, but others too. I believe that Theo, for reasons which probably emanate from his childhood, has always felt an insatiable need to be admired.

Not content with finding that admiration in his first, or subsequent marriages, Theo seems to have needed continual confirmation of it. In a way he was like an adrenalin junkie who thrived on the excitement of the next chase. The tragedy was that had he been able to pursue a career as a professional actor he would have drawn admiration from audiences and may have felt more fulfilled. If he could have found it in himself to be focussed and single-minded he could have been brilliant. It is a talent wasted.

When Theo left us my daughter was distraught. The children had no idea that anything was wrong. At first we delayed the full truth and explained that Theo had gone to live with a male friend for a while, to be nearer his work. It was the truth as far as it went. Andy appeared to be totally unaffected. He had been used to people disappearing before. He continued to eat, sleep and behave as though nothing had happened. His 'Waterloo' would happen much later.

My parents, although divorced by now themselves, were both furious. My mother penned Theo a scathing letter which I hesitated to show him and I was thankful that my father was now living on the other side of Sheffield some ten or twelve miles away. It was difficult enough to deal with the situation myself. I certainly didn't relish any interference by my father. My brother and his wife were shocked, and my step-aunt, who we saw little of, seemed unsurprised. There were a few 'I told you so's.' Nevertheless we were all impoverished by the split, and not just financially.

Self-obsessed, Theo had little awareness of the impact he had made on our lives. He assumed that friends, relatives and neighbours would all continue as before and he was surprised and disappointed when people shunned him. I couldn't bear to speak with him but I tried to be civil when I had to converse. The court had granted him unlimited access to the children, which I didn't oppose, but his visits were erratic and unpredictable. In time the children became variously anxious, bored, even reluctant to go out with their father. They never felt that they had him to themselves, there was more often than not another girl friend around. The visits became less and less and eventually stopped, along with any financial support. Suddenly, without warning the money deemed appropriate by the court, but in any case a totally unrealistic amount, stopped being paid into my account. The cruellest thing was that it happened during the school holidays when I had no other income. I applied for income support but was refused on the grounds that I had earned money before the holidays and would do so again afterwards. I was instructed to take court action to recover the due maintenance! But of course all of these things take time.

I was overdrawn at the bank, owing bills, and still had to feed and clothe two children. We spent a lot of time during that holiday period visiting people so they would feed us. I learned how to make jam and marmalade, and how to make one pound of minced beef stretch to make three meals (rissoles, spaghetti Bolognese and shepherd's pie). Kind friends who had been fruit picking, or blackberrying brought us some fruit. Another friend, a keen gardener with an allotment, brought us vegetables, washed and tied in plastic bags ready to put in the freezer compartment of the fridge. A neighbour brought us fresh lettuce from her garden along with some radishes and onions, and we tried to grow our own tomatoes in a few 'gro-bags'. The tomatoes were small and not uniform in size, but they were sweet and delicious. What began as a worrying time became a daily challenge which had its compensations, not least in the friendship and generosity of those friends who stood by us. You can't put a price on loyalty. It is beyond price.

Learning to live more economically was certainly easier during the summer months. Central heating was switched off and hot water used sparingly. I didn't use the washing machine. I washed my clothes by hand on the sink and threw sheets in the bath where we jumped up and down on them, washing our feet at the same time! Cooking of hot food was kept to a minimum and we had lots of picnics with days out at Cusworth Park (Doncaster), Millhouses Park where there was an open-air swimming pool and children's playground, and Weston Park, also in Sheffield.

I breathed a sigh of relief when term began again and there was some money coming in. New school uniforms were expensive but I managed to buy new blazers. For the rest I found a second-hand supplier and took shirts home in a Marks and Spencer carrier bag so the children would be none the wiser. With careful laundering the second-hand shirts came up like new.

To condense the tale, I was unable to do any repairs in the house. The roof needed urgent attention and the exterior painting. I couldn't renew insurances or use the telephone except for emergencies. I couldn't afford to pay for expensive school holidays or costly games equipment. The children had little pocket money. Life sometimes felt very claustrophobic. I had three attempts at court action to try and claim child maintenance. Each time Theo promised to pay a small amount, enough to satisfy the court temporarily. After the third time of being humiliated I gave up the fight, as many women do. Theo reneged on his children, and me, in every way. The final court appearance jolted me into action. I realized that everything was up to me.

I decided to move to a smaller, more manageable house. The big house needed a new roof, the inside bathroom wall was crumbling, the bay window leaked when it rained and then it fell into the music room. The problems escalated and I couldn't solve things any more by slapping a coat of paint around.

As luck would have it, and I reckoned I was due for some luck, the governors of the private school next door to us were keen to expand their library facilities. They were more than willing to buy the house. I didn't hesitate. I was able to buy a modern semi-detached house and pay for it outright. There wasn't a lot of cash to spare but I was determined to give the children a lovely bedroom each and a memorable Christmas, for that is the time we moved.

RENISHAW AVENUE – ROTHERHAM

The house on Renishaw Avenue was built in the late 1930's. It was part of a neat estate built on former farming lands belonging to the Sitwell family a far back as the seventeenth century. It was situated near the East Bawtry Road and Whiston, and close by to Broom Lane, a leafy mostly middle class area with mixed Victorian villas and some pre-war houses, built in the 1920's and 30's. The original owners of our estate house and their neighbours would have been in today's parlance, upwardly mobile, mostly white collar workers whose wives would mostly have stayed home to polish the furniture, cook the meals and look after the one or two children of the family. They would have had the traditional white wedding and the wedding photograph would have graced the sideboard, or piano if they had one, and the home would have had evidence of the wedding gifts in every room. There might have been a cut-glass or crystal fruit bowl or vase, lace bordered settee covers, embroidered pillowcases and tablecloths, maybe a companion set of brushes and dustpan by the fireplace, and a hallstand for umbrellas and with a small mirror to check one's hat on the way out! These houses were built without garages because in the 1930's family car ownership was rare. The gardens would have been uniform with neat lawns which the husband of the house would tend to on Sunday mornings. The wife would most probably have been in charge of the flower borders, always conscious of keeping her garden every bit as impressive as the one next door.

When we moved to the house on Renishaw Avenue in December 1981 snow was beginning to fall. In spite of the sense of relief at the easing of financial matters the moving in day was upsetting. I tried to remain calm and cheerful for the children's sake but I did have feelings of resentment that I was having to do this on my own and that we were very aware of our downgrading. Andy was disappointed that he had the tiniest room. My daughter's room had fitted wardrobes which were a novelty and a blessing. We all had to get used to living in a smaller space.

My friend Kate had helped me to wrap lightbulbs in newspapers at the old house and unwrapped them again in the new house. A couple of my taller students appeared unexpectedly in the evening to help put up curtain tracks and curtains and supervised the children as they made up their new beds and found places for their things. I made my new room and bed very pretty and feminine, a sort of liberation. The house lacked the character of our previous older houses, but there was a lot to be achieved in the skilful use of colour and furnishings. I think I improved in this respect as we went along, though choosing and hanging curtains still proves to be an irksome job.

We had to draw up a few house rules if I was to continue teaching at home. The children had a television and comfortable chairs upstairs and I bought a wonderful wooden summerhouse for the garden where the children could play in fine weather. A student's unemployed father and his friend assembled the little house for us. The children loved it. It was their secret world. Mums were not allowed.

The estate was fairly quiet, clean and pleasant, with level roads and pavements, good for riding bicycles and close to schools and bus routes. I found a super old-fashioned grocer from Whiston who was willing to deliver goods, and a small collective of friends who ferried my daughter to orchestra rehearsals and concerts. Cello lessons, for a while, had to be taken in school until we were able to pay for private lessons.

We were very fortunate to be living in Rotherham at that particular time. Opportunities for young musicians were excellent, due in no small part to the music adviser, David R., and the dedication and hard work of his team of instrumental teachers. My daughter had begun with the string groups on Saturday mornings but was delighted when she graduated to the Young Sinfonia where other instruments were in evidence. After that there was the opportunity to play with the Senior Youth Orchestra, Sinfonietta, string quartets and other small ensembles. Standards were high and during the summer there were intensive courses with guest conductors such as John Pryce Jones, Jonathan del Mar, and the pianist Peter Donohoe. It was inspiring for the young people to work with professionals prepared to give their time and expertise in this way. Music became a huge part of my daughter's life. I was pleased that she had found an outlet for her creativity and her emotions.

Andy didn't want to learn an orchestral instrument but was persuaded to join the prestigious Boys' choir when he moved to the comprehensive school. He sang in Ripon Cathedral, York Minster and at St. George's Chapel, Windsor. He enjoyed the trips away. I am not sure how much he enjoyed the singing. When his voice changed I think he was quite relieved not to have to pursue choral singing any longer. Boys did come in for some ridicule among their non-singing peers. Andy studied music theory and keyboard with Pippa, one of my former students. She was incredibly patient, just right for Andy. He didn't want to be compared with his sister. Pippa and I tried not to do this. We did our best to praise his individual efforts and qualities.

Unfortunately school teachers were less sensitive. Several of them were more than ready to compare Andy with his sister and quick to criticize his sometimes ebullient behaviour and limited concentration. Teachers rarely mentioned that Andy had a very kind nature and all he really wanted was to fit in. He seemed to get on best with the teacher of cookery who was surprised to learn that he had ambitions to be a chef!

Andy had a special friend, David, an only child of divorced parents who had managed to share their responsibilities amicably. David's father and his new partner often included Andy in trips out and holidays camping in this country and abroad in France.

We spent a fairly stable and happy two years in the small house and would have stayed but for two setbacks. The first was my worrying and continuing erratic income, although being in a lower cost house had certainly helped me to recover. The other set-back was the neighbours, welcoming at first, and declaring their love of music. They complained about my daughter practising in the mornings before school, but instead of talking about it they rudely banged on the adjoining wall. Of course they conveniently forgot about all the late nights when they played loud dance music on their hi-fi which we tolerated. The situation did upset and inhibit us. We put the upright piano in the hall and stuffed it with cushions to muffle the sound. When it came to cello practice my daughter played upstairs in her room and we tried to guess when the neighbours were not at home.

Times and attitudes certainly change. In my grandparent's time a piano would have taken pride of place in many front rooms, or parlours. Families would gather round the piano for sing-songs before the days of television and radio, and in middle class homes recital singers would be honoured guests. In the 1960's, living in my mother's small terraced house I used to practice for hours and no one complained, and next door to my mother lived a teenage neighbour who played rock and roll and pop songs of the day. He used to play through his repertoire every night and we knew the order of his songs so we knew when he would finish. Of course those noise levels were nothing compared to the awful loud amplified music of today's hi-fi's.

Work was very unpredictable, both in colleges and privately. Part-time hours varied, there was no security, no holiday pay and no possibility of paying into a private pension. The drawbacks of private teaching can similarly be just as disappointing and erratic. Pupils can begin well but may drop out for a number of reasons. They find the work becomes more difficult and time-consuming. Often they don't realize how hard or consistently they need to work. Parents sometimes don't realize what is involved in learning an instrument or they do the opposite thing and push too hard. There are parents and some students who feel that if they turn up for lessons the teacher can wave a magic wand and somehow miraculously make them into another Ashkenazy overnight and with the minimum of effort on their part. Occasionally one can have a pupil with little sense of commitment, who will cancel lessons suddenly and for very trivial reasons.

On the positive good side to piano teaching when one finds a family with a keen sense of commitment and realistic aims it can be a really fantastic partnership, with fruitful results. It is a great privilege to work with keen students on a one to one basis and especially if that student has the right kind of encouragement and support at home. I have never minded teaching beginners of any age, in fact it is probably better to take pupils from the very beginning than it is to acquire them from another teacher who may have left them with negative attitudes.

With all of these concerns in mind and a genuine interest in making a positive contribution to music teaching I decided to take the plunge and become completely self-employed. I needed a house where I could have a music school, developing my own syllabus and way of working with pupils and groups of all ages. It all had to be planned as carefully as a military operation. Second nature to me then!

I set about formulating and writing a proper syllabus of work for infant children's music classes. This incorporated all the work I had managed with the Sheffield children and the small pre-piano classes I had taught in the Broom Road house. The Introduction was devised so that school teachers, even without a lot of music knowledge or skill could use it with their own classes. I was invited to talk with teacher's groups and delivered a number of In-Service courses and 'Baker' Days in schools across South Yorkshire and Derbyshire. Copies of the workbooks were popular and sold in great numbers, with requests for a second one.

The second phase of my 'operation' involved finding rooms to hire where I could pursue work with other groups. The local Arts Centre had a number of suitable rooms, but only one with a piano if you didn't count the main hall and Steinway piano, which we used for pupil concerts. I advertised classes for Mums with Toddlers, Pre-Piano classes for 5 and 6 year olds, Recorder classes, Music Appreciation Listening Groups for

Mature People, Piano courses for Adults and Piano Accompaniment. I was inundated by prospective pupils for all groups and began a waiting list but also enlisted the help of students who would be trained along the way. Without their help I couldn't have coped with the numbers.

In 1982 a divorced, female parent who was self-employed or part-time employed was not considered to be a good risk by any financial institution. I had to think long and hard before approaching my bank. If I wanted a larger house where I could teach I would need to borrow about £8,000. Nowadays that seemed a paltry sum, but then it was a lot of money. The strategy I employed in visiting my bank manager had to be totally convincing. I worked on a feasibility study, compiled lists of waiting students and present ones. Accounts were properly prepared and presented along with a total work history of the previous twelve months. I bought a smart suit, had my hair done, acquired a new lipstick and briefcase, prayed, and off I went, hoping to impress.

I shook the bank manager's hand and smiled broadly. He let me talk and perused my papers more than once before he said 'I can't lend you £8,000.' My heart sank, but then he added. 'Our mortgages start at £10,000, will that do?' I was flabbergasted. I had asked for too little. I could have £8,000 as a different kind of loan, but at a higher rate of interest. A long term repayment mortgage would be much cheaper. I couldn't quite believe what had happened. We shook hands on the deal and as I moved towards the door the bank manager revealed that he knew all about my work and what he had heard had impressed him. He asked to be kept informed of my future activities and concerts. Gosh!!

GERARD ROAD, MOORGATE, ROTHERHAM

This being our third Rotherham house, and because the other houses are only situated a couple of miles from each other there is little value in repeating the pre-history and earlier history of the town. Each house has a character of its own with immediate surroundings which represent a particular part of Rotherham's history.

In 1905 when our house was just being built Rotherham was still a small town with its old street patterns radiating outwards from the fifteenth century Parish Church. Most industrial premises were in the Masbrough district, close to the river and railways. North of the town centre a pattern of long straight roads were built to house the expanding population after 1850 when privately owned land was released for house building projects. 1850 seems to have been an important year for Rotherham. There had been a devastating rise in cholera deaths during the previous twenty years due to poor sanitation and no running water or effective use of waste disposal. In 1850 the government held an enquiry under the Public Health Act and a local board of health was established. Work began to improve conditions in the town. Sewers and drains were laid and reservoirs enlarged. Piped water became available for the first time. Until then water had to be drawn from wells and either carried by hand or transported by horse and cart. Domestic rubbish was also collected in this way.

By 1902 the town had acquired County Borough status giving the council wider powers, which included education. Children from 11 to 14 years of age could now go to school, girls and boys, but usually in separate establishments. There had been schools for boys and the Grammar school of course, and some girls had been educated in private schools often held in the schoolmistress's own house. By 1911 all children could attend school. The first Director of Education was Spurley Hey, the name we now know as the school on Moorgate.

When our house was built on Gerard Road, Moorgate, the area was considered to be in the leafy stockbroker belt on the edge of the town. Beyond it were expanses of open country and common pasture land. There were a few other large houses and mansions such as Whiston Grange and Moorgate Grange, the old Vicarage and the Grammar School. Houses which infilled the spaces between the grand houses were smaller and of varying individual designs. Much later some small estate type semi-detached and detached houses were built on land behind Moorgate Hall.

Moorgate Hall, built on the site of an earlier house of distinction was home to William West, Chief steward for the Earl of Shrewsbury's South Yorkshire manors and legal adviser to the feoffees in the sixteenth century. The house was bought by Charles Tooker, industrialist, in 1627 and remained a Tooker family home until the nineteenth century. It was a family home until 1986 and then converted for office use. Five houses further down Gerard Road was our last family house.

Moving day was chaotic and tiring, but we were happy. As the day wore on and we became too tired to carry on the priority was to find some supper and the television aerial so that we could watch the American T.V. soap opera 'Dynasty' which gripped the nation!

The rooms in the new house were huge and although there was much work to do I could see that the house had potential. I had a music room again. The extra £2,000 I had borrowed paid for new double glazed windows which were long and elegant looking. The curtains from the smaller house wouldn't fit so I bought new ones. I chose dark brown velvet, and for the side window a gold William Morris design.

The red-brick house, Moorgate, Rotherham, 1999

It was wonderful to have a large second room and a breakfast kitchen. It was the kitchen which eventually needed most work. It was indescribably filthy and with old units, none of which matched either in size or colour. I had to buy a new gas cooker and washing machine, the rest had to wait until funds could be found. The children were delighted that the house was detached. It meant we could practice our music whenever we wished. They were also captivated by the garden.

In fact the badly overgrown garden paralleled my life. Recognizing and dealing with the horticultural problems proved to be very therapeutic. There were things which needed to be chopped down like the two giant sycamore trees which should never have been planted in a domestic garden. They had grown enormously making the whole place dark, and preventing the sun from reaching the lawn. After the two largest trees had been professionally felled and taken away I tackled the rose bushes myself. They had spread from the side border and covered almost half the thirty yard garden. The electric hedge-cutter was a fantastic buy and I was ruthless in charge of it. Roses were cut right back and shrubs like the eight foot fuchsias which had been allowed to grow wild. I needed a step ladder to reach the massive forsythia and flowering currant, laburnum and lilac, all of which had been neglected. Rhododendrons were being suffocated by honeysuckle and ivy growing along the red-brick wall which surrounded the garden. I was determined to rescue the rhododendrons because they reminded me of the lovely house Anton and I had lived in at Nether Edge in Sheffield.

After the big difficult jobs had been completed the children enjoyed helping me to mow the lawn and encourage the grass into a much healthier and green condition. They were looking forward to stringing a tennis net across the middle of it. We were a long time, many months in fact before we saw the benefits of our hard work. It was well worth it. Out of something nightmarish had emerged something good. The following Spring we had a concrete patio laid and planted a rockery. In the summer we bought garden chairs and a parasol table. The patio was a sun-trap until late afternoon. For the first time in years I felt able to invite friends in to share the garden, the sunshine, and home-made lemonade. Even our little King Charles spaniel Reuben (Ben), bought for my daughter's tenth birthday, enjoyed the company.

Ben was the dearest little dog. He followed me everywhere and liked nothing better than to park himself on the sofa next to you or on someone's knee. Sadly we were all devastated when we lost him because of a nasty bowel condition.

Having decided once and for all to leave the college and school work behind I had to be highly organized and motivated to make the private teaching practice work.

The Pre-Piano and Recorder classes continued. Piano pupils had to be accommodated between tea and my time to supervise the children's homework and music work. Daytime students came from the Thomas Rotherham Sixth Form College, just a short walk for them to my house. Mature students came in increasing numbers, some from training colleges and universities. Some mature students were late starters, or people who had learned in their youth and were re-starting. There was a lady in her sixties – Denise – who wanted to play for enjoyment and to keep her arthritic joints moving, my friend Alison, in her fifties who was pursuing her dream now that she was able to, and a GP who said that playing the piano helped to keep him sane! I taught a number of school teachers desperate to increase their skills and their C.V. There were parents keen to keep up with their children and some mature people who had 'graduated' from my listening groups in the Arts Centre. I had some serious Diploma students too, so I had the full range and ability range amongst my students.

It was easier to organize my own piano playing without fear of upsetting neighbours and having more time during the day to utilize. I had to work hard and to a routine wherever possible. I never gave a pupil music which I hadn't worked at myself and I was increasingly in demand as an accompanist. Accompanying other musicians really demands a chapter to itself, but suffice it here to say that for a busy pianist accompanying can be a very mixed blessing. When the other player is well prepared it is a real joy. When the soloist is not really ready, has never heard the piano part and in the case of exams the instrumental teacher might not have worked at Aural requirements it can be a real nuisance and very upsetting if one realizes that the candidate might fail. 'Will you just run through the Aural tests?' is a frequent request from teachers who should know better and candidates who are terrified of doing the tests. Aural work has to be a regular feature of lessons all the time and not just the week or so before exams.

Mercifully players in competitions and the BBC Young Musician of the Year rounds and also in college auditions have usually been very well prepared and a pleasure to work with. I must say that the pleasure has not always extended to the actual audition on the day. I once accompanied a talented young oboe player in a BBC competition where the adjudicators were extremely rude to both of us. We entered the hall, smiled and said 'Good Morning,' to which there was no reply. While the adjudicators were engrossed in their papers we were invited to tune. Then we waited and waited until one of them waved his hand in an irritated fashion, not even looking at us and said, 'Well start then!' We completed the performance. There was no response and no 'thank you'. The adjudicators continued talking to each other and a steward ushered us away.

I continued to organize an annual recital for my piano pupils. This gave them the opportunity to play on a Steinway Grand Piano and to hear other pupils of every level. No one was excluded unless they wanted to be. Sometimes if there was a particularly good year with advanced pianists we would hire two pianos and work on a concerto movement with myself playing the orchestral part. It was great fun and gave pupils a real opportunity to shine without being in competition.

I worked extremely hard. My whole life was teaching method and the children. There was no other life, no real social life outside of the home. There were no men in my life and I preferred it that way. I retreated from any further possible pain in that direction. When you have given your all to someone and then discovered that you were inadequate it doesn't fill you with encouragement to try again. I didn't have any inclination to repeat the experience. I had to learn to live and cope by myself. I've never regretted it for myself, but I am deeply sad that the children have lived without a good father figure in their lives. There have been many occasions, birthdays, Christmas, holidays, and especially school concerts and degree ceremonies when I have howled many private tears before facing the event as a lone parent. Envying happy and supportive families had been a feature of my own childhood. My parents never came to hear me play the piano in public or see me presented with prizes in my last year at school. It hurt terribly.

After three years in our big house and when my business had become well established I was nominated by one of my sixth form students and a parent for a national Music Teacher of the Year award. To my great astonishment I won the award for 'Private Music Teacher' of the year. I was very surprised and never expected such an accolade, but I was grateful that my work had been recognized.

There followed a period of frenzied excitement when local and national newspapers, radio and television producers swooped on me as though I was an important celebrity. Apparently the 'Times' newspaper which featured the event and a photograph was opened in the staff room at the college where I had previously worked. It caused great debate and expressions like, 'You shouldn't have left. The college could have benefited!' The lecturer who had been concerned about my loss of status if I left the post smiled hugely when he saw the news.

The presentation of my award was in London, at the beautiful Wedgwood showrooms in Wigmore Street. We were terrified to move around in case we should bump into the china. I was presented with a piece of engraved Wedgwood glass, and the reception, hosted by Guinness, was a really splendid affair. Wine was served, caviar, quail's eggs, salmon, melon balls and several other tiny finger foods which I can't quite remember now. I remember that we didn't care for the caviar! The biggest thrill was receiving my award from Lady Barbirolli who had no idea that I had formerly worked with her husband, the conductor Sir John Barbirolli. How I would have loved him to know of my success, not through any sense of vanity, but because he had been such an inspiration and so encouraging of my efforts during the early 1960's. Sadly Sir John died in 1970.

Back home once more and the neighbours were surprised to discover television vans, cables and crews on my doorstep. They wanted to film me teaching a lesson. My telephone rang constantly following the television appearances and radio interviews. There were many letters and calls of congratulation, offers of work and the opportunity to contribute to education journals. When all the fuss died down I had plenty of work to focus on. I was grateful for the extra work which the media exposure had generated but I was also thankful that I was able to slip back into anonymity afterwards. I couldn't have coped with that level of attention all the time.

Encouraged by my professional 'elevation', as one friend described it, and supported by my wonderful friends Rosie, John and Sib and John, and with the practical help offered by my mother I began to feel more optimistic about the future. Each new teaching year threw up new challenges. Younger pupils were just as important in my reckoning as older exam orientated students. Finding suitable, and new music for each one, solving their physical and reading difficulties, finding a way to make things interesting and most importantly teaching them to solve their own music problems was absolutely vital. I strongly believe that one of music's most important benefit is in developing children's ability to use their imagination, and to problem solve in a piece of music also helps them to think in a multi-dimensional way about other problems in their life or school work. As well as thinking skills music aids hand and eye co-ordination, memory work, and offers huge opportunities for children to co-operate with others. Before I leave this area of importance I must also elaborate a little further on music's basic role, that of self-expression and creativity. The conductor and pianist Daniel Barenboim frequently tells interviewers and audiences that through music he has learned so much about human nature and through music he knows that people from different cultures can learn to live and work in harmony. In these uncertain times I would venture to suggest that music should be very high on our list of priorities and would urge all parents to pressurise schools and education authorities and the government to make sure that it is.

My own children experienced the usual adolescent difficulties.

Friendships blossomed, others tested, feelings of insecurity from time to time, excessive demands from teachers or their careless, insensitive remarks and occasionally the frustration on all our parts was felt when we realized that money was tight. I am thankful now that all of this was before the age of computers and games consoles in every house. It was hard enough to deny the children the latest clothes or trainers without frantic saving, or a flat refusal. I remember feeling hard done by when schools demanded that they had the latest type of calculators for their maths lessons. I remember how hard I struggled as a child to understand maths and learn times tables.

My daughter survived the vagaries of school life and adolescence with the companionship of one or two close friends at school and a different set of friends in her orchestral life. My son survived by playing the fool because he thought it made him more popular. His school reports focussed on his poor concentration and occasional disruptiveness. We had many discussions about his behaviour and how it might affect his future. Sometimes I thought we were making headway but the effort was often short-lived on his part.

I tried to encourage Andy with his homework. He had all the books he needed, his own desk, equipment and all the art materials he could possibly need. I would read his work and offer suggestions for extending or improving things, but we argued. He resented my 'interference' as he interpreted it. In time he refused to let me see his work.

I remained concerned that he could simply complete homework tasks in just a few minutes. He had some artistic skill. He liked to draw birds, animals and especially cartoon characters. He had an eye for things and could draw much more skilfully than I ever could. Andy liked his art teacher and I had hoped that this small chink of interest might be fostered beyond school, but sadly it wasn't to be. My relationship with Andy deteriorated and he became increasingly un-cooperative, defiant and evasive. I'm afraid that I didn't handle the situation well and my patience was severely tested. Andy was not unintelligent, but he was unmotivated. At the time I didn't analyze things too deeply. I just felt that I was to blame. Now, many years later it seems clearer that Andy had always been resentful about the lack of male role models in his life. He had effectively been brought up, organized and ordered about by women. His birth father hadn't owned him, his foster parents had to relinquish him and then Theo had let him down. We saw little of my brother who was now working hard to establish his business after being made redundant from the steel industry. Sadly, we were all wary of my father who had always found it difficult to relate to children on their level. When he talked he shouted. He would order and he would criticize. He rarely encouraged.

As a small boy Andy would embarrassingly want to sit on the knee of any male visitors, or he would try to dominate the conversation. As a teenager he wanted to be treated as a man but was reluctant to learn how to behave in a grown up fashion. It was sometimes difficult to know how best to help and encourage him. I needed help.

Time passed. We had our first holiday in years but Andy refused to accompany my daughter and I to Edinburgh. He was ecstatic to be allowed instead to join his friend David, and his parents to France and a camping holiday. I thought it would be good for him. He had a wonderful time and so did we.

Our 'girls only' trip to the Edinburgh Festival was amazing. I could only afford a very third-rate hotel, which was disappointing, but we had such an interesting time that we chose to forget about the hotel. If we managed to come again we would be better informed. We went to concerts, plays, some rather risqué dance which shocked me, and some lighter events such as The Fairer Sax, an all girl saxophone ensemble. We were fascinated by the street theatre artists. More than anything we were entranced by the superb architecture, the stunning, elegant Georgian terraces and circuses where wealthy people live, and the leafy squares which reminded me of London. Edinburgh won over our hearts and it would be important to us again.

Andy enjoyed his holiday in France, riding bicycles, playing ball games, swimming, eating seafood. He even seemed to have enjoyed the domestic chores involved in camp life. I know that he enjoyed being part of a family group.

With his sister happier at Sixth Form College than she had ever been at school Andy seemed to have a more settled period. Certainly teachers referred less to his sister and I hoped he was beginning to think of his own future.

Andy was adamant that he didn't want to follow his sister to the Sixth Form College and we all understood that. It wasn't the right place for him in any case. At school we mentioned the possibility of him embarking on a City and Guilds Catering Course at a nearby highly rated further education college. The school was very dismissive and doubtful of his prospects of gaining a place. I was furious. I had tried my level best to interest Andy in thinking for himself about his future. I tried my utmost to encourage any spark of interest or inclinations he might have towards anything that was feasible, only to have our enthusiasm dashed. Undaunted we decided to deal with college applications without the help of the school. After an interview and meeting with the college tutors Andy was offered a place without question and he seemed quite excited to receive his list of equipment and uniform requirements.

After successful 'A' levels and university and college interviews my daughter had the most thrilling time of her life. She had been offered a place at every college, so much time and thought went into her final choice. She eventually discounted the colleges of music and accepted Hull University where she felt best able to develop her composition work. Until then she had been playing on a very poor quality cello. A professional standard would be required to see her through university and might cost thousands of pounds, which we didn't have. She applied to the Prince's Trust to see whether she was eligible for a grant towards a cello and this was very generously given. We had a fantastic day out in

Leeds trying every cello in sight. My daughter thanked the Trust and we thought that would be the end of it. Shortly after the thrilling new acquisition my daughter was approached by Yorkshire Television's producer Nick Lord and director Graham Robinson. They were making a film about the Prince's Trust and some of the recipients of the awards. Once again our house was invaded by a television crew and we nervously performed together for the cameras. I was very impressed not just with the highly efficient and professional way the film makers operated, but also with the great care and consideration they afforded my nervous daughter. They took her out for lunch and filmed her around the town as well as with her college teacher. The manager at WH Smith was thrilled to have a film crew in his store and presented my daughter with some record tokens. She had a wonderful and tiring day.

We all enjoyed the brief excitement and the whole experience gave us a much needed morale boost. Feeling quite mellow and encouraged by it all imagine the surprise to discover there was more to come!

Shortly after the film experience the regional director of the Prince's Trust announced that Prince Charles was planning to visit Sheffield and wanted to meet recipients of Trust Awards. We were invited. The Prince met dozens of young people and he had certainly done his homework. He knew in great detail about everyone, and spoke with knowledge to each of them. When he was introduced to my daughter he remarked that he had enjoyed the television film, and asked if she was enjoying the new cello. Astonishingly my usually shy, retiring girl replied that it was a lovely instrument and she was now saving for a decent bow! Surprised that she hadn't been given an adequate sum for both cello and bow the Prince immediately rectified matters and a further cheque was sent from the Trust within days.

The excitement subsided and eventually I needed to focus my attention on Andy. I needed to find a way of helping him. The list of requirements was huge. Chef's whites, shoes and kitchen knives in a professional case all cost several hundred pounds, not to mention textbooks. Spare cash was something I rarely had. I earned enough to live on and just about maintain the house. Juggling this bill with that and with severe economies through the summer months we lived comfortably but without luxuries.

The real down side of being a private teacher is that the income is very erratic. For approximately twelve weeks of the year pupils disappear on holiday. Sometimes they miss lessons through illness, school commitments or domestic crises. It's really a question of balancing one's income so that something is in the kitty for those lean weeks or months.

Trying to support two children, without financial help from other sources can get pretty desperate at times.

I spent many hours in the library sifting through directories of grant-making trusts. Many of them only award groups or organisations and many do not give grants to students who have a place in further education. I guess they think that the local authority will support them, but this is rarely the case for under eighteens who study in a different area when the same course is available on their doorstep.

When I had resigned myself to having to foot the entire bill I was casually turning the pages of the newspaper one day when I noticed an ad in the classified pages. The Savoy Trust were offering assistance to young people embarking on a catering career at colleges anywhere in the country.

I could hardy believe what I was reading. My son penned an articulate, pleasing letter to the Trust, filled in the relevant forms and found people willing to give him a character reference. We crossed our fingers and waited. Andy's face lit up when he received the reply letter together with a cheque. The money granted covered most of the uniform costs. He looked very impressive in his whites and also a little embarrassed as I admired him. I never saw him in the uniform after that.

Buying University books for my daughter almost crippled me financially but we made it eventually. The hardest thing of all was waving her off for the first time. Of course one is incredibly proud and delighted to help set one's child on their chosen path. It is what we all worked for, but the inexplicable feeling of loss when they finally leave home is dreadful. Suddenly the house seemed so big and empty, and the days cold and endless. Motherly concern would sometimes turn to sheer panic when we hadn't spoken for several days. There was a great deal of adjusting to do for all three of us. I'm certain that it is much easier when there are two parents to share the load.

It was clear that with one child at university and the other due to embark on his college carer I not only needed to earn more money in order to support them both, but I also had to expand my own life and career. Private teaching at home was great fun and satisfying work but it can also be very lonely. One can go for weeks without having an adult conversation. At the end of each day I would feel so tired and lethargic that I had little desire to do anything other than have supper, read a book, listen to music or watch television.

At times the house, in spite of its size, would feel claustrophobic. I had to make a real effort at the weekends to get out, to do anything that would convince me that I wasn't vegetating. Without a car everything took twice as long. Rotherham had little of cultural interest for me. Even the cinema had disappeared. I would sometimes travel to Sheffield to a concert, film or gallery. That proved to be very tiring and time-consuming, but the real downer was the unpleasant return journey at night. Trains, buses and the city centre could feel very threatening at both ends of the journey. Negotiating traffic and the full gamut of drunken yobs, drug addicts and pushers, pervy men and road racers and the possibility of being attacked or robbed could happen anywhere. When it is happening in your own street it doesn't inspire one with the confidence to go out at all. I became so nervous, and with real cause, that I wouldn't even walk the few yards to the letter box after dark.

A police helicopter circling my rooftop in the early hours of morning, then large scale police raids on nearby houses convinced me that I would have to find a way of moving, yet again.

The move away from an intolerable situation was of necessity a long term plan. It was still the children's home and until I was sure they felt happy and secure I had to remain. My mother began to have serious health problems and I was struggling to maintain my own health.

I decided to train as a music examiner. It would enable me to maintain and sharpen up my own skills. I would be able to travel, meet people, stay in comfortable hotels and do a worthwhile job. I could still retain my private teaching. It would just mean that for a short period towards the end of each school term I would have to re-arrange things so that I could escape!

I survived the training for my work as an examiner though once again feelings of inadequacy surfaced when I realized that most of my fellow trainees had been to Oxford or Cambridge, public schools, or were cathedral organists with upper class, polished accents. However I was reassured by the chief examiner, who was genuine and adamant in her desire to appoint examiners who were adaptable and able to converse easily with candidates. As I hadn't failed the training I must have achieved the required standard. The examiner trainers were very helpful and affable people and accompanied me on the first few assignments. My first solo engagement was rather nerve-racking. It is a very responsible job and examiners have to quickly learn the marking criteria and adhere to all the guidelines. It all works very well until examiners meet the unexpected. The need to be patient, pleasant and unflappable arises when candidate have some kind of crisis. Of course illness occasionally occurs, traffic is delayed, candidates might arrive without their music, the wrong music, or even without their accompanist. They may arrive late, in a nervous state or they might be very slow in performance, thus holding up the timetable and adding to the anxiety of other candidates waiting outside. Sometimes, rarely thank goodness, one might encounter an inexperienced steward or an unhelpful one, over fussy mothers, flustered teachers or petrified accompanists! I once had an adult candidate arrive several hours late and in an inebriated state. Nervous candidates and awkward teachers or parents can make the examiner's day very stressful. It became very clear to me why adaptability and the need to remain unflappable were vital requirements of the job.

My work with professional orchestras and musicians in Sheffield had prepared me for almost anything. Flashes of artistic temperament can occur at any age and can sometimes make or break a performance. Young players particularly need to be sensitively dealt with. The odd brusque or unfeeling look or phrase can soon adversely affect candidates who might interpret a look or a word quite innocently meant as something quite different. Many candidates enter the exam room in an already heightened sense of anxiety or simply excitement so anything the examiner can do to ensure that the exam proceeds happily and comfortably is absolutely necessary. Of course examiners try their very best to do this whilst also being aware that the best way for an examiner to achieve maximum efficiency is to know the material, the marking scheme and guidelines thoroughly. Having the mark papers in order, ready headed with details in advance is helpful as is a tidy, ordered desk on the day. Test books need to be kept in the same place after each use, and completed report sheets filed in a consistent order for checking later. I always had spare pens, pencils and a message pad in case emergency messages are needed for the steward, and if it is an unknown centre I discovered the wisdom of taking a packed lunch, and some loo paper!

I could write a lengthy book about my experiences in hotels and the strange venues where I had to work, but perhaps just a few short anecdotes will suffice to give the reader an idea of the conditions under which examiners have to work.

One wet November I had a special visit to a private teacher's studio in her London home. At lunchtime I was swiftly shown the door. 'Examiners usually go to the pub,' I was told. Not being in the habit of frequenting pubs on my own, and especially in a strange place I trudged around until I found a shop selling sandwiches and promptly returned to the house. By contrast the welcome I received at a house in Leeds couldn't have been more different. The teacher there had gone to great trouble to make things comfortable for teachers, accompanists and examiners. At lunchtime soup and sandwiches were provided along with a most congenial, friendly atmosphere.

Examiners soon learn that even in cities it can be difficult to find and eat lunch in the hour and a quarter allowed. It is important however to eat something in the middle of the day as it is hard enough to remain fresh-thinking at 5.00 p.m. as one was at 9.00 a.m. The best places to stay when working on assignments are definitely not city centre hotels which can be very noisy and cheerless places. Smaller privately-run and preferably recommended, (such as those in Guestaccom) are much better in every way. I've been very fortunate in some places, such as a charming country cottage in Cheshire where I was the sole guest and the proprietor grew her own raspberries and made the most wonderful desserts. There was a lovely guest house called 'Crimond' in Southport and two very welcoming guest houses in Edinburgh. By far the most memorable and fantastic places which I shall visit again at my leisure are run by Quakers. In central London the Penn Club is a quiet, safe haven and at Old Jordans, only twenty five minutes by train from Marylebone into the Buckinghamshire countryside there is a most comfortable, magical place with truly lovely, generous people to look after you.

By contrast I've also suffered in some really awful hotels where the standards of cleanliness and the food and service left a lot to be desired. Barnet was not my favourite place, nor was Jesmond in Newcastle though I had a very heart-warming reception at the school I went to during a particularly cold winter.

I had been warned that the area and school I was to examine in was rather tough. Like the hotel then, I thought! I felt more than a little apprehensive as well as cold, wet and hungry as I approached the school's reception desk. I was escorted by a large, lumbering boy who was wearing a hooded parka and plimsolls with holes in them. He opened doors for me and ushered me to the music room in a very polite manner. At break-time I saw the same boy again and two girls who vied with each other to present me with the school lunchtime menu. They took my order and promised to re-appear with the meal later. I found it challenging to understand the Geordie accents, some stronger than others. I had to ask one girl three times what the title of her first piece was. 'Muny Varrey' is the closest to phonetically writing down what she said. Eventually I had to scramble through the syllabus list to make sure what it really was. It proved to be a piece by Monteverdi! These children were mostly from relatively poor and unsophisticated backgrounds but their enthusiasm and attitude was really marvellous. The school was very well structured with clear aims and behaviour policies not just published on every corridor, but followed through. I had a surprisingly pleasant day.

At the other end of the social scale I have nightmare memories of one very exclusive private boys' school. Music rooms were named after English composers. I was allocated to 'Bliss'. I devilishly asked the Music

Master whether that was a promise to be revealed in the music exams. His face didn't alter. He didn't appreciate my sense of humour.

In Liverpool one exasperated teacher was in the waiting room with her pupils trying to teach them the correct way to announce their pieces, 'William Bird!' she said, 'you know, like the birds in the garden.' 'William Baird miss,' they chanted. 'No! William Burrrd!' the teacher persisted. This went on for several minutes until the first child came into the exam room.

I asked him, 'Are you playing the William Byrd piece?' The boy was greatly relieved and grinned. 'Yes miss!' he said.

In Suffolk I met a wonderful black American student who addressed me as 'ma-am' and in Newcastle a mature student who almost moved me to tears with his lovely rendition of 'The Waters of the Tyne'. There were many memorable performances and now years later I feel a nice glow of satisfaction when I spot some of the performers on various concert platforms giving audiences a great deal of pleasure too.

I would have continued my examining work for a few more years but it was sadly cut short after a frightening accident which resulted in my slightly damaging my spine and then the impossible task of sitting at a desk all day. I tried to continue but the pain in my lower back was excruciating, sometimes almost crippling and I would crawl back to my hotel room and just lie down.

The accident happened when I was travelling in the back of a taxi towards the hospital where my mother was a stroke patient.

The taxi slowed behind a car which was about to turn right, but the car behind the taxi did not slow down and crashed into us. So instead of visiting my mother that day I ended up in Casualty Department being X-rayed and examined.

I sustained whiplash injuries to my neck and a slight misalignment to my spine. The bruising soon disappeared but I had a terrifying blackout the morning after the accident probably caused by my getting out of bed too quickly and forgetting that my neck and back would still hurt. I spent many months undergoing painful physiotherapy, then visiting a private chiropractor. Eventually I achieved a sort of relief and some increase in mobility, but I have never felt completely recovered. Sitting on a chair for any length of time is difficult and back pain is only dealt with by large doses of pain killing tablets. I am now very nervous when I ride in a taxi!

To try and condense the 1990's. It was a horrendous decade in many ways. My daughter left home for Hull University and eventually to Edinburgh to complete a Master's degree in Composition. My son left to work in North Yorkshire and then to God knows where. He has chosen his own path and up to now he doesn't wish to share that with us. I hope that he is happy and well. For several years I continued to buy his birthday presents and cards and I saved them all hoping that one day he would come and visit. He had never given us a forwarding address though the Missing Persons Helpline has sent my letter to him. He knows where we are. I live in hope that one day he will let us back into his life and get in touch. It is a great sadness.

During the 1990's I had more than the occasional visit to the hospital. First there was a hysterectomy to sort out once and for all my crippling stomach pain and constant bleeding, then chest pains and high blood pressure seemed like a warning that I might emulate my mother and three grandparents all of whom suffered strokes and heart attacks. The road accident laid me low for a while but I had to get myself better. It was stiff upper lip time. Work through the pain, I convinced myself. Mind over matter. My mother needed me.

I didn't tell my mother about the accident and she didn't notice my neck collar. Old age and advancing senility can be so cruel, but in my mother's case her growing detachment from reality was a kind of cushioning. She didn't worry about the things that used to bother her. The awful fact was that we had hardly recognized that she was deteriorating mentally. She had lived alone in a council flat and had managed her own shopping, cooking and housework and until quite late on in her illness she was still visiting the public library and the hairdressers. She began to have a series of falls. At first she gave quite logical reasons for her accidents. She had stepped 'heavily' off a bus breaking her ankle. She 'lost her balance' one windy day and broke her arm, then the leg and eventually a hip which then needed emergency surgery. My mother was sent home to recuperate. My mother's step-sister helped with shopping and salon visits. Home helps were recruited and emergency alarms were installed. I had to visit more often, taking bus journeys of an hour there and an hour back again. Fortunately my mother had a very kind neighbour and my brother would visit when he was able to do so. My mother's mental decline was very slow, almost imperceptible to begin with. She had the odd forgetful moments but things usually returned to normal. Then she would forget birthdays, something she always looked forward to and kept a keen eye on her birthday book and diary. She wrote in a blank paged five year diary every day, little things, about the weather, who had called and whether she had been out. One day she admitted to having had a couple of 'dizzy spells'. She wrote it in the diary. We now know that these were what is termed 'transient ischaemic attacks'. The doctor said she had a blockage in the carotid artery. Then there was a mild stroke when my mother temporarily lost the use of her left arm and her speech. Her body resembled that of a rag doll. She was hospitalised for observations and investigations of a kidney problem. They kept her for seven weeks.

While my mother was in hospital I decided to give the flat a good clean. I discovered that she had attempted to boil water in a plastic electric kettle by placing it on a lit gas ring. It had melted all over the cooker. There were quite a number of other things which indicated that things were far from all right. I learned that she had allowed con men posing as water workers into her flat and they had robbed her of money, and possibly other things. She had become very confused about money and left incomprehensible messages out for the milkman.

Fortunately the milkman was honest and reliable. I was alarmed when I discovered the extent of her dementia and couldn't believe that we had missed many of the signs. It was clear that she couldn't be allowed home to live by herself again. She simply would not have been able to cope. She would need twenty-four hour care and supervision which I was unable to provide. After seven weeks in hospital, and by then almost completely disorientated my mother was placed in a very nice, comfortable care home. The day she moved in was St. Valentine's Day. She clutched the red rose that I bought for her and I cried and cried after I had to leave her. Sometimes she seemed content and at other times she became distressed when she remembered that she had once had her own home. She said that she missed doing things. Then she would lapse back into her detached state and all my suggestions that she might read, sew, knit or do her crossword puzzles or write in her diary, were in vain. It was too much for her. When I opened her diary she had written an entry on the previous Christmas Eve, then had numbered the days ahead ready for writing up, 25th December, 26th, 27th, 28th, 29th, 30th, 31th, 32th, 33th, 34th, 35th, and she had stopped at 36. I broke down when I read it. I felt so sad for her. There were several more strokes, stays in hospital and heart attacks until she was returned to the care home sixteen days before she died, on June 19th 1998 at 2.40pm. The only blessing was that she passed away in her pretty room with soft gentle classical music playing on the radio and surrounded by people who loved her. Even the domestic assistant and senior nurses came to kiss her goodbye.

I am glad that she didn't die in that awful, dirty, impersonal hospital environment where many of the staff seemed uncaring and abrupt. Elderly people suffered many indignities. I was present when my mother, a sweet, gentle and undemanding lady was shouted at, as was an old lady asking for a bedpan urgently. It never came. Some patients remained unfed because trays were placed out of their reach or they couldn't feed themselves. Requests for clean sheets or pillowcases were not always dealt with and personal belongings often disappeared when beds were moved or patients transferred to other wards. It was disgusting and not always because staff were over-worked. In my anger after my mother's death I did pen a letter both to Age Concern and to the hospital management. I suspect that mine was not the only such letter.

The loss of my mother was really the last straw. I decided to remain in Rotherham only to see through my sixth form students who were preparing for college. Then, instead of taking the train to Edinburgh several times a year to visit my daughter I would move there myself.

It was my time.

RETURNING TO ROTHERHAM

The penultimate chapter differs from the other descriptions of return visits to former homes. Most of the British houses were childhood homes but Rotherham is more recent. Ironically it is the place I've liked the least whilst living there but of necessity have lived for the longest period of time. This chapter is different also because I have only made one return visit to the other places but find myself still having to make fairly regular visits to Rotherham.

School holidays used to be the times when I looked forward to escaping Rotherham and having a wonderful time visiting my daughter in Edinburgh. Now I have to plan to visit Rotherham at some time during school holidays and whilst it is lovely to meet up with old friends I have to admit that once the train reaches South Yorkshire I am filled with a sense of gloom and despondency. These feelings do not disappear as the train pulls into Rotherham station. I always wonder if I'll be lucky and find one of the clean taxis waiting outside the station. On occasions I have preferred to walk the approximate mile to my father's sheltered housing complex. Now in his nineties and with all his mental faculties intact my father lives next door to his ninety-five year old lady friend. They look after each other and still try to walk the same distance into town as I have to walk from the station. They grumble about the filthy streets on their route into town but are grateful that they can still walk about. The slightly uphill walk back is too much for them so they pay for a taxi.

Although there are still some pleasant areas towards the edge of town such as Broom, Moorgate and further out towards Wickersley and in other directions there is Wentworth and parts of Thrybergh near to the country park, but the centre of town remains dirty and depressing. It's true that the smell of the pits and the steelworks have gone, but at least when the majority of people were in gainful employment there was some sense of purpose and vibrancy. There used to be interesting places to go and things to do. The trains, buses, streets and shops used to be cleaner. Now everywhere seems scruffy, smelly, litter-strewn and often graffiti-covered. The town centre is a miserable experience in spite of the newly re-furbished square and fountain. The quality shops such as Muntus and John Speed department stores and Horace Brook's high class greengrocer and delicatessen have disappeared. They have been replaced with shops selling cheap clothes and trashy goods, numerous charity shops and what seems like a pub or nightclub on every street corner. Takeaway food shops abound along with their grease-covered pavements. The chances of finding a decent restaurant serving anything but fish and chips and pizza is remote.

Marks and Spencer have withdrawn from the town centre and re-located to Parkgate Retail World shopping centre. This is fine for people with cars and plenty of time but no use at all for elderly folk such as my father who are too frail to negotiate bus station, hazardous road crossings and car parks just to buy their few little treats.

Clifton Park still exists near to the town centre and the Council Parks Department try their best to keep it blooming but the once safe and relaxed place loved by generations of families and elderly people at the weekends, and especially Sunday picnics by the bandstand, is now not a safe and pleasant place to be. People are wary and afraid of being attacked or robbed by disaffected or drug-crazed youths who might be any age from ten and upwards.

Culturally speaking the one saving grace in the town centre is Philip Howard Books situated near to the Parish Church and Merrill's coffee shop. These three places constitute the last bastions of quality, charm and grace, but this little quarter of old Rotherham could with a bit of foresight be transformed into an attractive area for all kinds of artistic endeavours. I truly hope that one day someone with a bit of vision will encourage a few enterprising business people to bring some culture and quality back into the lives of Rotherham people. One could of course blame the town's demise on the construction of the giant Meadowhall Shopping Centre. However if Rotherham had the Supertram, which currently only runs from Sheffield to Meadowhall, I believe that people might have ventured on to quieter Rotherham if there was anything worth coming for. At present there is little to entice people to the town.

Councillors could take inspiration from places such as Birkenhead, Leeds and Altrincham, to give just a few examples of re-generated and successful small towns who have created their own interesting identities. Rotherham seems to have lost its identity altogether. Ironic when one considers that Rotherham was once considered more important than Sheffield!

Visiting my three Rotherham houses brought mixed feelings, but no regrets about moving away. The first house now belongs to the local Preparatory School and supports a new, purple door. I mused whether the majority of the school's pupils actually lived in Rotherham and where their parents might work. The Renishaw Estate house seemed larger than I remembered but I noticed that the car port has been replaced with a proper garage. There was a kitsch ornamental wishing well in the front garden. I couldn't see through to the back of the house. I wondered whether the present owners had kept my children's little summer house. I hope they have.

My big, detached Edwardian house which sold for a paltry £65,000 in 1999 remains the same. I didn't linger, and I asked a friend to take the photograph. I didn't want to encounter anyone there. My hands were slightly trembling and I wouldn't have held the camera steady. I felt no desire to return there again but I was sad when I reflected on all the wonderful music which had been played in that house and all the marvellous students I had taught there. Before I became too emotional I also reminded myself how intolerable daily life had become when I was living there. The traffic, noise levels, congestion, intimidation, a house burglar whom I encountered on the stairs, unwelcome callers and police activity in the area all combined to reduce me to a state of depression and helplessness. I can't believe that I had allowed myself to reach such a state. My visit over I was more than happy to get back into my friend's car and drive away.

On a more optimistic note South Yorkshire Police reports show that house burglaries have plummeted by half during the past year, credit to a special unit set up in 2003. The unit is led by a Detective Inspector and Detective Sergeant together with seven other officers. They have detected 1,000 crimes recovering drugs and property worth almost a quarter of a million pounds. Police detection and arrests have been helped greatly by the fast-tracking of suspect DNA and the use of micro-dot technology, making property so that it can be easily identified. Three hundred homes on one crime-ridden estate were offered the microdot service and forty old people's bungalows have been fitted with burglar alarms.

Police have vowed to continue the fight against yobs, vandals and troublemakers after scores of complaints of damage, intimidation and violence. Anti-social behaviour seems to have been partially reduced through good police work, youth services aiming to give young people other things to do, and by the police securing nine ASBO's (Anti-Social Behaviour Orders) through the courts together with more than three hundred Acceptable Behaviour Contracts.

The Rotherham Crime Reduction Programme is one of the members of the Safer Rotherham Partnership which has an eleven point strategy to reduce crime and disorder. One of those eleven priorities is to reduce the volume of drug related crime. One of the Partnership targets is to establish a mechanism to strengthen the involvement of communities in resisting the impact of drug related crime.

There does appear to be a more concerted effort in Rotherham by many different agencies to make Rotherham a safer place though I was shocked to learn that residents in a private housing estate are actually paying a security firm to patrol their area at night. This in addition to their council taxes and contribution to police finances.

One can only hope and pray that these initiatives will continue to provide the Rotherham community with a greater sense of security. One hopes too that communities will grow in confidence and awareness and develop the skills to improve their own environment. Residents have to become more involved. The Safer Rotherham Partnership has to be just that, a partnership.

In the long term it must follow that when young people have a sense of purpose, some aspirations, and hope for their futures they will care more about the environment they themselves are creating.

EDINBURGH – CORSTORPHINE 1999

In Muriel Spark's wonderful story of a fictional, eccentric, and egocentric Edinburgh teacher 'The Prime of Miss Jean Brodie' Jean exhorts her girls – 'the crème de la crème' – to strike out as individuals, to have aspirations, and to do something useful with their lives. Otherwise, she feared they might end up living somewhere like Corstorphine!

When I first chuckled at this I hadn't even been to Edinburgh but I did remember it and when it seemed that Corstorphine would be my new home after leaving South Yorkshire I was intrigued to learn about this tiny corner of Edinburgh suburbia.

To most visitors Edinburgh consists of a castle and Palace, the Royal Mile, and the biggest Arts Festival in the World. However, there is much more to discover about Edinburgh's rich patchwork of rural life, history and traditions.

Until the mid eighteenth century there were as many as forty six villages spread over the area we now know as Edinburgh. Over the next two hundred years boundaries became less defined and merged. Some villages have simply become part of the extended capital as house building increased and the city became more commercial. Some areas, namely, Dean Village, Cramond, Colinton, Swanston, Morningside, Duddingston, Leith, Newhaven and Corstorphine still retain their independent histories, traditions and character.

Corstorphine is situated three miles to the north west of the city which can be reached within fifteen minutes by car or the Airport bus which runs throughout the day at ten minute intervals. Corstorphine is surrounded and interspersed by parks and open spaces including Corstorphine Hill, the site of Edinburgh Zoo. Corstorphine is a mainly residential area, and still retains its old village streets, green and ancient kirk. There are a number of interesting historic features including some eighteenth century cottages.

For many centuries farming sustained the population, mostly by the production of wheat and potatoes and later market gardening. The presence of a spring reputed to have had medicinal properties, until it became polluted as a result of the reclamation of the loch which once existed there meant that Corstorphine had its time as a fashionable spa. There were many concerts, balls and parties for the wealthy Edinburgh people.

In 1910 the son of William Morris set up an important industry in Corstorphine. This was the Edinburgh Tapestry Company, engaged in making the 'Dovecote' tapestries which were exported all over the world.

Corstorphine Castle, once the home of Adam Forrester, to whom the estate belonged no longer exists though the stone circular dovecot with over 1,000 nests is still maintained. This used to provide fresh food for the laird and fertilizer for his crops.

The seventeenth century Dower House in St. Margaret's Park displays characteristically Scottish crow-stepped gables. The building is now the home of the Corstorphine Trust who have preserved it and its archives. It is also a focal point for many activities within the community. It is a very much valued and used building, not just a museum. It is used for meetings of the conservation society and also hosts regular concerts and meetings of other societies. Coffee mornings twice a week seem like a time-warp in the old kitchen. The tiny room is always packed by the community-conscious inhabitants and their guests.

Ornamental gate pillars at the High Street entrance to St. Margaret's Park were thought to have been the entrance to the Castle. The village remained close to the protection of the impregnable castle during generations of the Forrester family.

The Kirk, another reminder of the Forrester reign, contains interesting early tombs of the family. There are a number of carved effigies and heraldic panels in the church which has been on the site in some form since the early fifteenth century. A lamp, high on the building, was once placed there to guide travellers along the marsh or loch at night. More recently, thanks to the Rotary Club, the old lamp has been replaced with a symbolic electric light. In 1905 the church was modernised to harmonize with earlier structures and is regarded as Corstorphine's heirloom, and a great source of pride to the community. The church and its village green and the community hall and youth centre are used frequently and provide a focal point for many village activities and celebrations. At Christmas a huge tree is erected on the green and lit for the community carol singing. The Youth Centre is a base for Drama productions and other activities including the annual Corstorphine Fair. The Fair involves hundreds of community groups and individuals who raise thousands of pounds for charities.

From the mid nineteenth century Corstorphine 'high' village, as it became known, grew up along St. John's Road and stretched outwards towards the Glasgow Road. Today it is the centre of the immediate district with numerous shops, offices, pubs, restaurants and guest houses. The most prominent landmark is the Gothic spire of St. Ninian's Church. Adjacent to it is the Roman Catholic Church of St. John the Baptist it's clean, modern lines providing an interesting contrast with St. Ninians.

Corstorphine has a rich heritage of churches and within a few minutes walk of my new home I counted at least ten churches of differing denominations.

Moving from South Yorkshire, where I had lived for over thirty years, was a huge undertaking requiring a huge leap of faith on my part. On a practical level I was moving from a large Edwardian villa to a tiny modern flat, so all of my large or unnecessary furniture had to be disposed of. Some was sold and much of it given away to charities. Books were ruthlessly sorted and excesses given to Oxfam. The physical part of dismantling the trappings of one's life wasn't as difficult as I had anticipated. After all I had done it many times before. Possessions, things didn't matter as much as people. The enormity of what I had set in motion didn't really hit me until the last day or two when there was a constant stream of friends and former pupils bringing me 'Good Luck' cards and gifts all given with love and a good deal of personal thought and care. It would have been quite easy to crumble emotionally and call the whole thing off, but I didn't.

I had spent a lot of time considering the pros and cons of moving so far at my time of life. I desperately wanted to improve the quality of my life. I wanted to be nearer to my daughter. Above all, I needed to feel secure. A deep sense of insecurity and subsequent lack of confidence had dogged my entire life. My students will find that very difficult to believe unless they read this whole story.

Moving to Edinburgh, no one's choice but my own, has been the best decision I ever made. That isn't to say that it was easy or that I have found Shangri-la! Far from it. But I now have more peace of mind. The few students I now teach, in order to eke out my pension, are a true delight. I have the time and the opportunities to go to concerts, talks and recitals every day of the week if I want to. I meet my daughter and friends in galleries and have embraced the café culture of ladies who lunch! I meet other teachers in professional groups and the Jewish Literary Society stretches my grey cells!

Writing this book and visiting former homes in pursuit of a greater understanding of my life has taken a great deal of time, but has been well worth the effort. In terms of emotional attachments I did not feel drawn to any of the places I re-visited. Although Portland was the most beautiful place I was very young when we lived there, and we were there for a very short time. I didn't regard this as home. None of the other places felt like home either. They were just places where we had stayed for a while. Some places clearly still held nasty memories of abuse, bullying or fear and the visits became an opportunity to face things head on. The word exorcism sprang to mind though things were not so dramatic as that would suggest. There were places which held happier memories of kind friends who, like me, had moved on. I only managed to find one friend from our army childhood and one from my last London school. My more recent Yorkshire friends now enjoy visiting me in Edinburgh so I haven't cut all the ties.

The initial quest to find a place which might feel like home seemed impossible, complicated, even futile. But after all the explorations it is quite simple really. Home has nothing to do with bricks and mortar, streets, schools or cities. Home is where you feel valued. Home is where you are loved.

March 7th 2005
Edinburgh

BIBLIOGRAPHY

BIRKENHEAD, MERSEYSIDE

Allison, J.E. 'Sidelights on Tranmere' Birkenhead Historical Society 1976

Boumphrey, I and M. 'Yesterday's Wirral' No. 7, Boumphrey 1997

Cammell Laird, 'Builders of Great Ships' C. Laird 1959

Dore, R.N. 'Cheshire' Batsford Books 1977

Hyde, Frances E. 'Liverpool and the Mersey Development of a Port 1700-1970' David and Charles 1971

McCarron, Ken 'The Fall and Rise of Birkenhead Docks' (Ed. Paul Rees) Merseyside Maritime Museum and Liverpool University 1977

Roberts, David 'HMS Thetis – Secrets and Scandal' Avid Publications 1999

Roberts, David 'Life at Lairds – memories of working shipyard men' Avid Publications 1993

Tomlinson, N.H.C. 'Walking Through the Blitz – in the Birkenhead area' I and M Boumphrey 1996

Warren, C. and Benson, J. 'Thetis – The Admiralty Regrets . . .' 'The Disaster in Liverpool Bay' Avid Publications 1997

Other publications

'Bombers Over Merseyside' – Authorized reprint from Liverpool Daily Post and Echo 1945, reprinted by Scouse Press Liverpool 1983

PORTLAND

Bettey, J.H. 'The Island and The Royal Manor of Portland' 1750/1851 1970 Bristol University

Houghton, Harry 'Operation Portland: the autobiography of a spy' Hart-Davis, 1972

Lonsdale, Gordon. 'Spy: Twenty Years of Secret Service' Neville Spearman 1965

Morris, Stuart 'Portland' The Dovecote Press 1998

Warren, J.W. 'The Island and The Royal Manor of Portland' by Order of the Court Leet and Court of the Manor 1939

White, Carol 'Discovering Portland' Panbourne Press 1989

Other publications

Various leaflets, maps and tourist guides from Weymouth and Portland Borough Council, 2002

ALDERSHOT – HAMPSHIRE

Lunn, Arthur E. 'Cove – a village at war' Footmark Publications 1998

Lunn, Arthur E. 'Our Hampshire Cove' St. Michael's Abbey Press 2000

Lunn, Arthur E. 'Sarsen – The Old Grey Stones of Hampshire' A. Lunn 2001

O'Dell, Noreen 'Portrait of Hampshire' Robert Hale 1979

Temple Patterson, A. 'Hampshire and the Isle of Wight' Batsford 1976

GILLINGHAM – KENT

Baldwin, Ronald A. 'The Gillingham Chronicles' Baggins Books

Harrison, Shirley and Sally Evemy, 'Rochester Upon Medway – The Tale of a City' The Word Team

Macdougall, Philip, 'A Chatham and Gillingham in old photographs' Alan Sutton

Macdougall, Philip, 'Royal Dockyards' David and Charles 1982

Penn, Roger 'Portrait of the River Medway' Robert Hale 1981

Presnail, J. 'Industrial Medway' North Kent Books 1977

Presnail, J. 'The Story of Chatham' Rochester and Chatham City Council 1952

Tomlinson, Norman. 'The Book of Gillingham' Barracuda Books

Other publications

Booklets, maps, leaflets, guide books from Royal Engineers Museum at Chatham, naval and Dickens collections, Medway Archives and local studies Centre.

GRAYS TILBURY – ESSEX

Powell, W.R. (Editor) 'A History of the County of Essex' Institute of Historical Research O.U.P. 1983

Raby, Peter 'Alfred Russell Wallace – A Life' Chatto and Windus 2001

Williams-Ellis, Amabel, 'A Biography of Alfred Russell Wallace' Blackie 1966

Other publications
Various papers from the Journal of the Thurrock Local History Society
Correspondence with Mr. John Ormston

TOTTENHAM – NORTH LONDON

Burnby, J.G.L. and A.E. Robinson 'Now Turned Into Fair Garden Plots'
Edmonton Hundred Historical Society Occasional Paper No. 45 1983

Collicott, Sylvia L. 'Connections – Haringey Local/National/World Links'
Haringey Community Information Service and Multi Cultural Curriculum
Support Group

Pegram, Jean 'Bruce Castle, Tottenham' Haringey Council

OTHER PUBLICATIONS

Local Herstory, Lives of Women in Haringey. Haringey Community
Information Service 1987

Articles from 'Haringey People' monthly council bulletin. Dec. 2003

Edmonton Hundred Historical Society Occasional paper No. 20 'John
Eardley Wilmot – a man of his time' 1965

PLUMSTEAD AND WOOLWICH SOUTH EAST LONDON
(BOROUGH OF GREENWICH)

Ackroyd, Peter 'London the Biography' Chatto and Windus 2000

Dalzell, W.R. 'The Shell Guide to the History of London' Michael Joseph
1981

Weinreb, Ben and Christopher Hibbert (Eds.) 'The London Encyclopaedia'
Macmillan 1983

Other publications
Official Visitor Guide to Greenwich, Greenwich Council 2002

South London Mercury Newspapers

Maps, pictures and guide leaflets, National Maritime Museum,
Greenwich

TINSLEY – SHEFFIELD

Hey, David 'Yorkshire from A.D. 1000,' Longman 1986

Pollard, S. 'A History of Labour in Sheffield' Liverpool Univ. 1954

Pollard, S. and Colin Holmes, 'Essays in the Economic and Social History
of South Yorkshire' South Yorkshire County Council, 1976

Wilson, C. 'Brinsworth and Tinsley' – A History of the area. Blackburn School, Rotherham 1994

VERDEN-ALLER – GERMANY

McLachlan, Gordon. 'The Rough Guide to Germany' Rough Guides Ltd 2002

Other publications

Military publicity brochures from Royal Engineers Regimental Museum, Chatham

Visitor Information provided by the Verden Tourist Information Office.

RICHMOND, NORTH YORKSHIRE

Godfrey-Faussett, Charlie, 'Footprint England' Footprint Pubs. 2004

Macdonald, Guy, 'England – Cadogan Guides' The Globe Pequot Press 2003

Other publications

Guide books from Richmond Castle and the Georgian Theatre

NETHER EDGE – SHEFFIELD

'They Lived in Sharrow and Nether Edge' Nether Edge Local History Group booklet, 1988

Old Ordnance Survey maps 1903 and 1905, Pub. Alan Godfrey

DONCASTER – SOUTH YORKSHIRE

Elliott, Brian (Editor), 'The Miner's Strike Day by Day – Diary of Yorkshire miner Arthur Wakefield' Wharncliffe Books, 2003

Ellis, Norman 'Yesterday's Yorkshire Series No. 2, Reflections of a Bygone Age', Keyworth Notts, 1999

Freethy, Ron and Marlene, 'Discovering Inland Yorkshire' John Donald Edinburgh, 1992

Hattersley, Roy 'Goodbye to Yorkshire' Gollancz, 1976

Pevsner, N. 'Yorkshire, the West Riding' Penguin, 1967

Pill, D. 'Yorkshire, the West Riding' Batsford, 1977

Pollard, S. (Ed.) 'Essays in the Economic and Social History of South Yorkshire' South Yorkshire County Council, 1976

Raistrick, Arthur. 'West Riding of Yorkshire' Hodder and Stoughton 1970

CROOKESMOOR – SHEFFIELD

Dawson, Simon and Paul Scarrott, 'Walkley Through the Ages' DS Print, Design and Publishing 2003

Dunkley, S. 'One cook, one parlourmaid, and one housemaid, the complete household' Hunter Archaeological Society, Vol 19, 1997

Other publications

'Crookes revisited' Crookes Local History Group. 1989

ROTHERHAM – SOUTH YORKSHIRE

Jones, Mel (Editor) 'Aspects of Rotherham' (three volumes) Wharncliffe Publications, 1995/6/8

Munford, Anthony. P. 'A History of Rotherham' Sutton Publishing 2000

Munford, Anthony. P. 'Rotherham – A Pictorial History' Phillimore 1994

Other publications

Articles from Rotherham Advertiser newspaper

Guides from Rotherham Parish Church

Newsletters, articles, press releases provided by South Yorkshire Police

Old Ordnance Survey Maps 1893/1901 Pub. Alan Godfrey

CORSTORPHINE – EDINBURGH

Blackadder, Kate (Editor) 'The Handbook to Edinburgh' Mercat Press 1991

Cant, Malcolm. 'Villages of Edinburgh' Vol. 1. Malcolm Cant Pubs. 2001

Oliphant, Margaret. 'Royal Edinburgh' – Her Saints, Kings, Prophets and Poets. Senate, 1999

Other publications

Tourist maps, guides and leaflets, Edinburgh Tourist Office, 2001/2